Belonging

A Memoir of Place, Beginnings
and One Woman's Search for Truth
and Justice for the Tuam Babies

CATHERINE CORLESS is married to Aidan, and they have four children, Adrienne, Alan, Alicia and Aaron, and nine grandchildren.

Her quiet, secluded life – rearing a family, farming, gardening, and enjoying her pastimes of art, crafts and family history research – changed drastically in 2014, after some research she had done into the Bons Secours Mother and Baby Home at Tuam was picked up by media and exposed worldwide.

Her research revealed the harshness, cruelty and discrimination of the mothers who gave birth there, and their offspring. It also revealed the terrible secret of 796 babies who had died at the Home from 1925 to 1961, whose remains had been laid in a defunct sewage tank. Resulting from this revelation, the Irish government was pressurised into setting up a Commission of Investigation into all Mother and Baby Homes in Ireland, whose final report was issued in January 2021. *Belonging* is her first book.

NAOMI LINEHAN is an author, journalist and documentary-maker. She was born in Dublin and grew up in Zambia. *Belonging* is her third book.

Her first book, *Nowhere's Child* (Kari Rosvall's story), was published by Hachette Books Ireland in 2015. It soon became a number one bestseller and has since been published internationally and translated into three different languages. Vicky Phelan's acclaimed memoir *Overcoming*, ghost-written by Naomi, was published by Hachette Books Ireland in 2019. It was a number one bestseller and the winner of the An Post Irish Book of the Year Award 2019. It was also named as the Sunday Times Memoir of the Year 2019.

Naomi worked in radio for many years, in flagship current affairs and features programmes on Newstalk. She has also written for *The Irish Times*, produced a series for RTÉ television and has worked in the areas of international development and social entrepreneurship.

Belonging

*A Memoir of Place, Beginnings
and One Woman's Search for Truth
and Justice for the Tuam Babies*

CATHERINE CORLESS

WITH NAOMI LINEHAN

HACHETTE
BOOKS
IRELAND

First published in 2021 by Hachette Books Ireland

A CIP catalogue record for this title is available from the British Library.

ISBN 978 1 52933 976 5

Typeset in Sabon MT Std by
Palimpsest Book Production Ltd, Falkirk, Stirlingshire

Printed and bound in Great Britain by
Clays Ltd, Elcograf S.p.A.

Hachette Books Ireland policy is to use papers that are natural, renewable
and recyclable products and made from wood grown in sustainable forests.
The logging and manufacturing processes are expected to conform
to the environmental regulations of the country of origin.

Hachette Books Ireland
8 Castlecourt Centre
Castleknock
Dublin 15, Ireland

A division of Hachette UK Ltd
Carmelite House, 50 Victoria Embankment, EC4Y 0DZ

www.hachettebooksireland.ie

Contents

For all the Tuam Home Babies
awaiting a dignified burial.

What Happened

~

This is the tale of two red-haired girls who lived on either side of a ten-foot wall.

One was trapped inside the Bon Secours mother and baby home.

The other was me.

I see them sometimes when I close my eyes. The 'home babies'. Not as they were, but as they could have been, at the end of their lives, instead of the beginning: with grandchildren of their own, perhaps, with white hair and weathered skin, recounting stories of the lives they've led, the places they've been.

Instead they lie beneath the soil, the bodies of those forgotten children. Dead before they'd barely started.

Above the surface, a seemingly normal Irish town: a children's playground, a church, a housing estate – the veneer of humdrum village life. But nothing could be further from the truth.

The story of how this came to pass, and how we came to know this dark secret . . . well, that is what I will tell you here.

796: the number of children taken from their mothers who died and were discarded. Remains found in a sewage tank on the grounds of the children's home.

Guilty of the greatest sin of all: to be born. Born to mothers without husbands, with no ring on their fingers. A shame to the parish.

What shame, now.

But who are these children? How did they get here? And who was meant to care for them?

When a child goes missing, the media shout for answers, for the Madeleine McCanns of the world. Photographs on milk cartons, search parties, distraught families. But when hundreds go missing in the care of an institution, there is silence. Mothers left to grieve alone.

I will not rest until every one of those children is accounted for. Each one some mother's son, or daughter.

They call me an amateur historian. But this story is not consigned to history. It nearly was. But the truth will not stay buried. What I am about to tell you sounds like fiction, but it is far from it. I will tell you how it all came to pass – the twists and turns of life that led to this discovery.

I have made a promise to myself that I will not stop until I know, until the world knows, what happened here, in the quiet corner of my little town, in the cradle of the Catholic Church.

What went on, on the other side of the wall.

The truth will be unearthed, if I have to fight 'til my dying day.

My name is Catherine Corless, and this is my story.

CHAPTER ONE

Beginnings

⌒

Everyone's life is unique, but they all begin the same way. It is the one thing we have in common, no matter who we are. We all had a mother, at some point. And our relationship with her shapes us in ways we may not even realise, until later in life. That is what happened with me, and my mother.

I always felt as though my arrival into this world was a bit of an inconvenience. Perhaps because I was often told as much by my mother.

She was in her forties when I was born. The year was 1954. I can only imagine I wasn't planned and perhaps not entirely wanted. I was the scrapings off the pot, as we called it, the last child born. My mother already had two boys and two girls. Each had been a home birth, delivered in the back bedroom of our family farmhouse; that is, until I came along. With high blood pressure, my mother very reluctantly agreed to go to the Galway central maternity unit some weeks before my birth.

In the ward she was stationed beside a friendly Traveller woman, who noticed my mother crying. 'What's wrong with you?' she asked.

'I just miss home,' my mother said.

'Ourra get out of that, you ol' fool,' she said, 'sure isn't this a chance to put your feet up, away from the other childer!'

My mother wasn't convinced. She left the hospital as soon as she was permitted. As was the way back then, the hospital ambulance delivered Kathleen Farrell and her new little bundle home to the farm. When the ambulance pulled up outside the house, my father came to the door with Anne, Michael, Martin and Mary, who were all eager to meet their new little sister, Catherine. And so it was that I would come to call this place my home, this farmland on the edge of Tuam.

And I was about to make my presence known, in a big way. I was a very restless baby, so I'm told, who cried a lot. And with four other children to look after, my mother didn't have much time for that.

Life was busy in our crowded little house. We were now a family of seven. We lived in what had once been a Royal Irish Constabulary barracks, situated on a former landed estate owned by the Henry family. Despite being old, the house was fit for purpose. It had a fine slate roof, a large kitchen area, a scullery with a Belfast sink, and a loft above the two small bedrooms.

But gone were the times of landed gentry. The new owner of the property was a man named Bobby Burke. He was a kind and decent landlord. He divided the estate among his employees, my father being one of them. They each received around 40 acres, and the landlord put in place a scheme where new houses were built to accommodate their families. My parents gladly participated, paying for the house in monthly rates.

I was six months old when we made the big move. The new house was spacious, compared to the old house. There were three bedrooms instead of two, which meant a new sleeping arrangement: a 'boys' room' and a 'girls' room'. It was decided that my mother would sleep in one room with me and my sister Mary, and my father would sleep in the other room with my two brothers Michael and Martin. Somehow, Anne, being 14 years old, got a room to herself.

I've never really known whether that arrangement was entirely due to the logistics of space or whether my parents preferred being in separate bedrooms. I've come to the conclusion, though, that I may have had something to do with it. My father couldn't tolerate any kind of loud noise, so the prospect of a crying baby in the night may have been more than he could bear.

My mother seemed quite happy with this set-up. I don't think she thought of my father in a romantic way. Of course, she cared for him and made sure he was looked after. Perhaps it wasn't quite love, but it was what she could manage. My father, on the other hand, was soft. He was the gentle one, the emotional one. He needed her more than she needed him. And her distancing seemed to make him need her all the more.

Though I was the youngest, I was often left to my own devices. Out of necessity, I suppose – not enough hands for all the children who needed minding. I had the bumps and bruises to prove it. All part of growing up. Or falling up, perhaps, in my case.

Though my mother did her best to keep an eye on me, my childhood seemed to be punctuated with tumbles and falls. I don't think I was overly clumsy. Just curious, perhaps. Always wanting to explore. The years flew by, and before they knew it, I was walking and getting up to mischief.

Life was simple back then. But it was hard work too. Every few days my mother would collect water from the stream that ran through our land and heave the heavy buckets back up the hill towards the house to be used for washing and cleaning and cooking. She fetched the drinking water from the well each day and was clever about harvesting the rainwater that ran from the drainpipes into barrels she placed beneath them. One day when I was about three years old, I was out on the farm with my mother and my sister Mary collecting water from the stream.

In one giant leap, I propelled myself forward in my wellington boots and tried to jump across the stream to the opposite embankment. I lost my footing and fell straight on to a sharp rock, hitting my head. I let out a piercing cry, then sat up, dazed and confused. My sister screamed when she saw the blood gushing from my forehead.

My mother dropped the buckets of water she was carrying. 'Jesus, Mary and Joseph! What is wrong with you?'

She scooped me up in her arms and brought me inside, where she placed a cold cloth on my head to try to stem the bleeding. A stern scolding followed, about trying to do things that were dangerous.

But, somehow, I didn't seem to learn my lesson. It was just a few weeks later when the dog incident occurred. I was playing in the kitchen with our family pet. After careful consideration, I surmised he was just the right size for 'horsey'. I threw my leg over his back and held on tight to the hair around his neck. 'Yeehaw!' I yelled as the dog took off across the room. I lost my grip somewhere near the hall and fell straight onto the concrete steps and was knocked unconscious.

My father saw me lying still on the floor. 'Christ!' he yelled as he ran to pick me up. 'Kathleen! Come quick! She's dead!'

'Nonsense,' my mother said. She brought me out to the back of the house and doused my head with cold water from the barrel in the garden, which quickly brought me back to myself.

My brother Michael came to check on me. 'Are you alright, Cat?' he asked, examining my head. He gave me a playful wink. 'Looks like you'll live!' Michael was always looking out for me. I adored him and looked up to him as my protective older brother.

I knew I could be a nuisance, being the youngest, but somehow he always had time for me.

And Mary too was very kind. She was often charged with taking care of me, and sometimes my mother asked far too much of her. As was the case the time I tried to make a whistle out of a small bicycle valve. It slid down my throat and I began to choke on it. My mother slapped my back in a panic, trying to release it. I went quiet for a moment, then swallowed it whole and down it went.

My mother wanted to ensure that the valve passed through my system and out the other end. So Mary, all of eight years old, was given the job of using a stick to examine my deposits under the bushes because we did not have a bathroom at that stage. Luckily, after several days, the valve appeared and we were able to put an end to that particular ritual.

I learnt a lot from Mary too. Like the day we heard that we were next in line for 'the stations'.

'What's going on?' I asked her.

'It's our turn for the stations,' she said.

'What's that?' I asked.

'Everyone is going to come and say their prayers in our house,' Mary explained.

I soon learned that it was a tradition whereby a kind of rota system operated in the village, and instead of everyone going to church for mass, they would come to a person's house. The priest would say mass in the sitting room and bless the house, with all the neighbours gathered around. And then we would have tea afterwards. It was a very important day, Mary explained, and it meant we had a lot to do to get ready.

My mother and father seemed to be taking it all very seriously. Work began immediately, as there was much to be done and not a moment to waste. In the quiet moments, I could sense that my mother was worried about it. One night I saw her counting out the money that she kept stashed in the metal box in the cupboard. No doubt it all came at terrible expense. But they had no choice but to go ahead.

My father began painting the house – inside and out. New furniture arrived and a linoleum floor covering was laid out in the sitting room. Being all but four, the new floor was the most exciting part for me. It seemed like an ideal ice rink to slide across. When no one was looking I took a flying run at it, but lost my balance and came down hard on my elbow. I let out a shriek and held my arm close to my chest, sure that it was broken. But a broken limb was the last thing my parents needed with so much to be done.

'Och Lord, what now!' My mother lifted me up and carried me into the kitchen, taking a jar of goose grease from the window-sill. The fat from roasting a goose proved to be an excellent remedy for most swellings. My mother always kept a jar of it to hand, from the leftover goose fat from Christmas dinner.

She sat me down at the kitchen table and opened the jar. The smell was pungent as she scooped it out with her fingers and rubbed the fatty goo on my elbow. The smell itself was enough to make you forget about the pain, if only for a minute. Whatever else you might say about my mother, she was a wizard when it came to home remedies, though in a way she had to be, as there wasn't much money to spare for doctors' fees.

After much preparation, the day finally arrived. My mother woke at dawn. I felt her moving in the bed. I turned over and closed my eyes tightly, hoping she might let me sleep on. I knew we would be needed though, especially today. 'Time to get up, girls,' she said, waking me and my sisters. 'We've a lot to do before they all arrive.'

I opened my eyes sleepily. I heard my mother stoking the fire in the kitchen.

Anne nudged me hard. 'Get up!' she said.

I jumped up and got dressed quickly. Our best clothes had been laid out on the bed. When I walked into the kitchen, Mam was busy setting the table and ensuring there would be enough food for everyone. We were hosting a sit-down meal for all the neighbours. Mary, Anne and I got to work helping her with seating arrangements.

Mam pointed us towards the white cloths and candles and asked us to dress the makeshift altar in the sitting room, which we did carefully, trying to get all the details just right.

Just then, my father came in from milking the cows with my brothers. 'You've done a fine job there, girls,' he said, taking off his muddy boots.

Once everything was ready, we waited for people to arrive. I stood watch at the front window.

'They're coming!' I shouted, as I saw the line of people making their way up the hill towards the house. Some walking, others on their bicycles. Everyone was dressed in their Sunday best.

'They're nearly here!' shouted Mary.

We took our places. We all knew what our jobs were for the day, to help things go smoothly.

Neighbours and friends from far and wide arrived. They were solemn and quiet, blessing themselves as they came through the door, as though they were entering a church. The candles were lighting in the room and a strong smell of incense filled the air. As more and more people arrived, we squeezed in tightly.

There was a mumble of chat as the farmers discussed their herds and crops and the women reunited with one another. Then, a hush moved through the room. 'Shhhh.' The priest was arriving. He was dressed in his stole and holy vestments. My mother went out to greet him and guided him into the front room where he would hear confession from those who wished to attend.

When that was done, the priest came into the sitting room to say mass. We all gathered around in a circle as he stood beside the fire. I watched, fascinated, as, row upon row, the adults clasped their hands and bowed their heads. When it was time to kneel, they bent double and dropped to the floor, even the tallest of men, made suddenly small. It was strange to see the adults, who were usually in charge, behaving like children in a classroom.

An elderly woman was seated on the armchair. She was dressed all in black. A younger woman, who looked like her daughter, gently helped her down to her knees by the fire, as she clasped her rosary beads in prayer.

The house was filled with the drone and mutter of prayers recited in unison. A cloud of incense wafted through the room, bringing with it the unmistakable smell of Sunday mass. The congregation followed the priest's lead, kneeling when cued and praying when prompted. Moving and speaking as one, all following instruction.

When the mass was done, the priest asked, 'Who is next to take the stations?'

There was a silence in the room for a moment, then a neighbour piped up and said it was their turn next. Mary told me it was bad luck to refuse the house mass, and that's why the tradition continued, year after year. I watched as some of the men stepped forward to give the priest a pound note for his trouble. And with that, the priest wrote down the name of the family to host the following year's gathering, making it official. That seemed to bring an end to the ceremony.

Then it was time for breakfast. The priest sat at a special table we had prepared for him, along with a few hand-selected men who would have the privilege of eating with him, my father being one of them.

People stayed for hours – talking and eating. No longer solemn, but casual, at ease with one another. When the meal was over, the men sat on one side of the room and the women on the other. I went to play with the children outside as we chased each other around the garden.

When it was time to go, one by one people thanked my parents and commended them on such an impressive 'stations'. When the last of them had left, my mother closed the door behind them and let out a sigh of relief.

We all looked at one another – we'd done it! I felt very proud in that moment to be a Farrell. To be part of something – family.

CHAPTER TWO

Beware of the Bull

I would soon learn that there were some things that even goose grease couldn't cure. I must have been about six years of age the day I decided to explore the forbidden field. I looked to see if anyone was around, then spotted a gap in the hedge and pushed my way through.

Out of the corner of my eye I saw something move in the hedgerow – a robin, perhaps. I hunched down, peering in through the leaves to catch a glimpse of it, when all of a sudden I felt myself being launched into the air. The world started to spin.

A bull had caught my dress in his horns and was trying to toss me into the air. I did the only thing I could think of: I held on as tight as I could to the bull's woolly head, then suddenly I felt a sharp pain in my leg as he bucked furiously. I tried to scream, but no noise came out. The pain was getting worse. Just when I thought I couldn't hold on any longer, I landed on the ground with a thud. I was crying and disorientated.

Next thing I knew I was in the arms of a man I didn't recognise.

'Are you alright, girl?' he asked, checking me for cuts and bruises.

I screamed.

'You're alright, you're safe now, you're safe now,' he said, trying to calm me down.

I tried to catch my breath through the tears.

He told me how he had been cycling past when he saw a bull tossing a little girl into the air. He jumped the gate and somehow managed to prise me from the animal, then escaped to safety, with me in his arms.

'You're a very lucky girl to have survived,' he told me. 'You were very brave, hanging on like that.'

When he was satisfied that I wasn't wounded, he asked me where my home was. I pointed to the farmhouse and the kind stranger took me by the hand and walked me back across the fields. My legs were shaking.

When my mother answered the door, he recounted the story, with horror. She thanked him, and he went on his way. Inside the house, my mother checked me up and down to make sure I was okay, then reprimanded me for going into the bull field.

I needed a hug, but I knew I wouldn't get one from my mother. I hoped Michael would be home soon so I could tell him what had happened.

Sometimes when life gets particularly tough I think of that little girl, in her cotton dress, holding on to the bull's head as he played bucking bronco. It makes me feel like I can take on anything, even if I'm on my own.

From a very early age I knew my mother wasn't like other mothers. She was always distant, never maternal. But she could be kind too, at times. I knew she was a good person, though she found it hard to show affection. I could see it in the things she did – for me and for other people.

The Kellehers were a poor family who lived about half a mile from us. And though none of us had much by way of money, they had even less. Their children would sometimes come to our house to play. My mother always showed great kindness to them. I would watch her load up each of their plates with slices of her fresh brown bread covered with butter and jam, served with a mug of warm milk, fresh from our cows, which they happily devoured. Even though I didn't understand my mother, I still wanted to be like her, in some ways.

One day I was playing with Jimmy, the eldest of the Kelleher children, in the garden. I turned to him and said, 'Follow me, I have an idea.'

We ran down the path, then stopped suddenly.

'Okay, I have a plan,' I said. 'But you have to promise not to tell anyone.'

He looked at me, wondering what I was up to.

'Promise?' I said.

He nodded.

'Say "I promise",' I insisted.

'I promise,' said Jimmy, sheepishly.

'Okay,' I said, 'come with me.' I brought him down to the hen house. 'Stretch out your jumper,' I ordered.

Jimmy obeyed.

And with that I carefully gathered each and every egg from the coop and placed them in Jimmy's outstretched jumper. 'They're for you,' I said, triumphantly, once I had completed the task. 'To take home for your tea!'

I watched as Jimmy waddled off, trying to walk the half-mile back to his house, carefully balancing the eggs in his jumper so as not to drop them. I wondered how many of the eggs might be broken by the time he reached home.

That evening as my mother was spooning out the stew for

dinner, she cleared her throat. I knew what was coming. 'Does anyone know what happened to the eggs today?' She paused, looking around the table to identify the guilty culprit. I looked down at my shoes. 'I went out to gather them earlier, but discovered they were already gone,' she said. 'Does anyone know anything about that?'

She was looking straight at me. I felt my face redden.

'Catherine?'

I had to own up. 'I gave them away . . .' I said.

'Away? Who did you give them away to?' she asked sternly.

'Jimmy . . .' I whispered under my breath, then added, defensively, '. . . because, Mam, you said we should be good to the Kellehers.'

I waited for the shouting to begin. But no shouting came. I looked up. She was looking at me with an expression I hadn't seen from her before. Something close to love, I think.

'Well, you didn't have to give them *all* away,' she said, catching herself, returning to form.

But I could tell she wasn't angry about what I'd done. On the contrary, she seemed pleased. Looking back, I think it was one of the only times I ever felt she was proud of me. Perhaps that's why I remember it so clearly.

I tell you this to explain how I came to be where I am today, how it all came about. My links to Tuam and the people here. It's in my blood, this land: the good and the bad of it.

CHAPTER THREE

Growing Up

When you're young, you think life will never change. Until it does, and it catches you off-guard.

This is what happened one night when I passed the boys' room on my way to bed, and saw my mother packing a suitcase full of Michael's clothes.

'What's that for?' I asked.

'Michael's leaving,' she said. 'He's found work in Dublin.'

'Leaving?' I said, shocked. 'For how long?'

'For good,' she said.

'When?' I asked.

'Tomorrow morning,' she said coldly, leaving the room to fetch something else to put into his suitcase.

My heart sank. I couldn't imagine life without Michael. I wanted so badly to ask him to take me with him, but I knew in my heart that wouldn't be possible. Especially if he was leaving for work. He didn't need his younger sister holding him back. I should be happy for him, I thought. That's what he would do for me. But happy was the furthest from what I was feeling. I couldn't sleep that night, knowing what was about to happen.

I wasn't proud of my decision, but the next morning, instead of saying goodbye, I went for a walk. I couldn't bear to face reality. I walked up to the top field to be sure I could look back at the house to see Michael when he was leaving. I sat on a rock and waited. I was sitting there a long time before I finally saw him emerge from the house, dressed in his best clothes. He suddenly looked like a man, no longer the boy I had always known. He was just 16, and even though I was only six, he was my best friend in the world. I knew at that moment that life was never going to be the same again.

I watched as he closed the front door behind him and walked away, suitcase in hand. He walked to the bend in the road, then waited there until the bus arrived and hissed to a halt. As he stepped on to the bus, he must have felt me watching him from high up on the hill. He turned and looked up towards the field. That's when he spotted me. He waved and I waved back. Then the bus disappeared around the corner, and he was gone. I wondered if I would ever see him again.

The house felt empty without Michael. He had always been my ally and was quick to stand up for me if ever I was in an argument with anyone else in the family. Even though I was the youngest, he always had my back. Now, without Michael around, I suddenly felt very alone.

Not long after that, Martin left too. He was headed for England. There was work there and he felt he could make a better life for himself across the water. It felt like the pillars of our family were disappearing.

My father must have felt the loss worst of all. The boys had worked by his side on the farm since they were small. Now he was left with his wife and daughters, knowing that, in time, his daughters would leave him too.

My mother disappeared into the fields the day Martin left. She went for a long walk, to be on her own. Her eyes were red and bloodshot when she returned. And yet none of us spoke of the heartbreak of losing the two boys. Instead, we just went about life, as if it was all normal, as if there weren't two empty seats at the table.

But you can't ignore those feelings, no matter how hard you try. They run deep within you – that love of family and the loss of them when they are missing. You feel it every day. Something I would grow to understand in adulthood in a way I never really appreciated as a child.

CHAPTER FOUR

The Gaps

~

Without the boys around, there was much more to be done on the farm. And we, the girls, were now needed, to fill the gaps, quite literally.

Mam was busy baking bread when she spotted something outside the kitchen window. 'Jesus, Mary and Joseph!' she said, wiping her floured hands on the dishcloth. She pulled on her wellies, which were stationed beside the range. 'He expects me to do everything – inside and out. Come on, Catherine, get your boots on; you're needed.' She gestured towards the door.

I looked out the window to see what was happening. And there in the distance, coming over the hill, was my father, with all our sheep running around him in every direction. The sheepdog was doing his best to keep them under control, but was having very little success.

We went outside and my mother quickly put some order on the situation, coaxing the sheep in the right direction, but despite her efforts, they kept escaping through the broken fences my father was always intending to mend.

19

'Catherine, stand in the gaps in the fence!' my mother yelled.

I jumped into the gap and created a barrier as a sheep ran in my direction, then diverted when it saw me. I watched as my parents worked together. Farming was the only time they worked in tandem, whether they were dousing sheep, milking cows or saving crops. It was comforting to see them working as a unit.

When the job was done, and the sheep were corralled into the correct field, Mam and I went back inside and my father returned to the farmyard. I felt a rush of excitement, knowing I had done something to help. It was nice to feel needed.

But there was no rejoicing over the success. My mother went straight back to her baking. I could see she wasn't in good form. She had a way of changing the atmosphere in the room, depending on her mood. Our world revolved around how she was feeling.

It was only when I started school that I really began to get a sense of life outside of our smallholding, of the world beyond the farmyard gates.

CHAPTER FIVE

Sweet Temptation

ᴄ

Childhood memories are like stepping stones. We jump from one to the other in our minds to make the story of our lives.

But there is one moment in particular that changed my life entirely. I was all but six years old when I came to know of the home babies.

My sister Mary and I attended the Mercy Convent primary school and we walked the three miles there each day. When we reached the road, we walked along its grassy verge, past the fields, then down by the high stone walls of the mother and baby home, into the heart of Tuam.

The mother and baby home was a strange place. It was a huge building, much bigger than anything else in Tuam, apart from the cathedral. It was where all the babies with no mammies and daddies lived. Or at least that's what I believed back then. I used to stop outside a while, to see if I could spot the bread man or the milk cart arriving to the home, for the chance to catch a glimpse inside.

One morning, as we passed the home, I noticed that the gates had been left slightly ajar. I checked to see if anyone was coming. No one. Now's my chance, I thought. I looked up at the glass shards embedded in the top of the wall, glistening in the early-morning sun. I wondered if the purpose of the glass was to keep people from breaking in, or to stop those inside from escaping. I approached the gate, slowly, carefully, hugging close to the wall, so as not to be seen.

'Pssstt, what are you doing. Catherine!' Mary hissed. 'You're going to get us in trouble!'

'Shh,' I said. 'There's no one here. I just want to see what's in there.' I prised open the gate. It was heavier than I imagined. I peered, cautiously, into the yard, studying the building, searching for some sign of life inside its many windows.

Suddenly the gate clanged shut. We both jumped with a fright. Then caught our breath. Just the wind.

'Let's get out of here!' said Mary.

We ran the last half-mile to school. If we were late, we would get a slap. We got there just in time, panting.

'Good morning, Miss Farrell,' said the head nun, standing in the doorway.

'Morning, Sister,' I said, hurrying past her, as she tapped a ruler in the palm of her hand.

Mary came in just behind me. I heard the tap, tap of the ruler again as Mary slinked in.

I hurried to the classroom, found my seat and pulled out my copybooks, ready to start. Then, ten minutes later, as was the daily routine, the home babies arrived. I watched them as they shuffled in, one by one, with their heads down, the click-clack of their hobnail boots tapping the floor, as they took their seats at the back of the class.

The teacher entered the classroom. We jumped to our feet.

'Good morning, class.'

'Good morning, Sister,' we replied in unison. The daily ritual.

She placed her things on the desk, then bowed her head and clasped her hands. 'Our Father . . .' The cue for us to begin.

'Our Father . . .' We recited the Lord's prayer.

'Take out your copy books. Spellings . . .' she said, and the class began.

For the rest of the day the home babies remained at the back of the room, quiet and unengaged. The teacher never called on them. It was as though they weren't even there.

Something about the separation, the segregation, was having an effect on our young, malleable minds. We saw them as 'different'. We were taught that we were not the same. I can only imagine that's what drove me to do what I did next. I had seen another girl in the class doing it. My friends egged me on.

It was break time and we were in the cloakroom. I took a sweet wrapper from the pocket of my jacket and scrunched it up in the palm of my hand. 'Hey! I've got something for you!' I called to one of the home babies: a red-haired girl with big green eyes.

She turned her head towards me, cautiously.

I presented my outstretched hand. 'Here,' I said, 'a sweet.'

Her eyes lit up. She reached out to grab the sweet, ready to relish the taste in her mouth, only to realise seconds later that it was nothing but a scrunched-up piece of paper.

The other children erupted in laughter. I'll never forget the look on the girl's face. I regretted my prank immediately. I couldn't concentrate on my lessons for the rest of the day. I kept replaying the moment again and again in my mind.

When class was dismissed, as usual, the home babies left first. The red-haired girl was among them. I looked up and tried to catch her eye, willing her to look my way. I wanted to show her that I was sorry. But she walked with her head down. I could feel her nervousness as she passed me. It was a horrible feeling –

thinking someone was afraid of you. She exited the classroom. I watched her go.

I gathered my things and flung my schoolbag over my shoulder and left the school behind me. Walking past the fortress of high walls, I quickened my pace as I headed into the surrounding farmland, towards home.

When I was far enough away, I looked back towards the mother and baby home, wondering what those children were doing behind the high walls. What happened to the red-haired girl when she went 'home', back to the institution run by the Bon Secours nuns. I wondered if she was upset about what had happened. I sighed and tried to shake it off. Just another day at school.

But it wasn't that easy. The guilt was weighing heavily on me and I had to do something about it. I needed to tell my mother. For some reason, I felt she ought to know. I just didn't realise how much it would affect her, and why.

CHAPTER SIX

Home

⌒

As I reached home, I saw Puppy bounding up towards the
gate to greet me.

'Hi, Puppy!' I said, petting her golden brown coat as she turned
onto her back for a belly rub. 'You're my best friend!' I said. She
seemed to understand what I was saying. She wagged her tail and
gave me a lick. I laughed. She always knew how to make me
smile.

But as I went to turn the front-door handle, I felt that familiar
heaviness come over me. I went inside and took off my shoes.
Already I could feel the tension in the house. I heard my mother
scolding my sister Mary about something or other.

I walked into the kitchen. 'Hi, Mam,' I said, as I reached for
some leftover soda bread on the kitchen table. 'Something
happened at school today, Mam . . .'

I wanted to get it off my chest – to tell someone what I'd done.
Mam didn't look up. She continued washing the dishes, but I
could tell she was listening.

'I played a trick on a home baby,' I said.

I saw my mother flinch a little. I continued, 'I scrunched up a piece of paper in my hand and pretended it was a sweet, but when the home baby went to take it, there was no sweet there, and she was very upset,' I explained. 'I don't know why I did it, Mam . . .'

My mother said nothing. She stared at me for a moment, a kind of cold stare, then turned on her heel and left the room.

I sat at the kitchen table, waiting for Mam to return. Though she rarely hit me, I was fearful of what she might say the next time I saw her. Her words were often the most hurtful thing of all. I thought back to a memory which always felt close to the surface. One afternoon when I was five years old my mother and I were in the kitchen. She seemed particularly angry that day, for some reason. I couldn't help but feel I was the cause, but I didn't know what I had done to anger her. I was standing beside the clothes press when in a moment of frustration she stopped and stared at me and said, 'I rue the day you were born.'

I didn't understand what she meant at the time, but the look in her eyes told me that it wasn't a good thing. Maybe that's what she was thinking now, behind that cold, listless stare. Bruises healed, but some of the things she said to me still echo in my mind. They stay with you forever, words. Not just for childhood.

All of a sudden I felt as small as I had felt when I was five years old. I went to collect the turf, hoping that doing some chores might win Mam back. I missed Michael in that moment. I missed both my brothers. The house still felt empty without them.

I was thinking of them that day as I went out to the back shed and piled the turf high in my arms and carried it into the house. As I passed my father's room, I peered in through the gap in the door. My mother was placing some tea and toast on the chair beside his bed. I could see the shape of Dad under the blankets.

He wasn't moving or responding to Mam. That meant he was

having one of his bad days. I wasn't sure what bad days were exactly, but I knew to stay away from him and let him sleep. My mother was always in worse humour when he was in bed. It meant she had to take on all the farm work – milking the cows and feeding the sheep – as well as tending to us and doing all the cooking, cleaning and washing.

I missed my dad when he wasn't around. It was like he was gone away and there was no telling when he would be back. Sometimes he stayed in his bedroom for weeks at a time.

At that moment the floorboard under my feet creaked. My mother looked towards the door. I hurried on so as not to be seen. I dropped the turf by the fire, then slipped out the back door. It wasn't a day for being inside. I needed to get out of the house.

I ran to the bottom of the garden and slowly prised open the back gate, hoping it wouldn't screech. It was old and wanting oil. I closed it behind me and ran down through the fields, out towards the woods. I could feel my heart lifting. It was springtime and everything was in full bloom. I was free. I felt like I could breathe again.

When I reached the edge of the woods I collapsed onto the grass, into my favourite little hollow, and closed my eyes. I could feel the warm sun on my skin. All of a sudden I felt something wet on my face. I opened my eyes. 'Puppy!' I giggled. Somehow Puppy had found me hiding in the long grass among the buttercups. He always had a way of finding me.

'Let's go, Puppy!' I said, jumping up. Though he had long outgrown the name, we still called him Puppy. And it suited him. He had the bounce and joy of a puppy. Sometimes I worried what life would be like if anything ever happened to him. He was the best thing about home, most days. And my only friend a lot of the time.

I stayed there in the woods for hours with Puppy in tow, exploring the well-trodden trails, the scent of wild garlic in the air. I needed the escape, especially that day. As far back as I can remember I have found solace in the quiet solitude of nature. There is a rhythm to it and a stillness. You are alone, and yet you are never alone.

The birds were out in song. The colours were bright and the air was crisp. It was among the wood anemones and the trees that I found myself at peace. Well, usually. That day was different. I thought by getting away from the house – away from my mother and my confession – that I could escape my sense of guilt. But it wasn't working. I couldn't stop thinking about the red-haired girl. I wondered how she might be feeling, locked away in the mother and baby home, remembering how everyone had laughed at her.

I was afraid to go back into the house. I knew I had upset Mam. I had often felt the brunt of my mother's anger. I knew how to channel that. When she hit me, I would crouch down on the floor and cover my head with my hands, rather than escaping out the door, because I always thought it was better to stay and let her have it out. I knew that once it was over, we would be on better terms. It was a vicious cycle, but I had a method, a way of dealing with it.

But this wasn't anger. It wasn't disappointment either, because I knew what that looked like too. This was worse. I felt I had hurt her, and I couldn't understand it.

What I didn't realise then was that that day would stay with me for the rest of my life and that many decades later, that memory would haunt me, and lead me to do something I never thought possible.

CHAPTER SEVEN

Steps of the Stairs

﹌

As I grew up, I spent more and more of my time at the Ryans' house. They lived about half a mile from us. The Ryans had twelve children, who had arrived steadily, one after the other: seven girls and five boys. They were like the steps of the stairs when stood side by side. Of course, I had a favourite: Geraldine, eighth in line. From the age of twelve, I would go and help look after the children. I often took them down the fields for walks or helped them with their lessons.

One day, as I rounded the corner, the children ran towards the gate. Geraldine was out in front, waving. 'Catherine, Catherine!'

I smiled and waved back. I reached into my jacket pocket to take out some sweets – a nice treat for them, I thought. Treats were scarce in those times, and I knew they were even scarcer in the Ryans' house.

I didn't know how Peg, their mother, managed it all. She had been raised as an only child, but here she was, raising twelve children. We went inside the house. 'Hello, Peg,' I said.

'Ah-gee, how'ya, Catherine?' she replied.

She was busy making flaky pastry apple tarts for the children – a little treat to make the day special. I watched her rolling and stripping the dough and rolling it out again and again. The radio was blaring, the baby was crying and the toddlers were wrestling on the floor. And yet somehow she was able to do everything she needed to do.

I saw where I was needed and began playing with the children, trying to entertain them. 'What's the matter with John, Peg?' I asked eventually. One of the youngest had worked himself up into a full-blown tantrum and was pointing at the coat hooks in the kitchen.

Peg dropped her saucepan, brushed past me, took one of her old coats off the hook, threw it in a corner on the floor and said. 'Here! That should work.'

And sure enough, the little lad lay down on the coat, finished his bottle, and drifted into a sound sleep, amid the pandemonium of the noisy kitchen. They were in a happy kind of chaos all the time, knowing their mother was there to look after them.

And Peg, with everything else she had to contend with, somehow managed to do that for me too – to be a mother to me. To make me feel safe and useful, to make me feel that I was needed, that I would be missed if I wasn't there.

I played with the children a while longer, as we went outside to run around the yard.

'Dinner time!' Peg called from the door and they all filed in, clambering to get to the table first. 'Thanks for minding them, Catherine. You're a topper.'

I loved how she called me topper. She always made me feel like I was doing a great job. In the Ryans' I felt useful – like I had a place, and purpose. They felt like family. I had been there to witness each and every child arrive home from the hospital.

I thought back to when Angela was born. I was at the Ryans'

minding the children, when the baby decided to come a little earlier than planned.

'I need to go to the hospital,' Peg said to me.

'What?' I said. 'Is everything alright?'

'Will you hold the fort here until Sean gets home from work? My water's breaking,' she told me, though I had little idea what that meant.

I nodded. 'Of course,' I said.

And with that she strapped her bag on to her high nelly bicycle and cycled the three miles to the Bon Secours maternity unit in Tuam. She would stay there for a week, and return home with another little bundle.

For Peg, that week in hospital would be a break, if you can call delivering and caring for a newborn baby a break. It was time away from all her other children, a little time to rest and repair.

I looked at Peg with the twelve children gathered around her: such a pillar of strength for all her children. I had so much admiration for motherhood in that moment. I hoped one day I could be a mother like Peg. I wanted to tell her that, but I didn't know how. Instead I said, 'Thanks, Peg. I'd best get home.'

'Will you come again tomorrow, Catherine?' asked Geraldine, hopefully. 'Please come tomorrow!'

'I'll try my best,' I said.

'Promise?' said Geraldine.

'I do,' I said.

'Say "I promise",' she said. It was a game we played.

'I promise,' I said.

And with that I ran all the way home. I didn't want to be late for dinner. I skulked inside and heard my mother calling us. Home just in time, I thought.

We sat at the table and Mam dished out the dinner – potatoes, veg and a little bit of beef for each of us. One plate was left aside. Mary picked it up and carried it out of the room. She was bringing it to Dad to eat in his bedroom.

'Tell him he's to eat that now,' my mother called out after her. 'I don't want to see that coming back into the kitchen.' My mother seemed very agitated that evening.

As I grew older, I was starting to challenge her more when she was in that kind of mood. 'What's the matter?' I asked.

'There's nothing the matter.' She scowled. 'Why would anything be the matter?'

'Why are you angry?' I persisted. I knew it would vex her, but I did it all the same.

'Why? That's why.' Her favourite response. It closed down any conversation.

I know now that it was all a defence. The only way she could keep her secrets locked inside her.

CHAPTER EIGHT

Cycling Out

The childhood years went by quickly, as childhoods often do, and soon I was a teenager. This brought a new kind of freedom: a life of my own, away from home. They are halcyon days in my memory – filled with cycling and friends and long summer evenings. The winters were harsh in Galway and the summers often not much better, but when the sun shone, it was like no place on earth.

On sunny days, I would jump on my bike and meet my friends at the edge of town. With our picnics packed into our knapsacks we would ride out into the country, exploring all the back lanes and lakes. When we found a scenic spot, we would throw our bikes by the old stone walls and settle in a field or by a lake or river to eat our lunch. The boys, playing to the audience of girls, were always up to some kind of mischief. We laughed a lot, I remember that much. And the days seemed endless. When the sun was finally setting, we jumped back on our bikes and headed home again. We did this a lot. Those days all blur into one – a kind of heavenly glow of summertime in adolescence.

But one day in particular stands out. I was about nineteen at the time and had just finished my Leaving Cert. I was delighted to put school behind me after all that time cooped up indoors studying. It was liberating to be outdoors again. It was a beautiful sunny day. There were about a dozen of us out for a cycle – some of my girl friends and the boys from the school across town. We met at our usual spot, just outside Tuam.

'This is Aidan,' said one of the lads, introducing a new boy in the group.

Aidan smiled. 'Nice to meet you,' he said, as he went around the circle shaking hands with us all.

'Catherine,' I said. 'Nice to meet you.' Our eyes met, and our handshake seemed to last just a little longer than all the others. I smiled and shrugged it off. 'Come on, let's go,' I said.

With that we all grabbed our bicycles and cycled out into the countryside. When we reached the old castle ruins we threw down our bikes and climbed over the crumbling stone wall. I found a comfy spot and placed my jacket on the dewy grass to sit on. I rummaged through my bag to find my sandwich. I felt as though someone was watching me.

I glanced over. Aidan and I made eye contact for a moment, before he swung his head around to look out towards the river. I blushed. There was an awkward energy in the air all of a sudden. I started a conversation with my friend Aoife, just to break the silence. 'What did you pack?' I asked her, desperate to move the attention away from what had just happened.

'You're very red,' she said, laughing. 'What's going on?'

'Aoife!' I said. 'Shhhhh.'

I looked back towards Aidan. He was still looking away, though I could tell he was listening.

When our picnic was over, we got on our bikes and cycled

towards home. I was struggling up the hill when I noticed Aidan coming up beside me.

'It's a tough one, isn't it!' he said, as he pumped hard on his pedals.

'It's not too bad!' I replied, determined not to let the boys get the better of us.

We started talking – about school first, and then about other things. We talked the whole way home. I wasn't used to making new friends, but there was something about Aidan that made me feel safe in his company. A warmth I had never felt before.

'See you soon, hopefully,' he said, as we all said our goodbyes.

'Are you meeting Paul later?' Aoife asked me, with a cheeky smile.

'Who's Paul?' asked Aidan.

'Ehh,' I said, feeling embarrassed, 'Paul is . . . well . . .'

'He's her boyfriend,' said Aoife.

'Oh . . .' said Aidan. 'I didn't realise you were . . .'

'Well, we're not really,' I said. 'We're just . . .' I couldn't think of what to say. I felt foolish all of a sudden. I had been seeing another boy for a few weeks. It was all very innocent, as it tended to be back then, but somehow I felt I needed to explain myself.

'It was nice to meet you,' said Aidan, breaking the awkwardness. 'See you soon.'

But I didn't see him soon, and the weeks passed and the summer wore on. I wondered each time we went for a cycle if he would be among the group of boys we were meeting. And each time I felt disappointed when he wasn't.

Then one day, my Aunt Mary-Ann, who lived nearby, asked me to help her paint her house. So that Saturday, I put on my painting clothes and hopped on my bicycle. I was looking forward to spending the day with Mary-Ann. She was a character, and always in good humour.

As I rounded the bend towards her house, I noticed a yellow estate car parked outside. My aunt was taking buckets of paint out of the boot with the help of a boy I immediately recognised. It was Aidan! What was *he* doing here, I wondered. I was suddenly very aware of my oversized t-shirt and messy hair.

'Hi!' He waved, nervously.

'Hi . . .' I said, leaving a bit of a question mark in the air. I was panting a little, trying to catch my breath.

'I'm just delivering paint to Mrs Jennings,' he said, in a way that seemed rehearsed.

'That's my aunt,' I said.

'Oh, really?' But something about the way he said it gave him away. I knew he must have known Mrs Jennings was my aunt. It was a small town, and we all knew who was related.

I played along. 'I've come to help her with some painting she's doing to the house.'

There was an awkward silence. 'I better go,' I said. 'I'm very late.'

'Don't go just yet,' he said. His face turned red.

I raised my eyebrows. 'Why?' I asked.

'I was just hoping . . . to ask you something,' he said.

I shifted awkwardly.

'I was wondering . . . there's a dance on in the Ranch House next weekend . . . would you like to go?' He gulped as he said the words, looking at me for a moment and then down at his feet. 'We could go . . . as friends, you know. There's nothing wrong with that. There's a great band playing, I hear . . .'

'I'll think about it,' I said, before I could gather myself.

'Does that mean yes?' he asked, smiling. I hadn't noticed his smile before.

'Maybe . . .' I said, smiling back. And the tension was finally broken.

'I better get back to work,' he said, a new pep in his step. He turned to leave. 'Maybe I'd meet you on the top road then, next Friday night . . . seven o'clock?'

'Maybe . . .' I said.

I turned to go inside the house. When I thought it was safe, I glanced back over my shoulder. But Aidan caught me looking. He waved from the window of the car as he pulled away, smiling from ear to ear. I couldn't help but smile too.

'Hi, Catherine,' my aunt said, opening the door. I suspected she had been watching our encounter.

'Sorry I'm late,' I said, grabbing a paint brush.

'That fella from the hardware store was hanging around here a long time,' she said.

I could feel my face going red again. My aunt noticed, but pretended not to. 'Seemed like a nice young lad . . .'

I could tell she was teasing me. I didn't respond.

'Right,' she said, 'this painting won't do itself!' And with that we got to work. As I rolled the paint brush up and down the wall, I replayed the conversation with Aidan again and again in my head. Was I going on a date?

Friday came around very quickly. I went to the meeting point on the old Dublin road. It was five to seven. I looked up and saw Aidan coming over the hill.

'Hi!' he said, waving. He looked relieved to see me. 'I wasn't sure if you'd make it . . .'

'Hi,' I said, smiling.

'Good to see ya!' he said. He was suddenly very confident. Or at least he seemed that way.

'Where's your car?' I asked.

'What car?'

'Well . . . how are we going to get to the dance?' I asked.

He looked at me with raised eyebrows, smiled, and stuck out his thumb.

'Hitch-hiking?'

'Works every time!' he said, turning his attention to the oncoming traffic.

I watched and waited. And sure enough, before too long, a van slowed down and a man rolled down his window. 'Where are you off to?' he asked.

'Ranch House in Cummer,' said Aidan.

'Hop in,' said the man.

'Ah, sound,' said Aidan, 'thanks a million.' And he gave the driver a wink. Everyone seemed to love Aidan. Already I could see he had a way with people.

We chatted to the driver as we made our way towards the dance hall. He told us about when he used to go dancing with his wife. 'Back in the early days,' he said. 'Who knows,' he added, with a twinkle in his eye, 'maybe you two might be married one day too – if you're not careful!' Aidan and I shuffled awkwardly in our seats. 'Here we are!' he said, as we pulled up outside the Ranch House.

It was the most popular venue in the county. From the outside it looked like a big old farm shed. It was always teeming with people and tonight was no different. Some of the best showbands in the country played at the Ranch House in Cummer, and Tuam was fast becoming the showband capital of Ireland.

When we arrived, Aidan's friends were all at the bar waiting for us. Suddenly I felt like I was on show – the new girl on the scene. What had seemed like a friendly outing suddenly felt like there was more at stake. Aidan sensed my discomfort. 'Let's dance!' he said, as he grabbed me by the hands. He pulled me across the dance floor and spun me around. I laughed as we twirled and dipped to the sound of the music. We danced through the night as the band played on. I had never danced so much in my life.

And so, the Friday night dance became a weekly affair, and before we knew it Aidan and I were 'going steady', as they say, full of the innocence of youth and the excitement of new love. Our lives were full from then on. Suddenly everything seemed to go our way.

I applied to an art college in Galway and got accepted. From the very first day, I loved being there and immersed myself in the creativity of it all – spending my days painting and drawing.

After a year, though, I decided to leave art school as I wanted to earn my own keep, to be able to stand on my own two feet, rather than spend the next few years in college. I didn't feel like I could be independent until I got a job of my own. Aidan was working as a salesman for a paint and décor company and was very happy in himself.

I tried my hand at a few different things, but they were all part-time nixers and didn't really amount to much. My mother suggested that I take a typewriting course, saying it might open up other opportunities for me. I dismissed the idea initially but then decided to give it a go. And sure enough, soon after I'd finished the course, I applied for a job as a receptionist in a textile company, and got it. Finally I was in a job I enjoyed, a job where I felt useful.

Aidan and I both worked hard and enjoyed spending our time off together. We would meet most evenings, except when I was at the Ryans' helping the children with their homework.

The years went by and we were very happy. There was a rhythm to our lives and we were enjoying all the rituals that come with being a new couple in love – as old as time, but new to us, as it is to every couple when they're starting out. We were feeling out our new reality, finding our feet as a unit, getting to know one another as our two lives were slowly becoming one.

I had grown very attached to Aidan. But as time wore on, the closer we became, the more I began to feel uneasy, as if we'd missed a step, had slipped into the routine of 'us' without ever discussing what we were. I assumed we were both heading in the same direction, but somehow four years had gone by and there was something missing. And much as I tried to ignore it, the uncertainty was starting to get the better of me. I needed some reassurance that he felt the same way.

One night we were out for a walk. I was unusually quiet.

'Is everything alright, Catherine?' he said eventually.

'Well . . . it's just . . . us . . .'

'What do you mean, "us"?' I could hear he was getting a little anxious.

'Well, you never talk about us . . . about where we're going.'

'Oh,' he said. He looked taken aback. 'Well, I have my plans,' he said.

And sure enough, he moved pretty quickly after that. A few months later we had arranged to get married. We picked a date and venue. All that was left was to tell his mother.

CHAPTER NINE

Family

Josie could be difficult about this kind of thing. She was suspicious of anything that took Aidan away from home, away from the nucleus of his family. I think she could sense that things were starting to get serious between us. One night, Aidan was on his way out the door to see me.

'Where are you off to?' said Josie, knowing well where he was going.

'Out,' he said.

'With who?'

'Catherine, Mam, sure you know that.'

'But you're not well,' she said, referring to a cold he had. 'Would you not stay in tonight?'

'Mam,' said Aidan, 'I'm going out.'

'Would you not think again about that girl?'

Aidan ignored her and headed out the door.

'Don't you be out late now!' she yelled after him.

I was surprised to see Aidan's car pull up outside our house that evening, as I knew he hadn't been feeling well, but I was really pleased to see him. I got into the car and we started chatting. We stayed there for hours talking and making all sorts of plans.

'Oh God,' Aidan said, catching sight of his watch. It was approaching midnight. 'I better go. I promised Mam I wouldn't be late.'

We got out of the car and Aidan walked me to my door to say goodnight. He was leaning in to give me a kiss, when all of a sudden we saw two headlights hurtling towards us. We both looked up, surprised to see anyone out at that hour of the night. But as the lights got closer, Aidan recognised the car. 'I don't believe it!' he said.

The car screeched to a halt and out jumped Josie. 'Who do you think you are keeping my son out this late,' she scolded, 'and he with a head cold!'

I didn't know what to say. I was stunned, rooted to the spot.

'Mam! You can't be going on like this! Christ, I'm 25 years of age!' Aidan yelled.

'Get into your car, Aidan – we're going home!'

Aidan gave me a look as if to say, 'I'm sorry about all this' and dutifully got into the car. He knew it wasn't worth the fight. His mother was worked up and the easiest thing to do, for everyone's sake, was to calm her down.

Josie was only five feet tall but she could tower over most men twice her height. She was kind at heart and meant well, but she had a hold over Aidan, her only son, that was hard for him to break free of. I watched them drive off into the distance.

We talked it over the next day and decided it was time to move forward, together. No matter how hard that might be. That evening Aidan told his mother the news of the engagement. As expected, she protested. 'You're far too young for that,' she said, though back then, in 1978, 25 was considered a fine marrying age.

He let her know that the wedding would be going ahead, with or without her blessing. I was proud of him for that. It took a lot out of him to stand up to her. He wanted to keep everybody happy. Little did we know quite what that would entail.

We were married at a small hotel in Galway. Our wedding was a very quiet affair, with just our families there – the way we wanted it. I wore a mix-and-match bohemian-style cream outfit. It was a beautiful day with very little fuss, which was very us.

Everything seemed to be happening quickly. We had been looking at houses, hoping to buy something in the village. We found the perfect house and put a bid in. But when Josie caught wind of this, she was not pleased. She wanted to know why we didn't move in with her and Paddy and Aidan's sister, Carmel. 'There's a fine big room there – plenty of space,' she said.

When Aidan told me this I let him know that there was no way I was going to move into his parents' house. He agreed. It was not what either of us wanted.

I could see the pressure of it all starting to take its toll on him. He felt a sense of duty to his parents, to ensure that they were safe and happy, and I understood that. But at the same time, we were trying to start our new, separate lives, as our own unit. Eventually, Josie conceded. We were not going to move into the spare room. At this point we had pulled out of the house we were trying to buy as the pressure of the indecision was getting to us both.

'Mam had another idea,' Aidan said to me one evening.

I could only imagine what Josie might have thought of next.

'Somewhere independent that we could live,' he said.

I could tell he was nervous. I raised my eyebrows, prompting him to continue.

'Well, she suggested that we set up a mobile home . . .' he paused '. . . in their garden.'

'A mobile home?' I said, checking to see if I'd heard him correctly. 'In their garden?'

'Yes,' he said, grimacing.

In a million years this wasn't how I'd pictured my first foray into married life. I paused for a moment, then said something Aidan wasn't expecting. 'Okay.'

'What?'

'I said, okay, that's what we'll do.'

Aidan looked at me in disbelief.

I was tired of the constant battling and I could see it was really starting to have an impact on Aidan. He wasn't himself, trying to juggle everyone's needs. If this was really what would keep Josie happy, I was willing to do it, and it sounded a lot better than moving into someone else's house. At least in the mobile home, we'd have our own space. So it was settled, that's what we'd do.

'It won't be forever,' Aidan said, apologetically.

'I know,' I said. 'But for now, let's go ahead.'

Doing something felt better than doing nothing – the limbo we had found ourselves in. At least now we could move forward. And that's how we found ourselves living in a mobile home parked at the bottom of Josie and Paddy's garden.

We chose a big mobile home – something with a couple of bedrooms and a bathroom and kitchen. It was grand, actually, like a small house. And it still felt like moving in together. We were nesting. We were just in a different kind of nest. We were happy there. Though it never felt quite right.

Every night Josie insisted that Aidan come 'home' for his dinner after work, 'as he'd always done'. So that's what we did – each night Aidan went into the house for his dinner. I didn't like to eat late at night so I stayed in the mobile home and had a cup of tea and waited for him to come back. I was okay with it, but I wished it could be different. I wanted to cook for us both and sit over supper as I'd imagined we would as a married couple. It was strange, at times, feeling like an add-on to another person's family. But we did have each other and I knew things wouldn't always be this way. It was a stepping stone to becoming our own unit. I cared for Josie, and I wanted her to be happy too.

We were enjoying our newly wedded bliss, spending our evenings and weekends doing the gardening and meeting up with friends and family. Then came another surprise, a happy one. One day at work, I started to feel nauseous. I excused myself and went to the bathroom. I hovered over the sink, feeling like I might get sick. And then it dawned on me that my period was a little late too, come to think of it.

That night, I mentioned to Aidan that I thought I might be pregnant. We were both very excited, but cautious too. We didn't want to get our hopes up, in case I wasn't. A few weeks later, I was still feeling nauseous, so I knew for sure. 'Aidan, we're going to have a baby!' I said excitedly one night.

He hugged me and felt my stomach. 'Our little one,' he said, beaming. Our band of two was soon to become three.

Over the next few months I began to feel the toll of pregnancy on my body. Morning sickness and fatigue were getting the better of me, especially during the long days in work, in a job I was growing to dislike more and more. After weeks of deliberation, I finally made the decision to hand in my notice. The moment I was released from the job, I knew it was the right decision. I felt a huge weight being lifted.

Aidan had hoped I might hang on a little longer, as we needed the money. I worried I was letting him down, but he understood and reassured me that we would manage. I loved him for that. He was always so supportive.

I could concentrate now on the baby and the joy that it was going to bring to our lives. Instinctively, it's what I wanted to do. I'd heard about nesting – how you begin to make a home for your child, knowing that soon they will leave your body and enter the world. It was true! It was exactly what I was doing. I wanted to be my best self for when the baby arrived. Some people find it hard being pregnant, but I was happy to be at home, getting everything ready.

Josie hinted her disapproval at my decision on more than one occasion, but I knew in my heart it was the right thing to do. And in a peculiar way, things worked out for the best, as they so often do. Not long after leaving the job, I got a call from my brother Martin, who had moved back to Ireland from England a few years previously. He wanted to know if there was any way I could help out with their three children, including their three-month-old baby. His wife Margaret had been unwell, and now she needed a spell in hospital for tests. I was delighted to help and wanted to spend time with the children. I knew it would come easy to me after all my time at the Ryans'. I was also trying to soak in everything there was to know about babies, as I prepared for my own to arrive.

It was around this time that Josie became ill. A trip to the doctor's turned into a few more appointments and then a hospital stay. She needed to have a hysterectomy, she told us. She made little of it, and didn't say much about the diagnosis or how she was faring with it all. She could be like that. Very proud. Old-fashioned, I suppose, the way that generation can be.

By not telling him, Josie was trying to protect Aidan, like he was a child. But Aidan wasn't a child. He was an adult. And the not knowing was worse. It made him imagine all kinds of possibilities. Though, in a way, I could understand. He wasn't a child, but he was *her* child, and he always would be. I rubbed my pregnant stomach. Perhaps I would do the same thing, one day.

It seemed like no time at all before I was full term. It was May 1979. We had been married for just over a year. I was to deliver in the Bon Secours private maternity unit in Tuam and had agreed to follow their method of childbirth. It was all planned out. No spontaneous labour. At my last appointment I was given a castor oil mixture and told to take it early on the Monday morning. I was admitted that afternoon. Then followed many hours of pain until I was wheeled into the delivery room, where my feet were put in stirrups.

'Time to push!' said the midwife.

She coached me through. I pushed, and breathed. Pushed and breathed. Pushed and breathed.

'Come on, Catherine!' she said. 'One. Last. Big. Push!'

I pushed and screamed with every atom of my being. Then I passed out. It must have been the anaesthetic they gave me to help me cope with the stitches.

When I finally came to, Aidan was sitting beside me. He placed his hand on mine. 'We've got a little girl!' he said, with tears in his eyes.

The nurse came into the room with our beautiful baby girl swaddled in a blanket. A girl. Our girl. Our daughter. She handed her to me. In that moment I felt happier than I could ever imagine. She looked up at me as I held her. She had big blue eyes. Just like her dad. We named her Adrienne.

I'll never forget bringing her home, walking through the door of the mobile home with her in my arms. 'Welcome home,' Aidan said. We had everything ready for her arrival. Her Moses basket next to our bed, the drawer filled with all her little clothes. The teddies and soft toys from friends and family all lined up, ready to welcome her. Suddenly the place felt like home, in a way it never really had before.

I studied her as she lay sleeping in my arms, the contours of her face, her little nose, her delicate lips. So peaceful. I couldn't believe that Aidan and I could have created something so precious, so beautiful.

We soon settled into our new routine. For a few days we had our own little bubble, the three of us, as we watched her and loved her and learned how to mind her. Then friends and family began calling in to see her, to lend a hand and to wish us well.

But there was still one very important person who had yet to meet Adrienne: her paternal grandmother. We dressed Adrienne up in a special outfit. I sat in the back seat to keep an eye on her as we drove out to the hospital.

In the corridor, we spotted the nurse who was looking after Josie. She had just stepped out to get something.

'How is she doing?' Aidan asked.

'She's being very brave,' the nurse said.

'Is she getting better?' he asked, hoping the nurse might tell him something about her condition.

'Well . . . I suppose everyone's different when it comes to cancer.'

'Cancer?' Aidan was taken aback.

'Didn't you know?'

Aidan shook his head. 'How bad is it?' he asked.

'I don't think it's my place,' she said, and with that she promptly left.

I put my arm around Aidan. He took a deep breath. 'Let's bring her in,' he said, looking at Adrienne asleep in my arms.

We walked into the room. 'Look who's here to meet you!' I said.

I presented Adrienne to her grandmother. Josie sat up in the bed, propped up with pillows as I handed her first grandchild to her.

A nurse passing through the ward looked over at the scene. 'Ah, she's the image of her dad!' she said. 'I've never seen a baby look so much like her father.'

Josie beamed with pride as she kissed Adrienne on the forehead. From that moment on, they shared a special bond, grandmother and granddaughter: the eldest in the family and the youngest.

Aidan took the news of his mother's illness very badly. I could see how much he wanted to help, because he was always trying to fix things, for everyone, always trying to make everyone happy. But cancer was often unfixable. And Josie was old and her body tired. Deep down, we all knew that, though we tried to stay positive.

'They know a lot more now than they used to,' we told ourselves. We clung to stories of people who had survived, against all the odds. There seemed to be a lot of them. Positive stories. Especially when they were what you needed to hear.

We decided not to tell Josie that we knew. But at least now we were in a better position to help her, in whatever way we could.

It was a time of mixed emotions. Through the difficult days, we were still embracing all the joy that Adrienne had brought us. Becoming parents for the first time was wonderful. But it was exhausting too. Each night I woke to the sound of Adrienne crying. I picked her up and held her in my arms. The crying stopped momentarily, and then started again. I went to the kitchen and heated the bottle. Our nightly ritual. I took the night shift, as Aidan was on the road all day with work, and I worried he might have an accident if he didn't get his sleep.

Adrienne and I found our rhythm. We had our little routines. We spent the mornings feeding and napping, and I spent the afternoons gardening while Adrienne lay in her pram, wrapped up in blankets, taking the fresh air. Sometimes, I would carry her in my arms up the fields on my walks, as she slept.

I washed her clothes by hand in the sink, twisting the little white vests, ringing out the water. It was something I remembered my mother doing – washing our clothes by hand in a washtub. As I stood over the sink, for just a moment I felt there was a little bit of my mother in me – I wondered if she might be proud to see history repeating itself in that way. That I, her child, was now a mother too. Doing the things that mothers do.

When Adrienne was about four months old, a neighbour who had six-week-old twins was desperately looking for a babysitter as she had to return to work after her six-week maternity leave. I thought of Adrienne at that age. Still so new. So little.

She asked if I could mind the twins for a week or so until she could sort out a longer-term arrangement. I obliged as she seemed in such distress. The week went very well. Somehow, to my surprise, minding three babies didn't seem too much harder than one. I loved being around the babies all day and watching over them. I was able to get them into a relaxed routine and we were all happy.

And so the week of minding them turned into a couple of months, which turned into a year. Working with children suited me well. Of course it could be difficult at times, but somehow I loved it, in a way that I hadn't loved any other job before.

And so life continued, as Adrienne grew with each passing month. Before we knew it, she was 18 months old and I was pregnant again. Alan, our son, came next. A beautiful little boy. Now we had one of each. We felt very lucky. Two healthy children.

But this time I found it all a little harder, for some reason. After giving birth to Alan, I became very emotional. I could be irrational, angry about the simplest things. Motherhood was complicated. You don't know what that means, really, until you've experienced it. It was the best thing in the world, and the hardest thing in the world, at the same time. Like nothing else I had ever experienced. And it ran deep within me. Every emotion attached to motherhood.

'It must be my hormones,' I said to Aidan one night. I knew it wasn't the normal exhaustion of having a new baby and toddler. I was well used to coping with toddlers. And Alan was such a good baby, a good sleeper and feeder. And Adrienne was a great toddler, sleeping through the night. I really should have had nothing to be stressed about. I felt so guilty for feeling this way, knowing the blessings that were in my life, but not being able to fully appreciate them.

There was a darkness in my mood a lot of the time. I was irritable and fearful. I had a fear of not being in control, a fear of not being able to mind our family. Privately I worried I might have postnatal depression and I worried about what that might mean, if I told anyone; if I said it out loud.

I thought of my own mother – her irritability. The darkness that surrounded her. Was that what I was becoming? The thought terrified me. Perhaps that darkness was in me too. I wanted with every part of myself to be a good mother. To be the mother they deserved.

Aidan could see I wasn't myself. Maybe a change of scene might be a good idea, he suggested. We decided we needed to move somewhere with a little more space. We found a bungalow a half-mile away. We had saved up as much as we could and we were just about able to afford it, with a loan from the bank. The house needed work, and the garden was wild and overgrown – plenty for Aidan and me to do. We relished the thought of the challenge. I felt we would be happy there, comfortable. It felt more permanent, more settled. So we packed up our things and moved bit by bit into the new house. There were jobs to be done – painting and decorating and sorting the furniture. We busied ourselves nesting, making a new life for our family.

And then, we got the news: 'Come quick. Josie's not well.'

We went to the hospital to be at her bedside, and didn't leave. She passed away several days later. On the day of the funeral, Aidan was very emotional.

When the formalities were over and people returned to normal life, we tried to continue where we left off, somehow. But there was a big gap in our lives, a huge missing part, especially for Aidan.

We went on to have two more children: Alicia and Aaron. Not all planned, but all very much wanted and loved.

Then some years later, Aidan's father Paddy passed away too. It was a time of change, a lot of transitions and starting anew – the children learning to live in the world, and Aidan and I learning to live in a world without his parents, and the hole that was left in all our lives.

Then came the question – who would take over the family farm? It was decided that Aidan was best placed to take on the responsibility, and so we packed up and moved our lives back to Josie and Paddy's.

CHAPTER TEN

Life on the Farm

Life had come full circle. It felt strange to be back again, though on very different terms. Waking up in Josie and Paddy's house every morning was difficult to get my head around. We were surrounded by reminders of who they had been. I don't know if it was harder for Aidan or more comforting to be there.

After a while, life seemed to take on a new rhythm for us all. We took on the running of the farm and all the responsibilities that came with that. It took time, but as we became settled into our new home, the farm gave us all a tremendous sense of place and purpose. We felt we owed it to Josie and Paddy to do our best with it – to keep it ticking over as best we could.

Aidan was on the road a lot with work, so I tended to the farm. I took it very seriously. It suited me to be back working with animals, out in nature every day. In a sense, I think it's what kept me going. Being outside. Having jobs to do. I needed it. And I had the children to help me. They loved the farm. They ran barefoot in the summers, and they were hardy. But, best of all, they were great friends. That is what I wanted for them more than anything.

I would swing open the doors of the kitchen and let them run into the woods, where they built their dens and had their own little adventures. I watched from the kitchen window as the four of them ran across the field with their two pet lambs, Ricky and Lazarus, in tow. The lambs seemed to think they were the family dogs, running after the children.

Though the kids kept me busy, I always tried to maintain a little hobby going, as an outlet. Whenever there was a community event on I volunteered to do the artwork for the posters. It was a way of being involved without having to be overly sociable. I preferred it that way. I had a few good friends that I liked to meet up with, but I was always best one on one. I wasn't very comfortable in a big group of people. Some people light up in a crowd and become the life of the party. Aidan was like that. But I liked to take more of a back seat, to listen and take things in. We balanced one another out that way.

As word got out that I was doing bits and pieces for the community, the priest asked me if I would paint some worn-out statues from the altars of nearby churches and give them a new lease of life. He would drop them into me if they ever needed painting. Soon I found myself painting the grottos around the town too, whenever they needed it.

I loved it. Art was an escape for me. And it soon became a big part of the children's lives too. On the weekends, there could be a dozen or more kids in our house running around with pots of paint and paper and glue. We seemed to attract all the neighbourhood kids, who came to play with our brood regularly. I didn't mind, though, I found children to be the best kind of company. Their chatter and laughter helped to ease my anxiety. Children are themselves, no matter what, and I loved that. There was no nuance, no second-guessing. The way people ought to be. Before the insecurities kick in, and the doubt starts to seed.

I also joined a FÁS scheme, to keep me busy while the children were at school. It was a project that was focused on surveying cemeteries. A few hours a day, my job was to transcribe all the headstones in various local graveyards. This information was then collated by the Galway branch of the Irish Historical Society to create a digital archive.

It certainly wouldn't be for everyone, but I loved it. I especially enjoyed trying to decipher the wording on the old slab stones. Sometimes, when I couldn't work out what they said, I would pour water over the indented writing, which made it easier to read. I found a peculiar sense of peace in those graveyards and a sense of worth, knowing that those long buried were to be written into history.

And though we were happy, I could feel that heavy feeling creeping in, trying to pull me back down. I was managing to suppress it, enough to keep things normal, to keep things happy. I was glad I was able to do that. What I wanted more than anything in the world was for my children to be happy. For us to have a happy home. And for many years, we achieved that.

Not like the home I had grown up in. Full of secrets. Some of which were about to resurface.

CHAPTER ELEVEN

An Unexpected Visitor

T here was a knock at the door one Sunday afternoon. When
I answered it, to my surprise it was my sister Mary and a
woman I didn't recognise.

'This is our relative!' Mary announced, smiling at me.

I could hear the children squabbling inside. 'Pardon?' I said.
'Come in.' I beckoned them to follow me. 'Sorry,' I said, when
we were in the kitchen. 'What did you say?'

'This is our cousin, Meena, from Keady in Armagh,' Mary
repeated.

'Armagh?' I said. 'Mam's side?'

Mary nodded enthusiastically.

'I was in the neighbourhood and thought I'd come and visit,'
Meena said. 'It's lovely to meet you all.'

I had never met or heard of anyone related to my mother
before. It was all very peculiar. I made a pot of tea. 'So, how are
you related to Mam?' I asked.

'I'm her niece. Well, step-niece, I suppose,' she said, correcting
herself.

'Step-niece?' I asked.

'Well, yes,' she said, surprised by my reaction. 'I better not say much more,' she added, sipping her tea.

'Why not?' I asked.

'Well,' she said, looking embarrassed, 'your mother asked me not to.'

She explained that when she had first arrived at my parents' house my mother had taken her aside, into the next room, and warned her: 'You're not to tell them anything about me, do you hear?' Meena explained that she didn't want to disobey. Mary and I looked at one another. It was all very mysterious.

That afternoon when Mary and Meena had gone and the children were with Aidan, I decided to call up to see my mother. We had kept up a relationship since I'd left home, but it was always the same kind of distant discourse whenever I visited.

'Well, you never told us we had a cousin, Mam!' I said jokingly, trying to make light of the situation, hoping it might entice her to open up.

She didn't rise to it. She didn't even look up. I watched her as she continued kneading the bread she was making. What was she trying so hard to hide? I wondered. What part of her did she not want us to see? She hadn't changed in her old age. You sometimes think people will soften with age. She got harder, if anything, more reclusive.

I wanted so badly to question her – to ask her to tell us why she didn't want to talk about her past. But, instead, I changed the subject and talked about the weather. I stayed for a short chat, then went back home. I felt she wanted her space.

Meena was never mentioned again. My mother continued as if nothing had ever happened.

I found it harder to let things go. I called Meena a few days later. I wanted to see if she might be more open to talking, now that she was back home and away from the prying eyes and ears of my mother. But Meena said very little. She either didn't know very much about my mother, or didn't want to break a confidence. And so my mother remained a mystery.

I didn't fully understand then just how complicated life could be. How much hurt and pain from the past my mother was harbouring. All within the small frame of her body. Little did I know how much I would come to understand, and how quickly. How much our lives were about to change and how complicated things were about to become, and in so many different ways.

CHAPTER TWELVE

Darkness

⌒

The children were growing up fast, as they do. We were always trying to think of new ways to amuse them, new experiences for them, things we could do together. We loved bringing them on adventures – family days out. We tried to do it every weekend, if we could. And they were usually very happy occasions, but one outing in particular stands out in my memory.

It was a beautiful day in the spring of 1990. Aidan suggested we go for a drive to Claregalway to see Cloonacauneen Castle. Anne, one of my closest friends, had told me how surprised she'd been that her husband Sean had bought the castle on a whim. He had told her casually over the dinner table that they were now the proud owners of a castle.

'I wouldn't put it past him!' Aidan said, when I told him the news. Sean was like that – wonderfully spontaneous.

'You must go and have a look at it,' Anne had said. And so, it seemed the perfect outing for the kids – a ramble around the castle grounds and a chance for us to escape for a few hours. The usual Sunday afternoon chaos was in full flow and we needed to get out of the house.

'Right, everybody into the car!' Aidan shouted. 'We're leaving in five minutes!'

The kids scrambled around, running up and down the stairs.

'Mam! Where are my shoes?'

'I've lost my jacket!'

'Give that back!'

And 15 minutes later we were off – all clad and shod and buckled into the car.

Aidan turned on the radio. We all sang along and the music kept everybody happy. We headed out towards Claregalway, weaving through the back roads, the sun beaming down on us.

'Look, there it is!' shouted Adrienne, pointing out the window. The castle had just come into view. 'Is that it?' she asked excitedly.

'I think it is,' said Aidan. 'And you know how it works, don't you?' Aidan joked with the children. 'I'm the king of the castle, and you're the . . .'

'Dirty rascal!' they yelled in unison.

'Well, at least we know where we all stand,' said Aidan, winking over at me.

We pulled up outside the castle gates, and clambered out of the car, deciding to approach it by foot. It was much bigger and more impressive than I could have imagined.

'Can we go in?' asked Aaron, eager to explore.

'Let's go!' said Aidan, picking Aaron up and hoisting him onto his shoulders as they opened the gate and started to walk down the avenue.

I'll never really know what happened next. Suddenly, I felt my legs give way. I tried to grab on to the gate but lost my balance and fell to the ground with a thud. Everything went dark. All I could see was static. I could hear a ringing in my ears.

'Catherine, are you alright?' cried Aidan.

I could hear him, but his voice was becoming more and more distant. My hands and feet were tingling. I could feel Aidan's hand on my forehead. The next thing I knew I was laid out in the front seat of the car. I was sweating.

'Catherine, are you okay?' Aidan repeated over and over, trying to keep me conscious. He packed the children into the car and drove at speed towards the hospital. 'How are you, Catherine? Can you hear me?'

I tried as hard as I could to answer, to make even just a small noise, to reassure him I was still conscious.

We pulled up outside the A&E. Two paramedics arrived with a wheelchair. I was disorientated. I heard Aidan telling them my details. 'Corless,' he said. 'Catherine.'

'Any known medical issues?'

'None.'

And with that I was wheeled inside. The children were not allowed in, so Aidan had to stay with them. I was placed on a trolley. Doctors came and went, checking my blood pressure and asking how I was feeling.

Eventually I saw a consultant, who referred me to the psychiatric unit for assessment. I met with the doctors there, and we talked through what had happened. They asked me questions about my life and my childhood and I tried my best to answer. For the first time in my life I opened up about things that had happened when I was a child and about my relationship with my mother. I didn't know why I was confiding in these strangers. Somehow their questions had led me there.

There had been a darker side to my childhood, one that I told no one about, until now. I told them of how, from the time I was very young, a frequent caller to our house was often drunk and rowdy. He had a way of changing the atmosphere in the house

– of making home a frightening place for a child. He was there a lot, coming and going as he pleased. I couldn't understand how my parents allowed him to keep on visiting.

As the years went on, he seemed to become more of a permanent fixture in our house. I hated being at home when he was there. If he arrived after being in the pub, there was a stench of alcohol and the atmosphere was tense. He had a terrible temper, and could take it out on anyone in the family. I was frightened of him, and as I grew older I began to be more wary of him. Perhaps I was right to be.

One night, when I was about 23 years old, I woke to find him sitting at the end of my bed. I was terrified. What was he doing in my bedroom? I yelled at him to get out. He drunkenly stumbled back towards the door and left the room.

After that, I didn't feel safe in the house anymore. I told my mother what had happened. She listened. I don't know what I expected her to do, but I didn't expect her to take his side. 'Ah, sure, he'd never harm ye,' she said, excusing his behaviour.

That night I placed a chair up against my bedroom door. It was very late when I heard him coming in from the pub. I listened to his footsteps as the floorboards creaked beneath him. My heart was pounding. I held the duvet close and waited. I heard him go towards the sitting room, but I couldn't sleep for the rest of the night out of fear that he might come back.

This was a turning point in my life. I decided I couldn't take it anymore. I had been frightened for long enough. I packed some clothes into a bag and told my mother I was leaving.

She barely reacted, as if she didn't care that I was leaving home. I was so angry at her. All those years of fear and anxiety had built up inside me. How had she allowed this to go on? How had she allowed me to feel so unsafe in my own home? Her own child. I thought all these things, but somehow I couldn't express them to her, because I knew she wouldn't communicate. She would just be defensive.

That was the day I finally walked away. As I closed the farmyard gate behind me, I knew in my heart I was leaving my childhood home forever. I felt a sense of relief as I made my way up the lane, towards my brother Martin's house.

Martin was surprised to find me there on the doorstep, with my suitcase. I asked him if I could stay with him and his family for a little while, just until I found something more permanent. Of course, he said. I was always welcome there. I felt safe in Martin's house, knowing that I had left all that darkness behind me. A few months later Aidan and I got married and moved into the mobile home.

After a long chat, the doctors suggested that I may be suffering from post-traumatic stress disorder, from having experienced a lot of fear and anxiety as a child. They explained that childhood traumas can often resurface in adulthood, and can manifest in panic attacks and anxiety, which may explain what I was experiencing.

In a way I had never allowed myself to fully acknowledge how hurtful that was – feeling that my own parents didn't care if I stayed or went – but as I thought back on that time, I remembered how it really was, feeling like I had no place in the world, no home to call my own. I had to make my own way, my own life with Aidan. I think that's why I dropped out of art college. I knew I had to be able to stand on my own two feet.

I was exhausted from talking to the doctors. I thought I had put all that pain behind me, years before, that I had succeeded in moving on with my life, but now here they were, telling me that I couldn't escape it, that that darkness still held a power over me. I felt very drained and I didn't know what to think anymore. I wanted to go and find my husband.

'Are you sure you're feeling up to it?' one of the doctors asked.

I insisted that I was. The nurse pointed me towards a restaurant down the road. She had directed Aidan and the children there so he could get them something to eat. She could send for Aidan, she suggested, if that was better for me. I insisted I wanted to go and find him.

Stepping out of the hospital, I drew the air deep into my lungs. I walked slowly and carefully, cautious that I might fall again. As I passed strangers on the street, I felt as though, by looking at me, they might know what I had discussed with the doctors. I felt vulnerable all of a sudden, as though I was giving it all away. But of course, they didn't know. Because you never know what someone else is going through – someone you pass on the street some quiet Sunday afternoon.

I was deep in thought as I tried to make sense of everything that had happened. I replayed it in my mind: how I had lost all feeling in my legs as I had approached the castle gates. As the lights at the crossing changed from red to green, I stepped out into the road and suddenly an image flashed before me from when I was a child. It was of an old iron gate with a rhododendron branch hanging over it. It was the gate to my parents' farm. I wondered if that's what had triggered the anxiety attack – seeing a similar gate at the castle. Deep down, I knew that's where my fear was hiding – behind those old iron gates of my parents' farm. Somehow I had managed to keep them shut all these years, but now they seemed to be opening up again.

I arrived at the restaurant. As I walked through the double doors, the kids spotted me. They looked relieved, as did Aidan. He pulled a chair over from the next table. 'Sit down,' he said. 'How are you feeling?'

'Much better now,' I replied, sitting, and smiling at the children. 'Mammy just had a bit of a fall, that's all.'

Aidan waited until the children were engrossed in their chicken nuggets and chips before whispering to me, 'What did the doctors say?'

'A panic attack.'

'Thank God,' he said. 'I thought you were having a stroke.'

'I felt like I was dying,' I told him, quietly, so as not to alarm the children. 'They think it might be post-traumatic stress disorder.' I saw Adrienne look over, trying to listen in to our conversation. I hoped she hadn't heard me. As I reached to take a sip of water, my hand was shaking.

'Let's get you home,' said Aidan. And with that we packed the children into the car and headed off.

I had no idea then that my life was about to change. Nothing would ever be the same for me, or for Aidan, from that day on.

When we got home I went to lie down. I closed the curtains and made the room as dark as possible. My head was hurting. No matter how much water I drank, I couldn't seem to get rid of the headache. I lay in bed, trying to focus on the feeling of the cool crisp sheets and the softness of the pillow. I felt nauseous. I practised the deep breathing they had shown me at the hospital.

Aidan came in with a cup of tea. 'How are you?' he whispered.

'Still shook,' I said, propping myself up on the pillows.

We decided it would be best for Aidan to take the following day off work, just in case I fell again. A day turned to several days. I couldn't trust my body anymore. I felt like my legs may give way at any point. The thought of falling prompted the tingling in my fingers and feet all over again.

A week went by. 'I'm going to have to go back to work tomorrow,' Aidan said.

It was Sunday evening. I knew this had been coming. The thought terrified me. I still wasn't feeling right and I was afraid of being on my own with the children, worried that I might pass out while looking after them or, worse still, if I was driving them somewhere.

We made a plan and decided I would keep it simple, stick to the house, at least for the first while, in case another panic attack struck. And somehow, very quickly, that became my new normal. I stayed close to the house – all day, every day.

As invitations came in from friends, I politely declined. I came up with excuses for why I couldn't go. I just couldn't bring myself to meet people.

'Anne and Sean would love to see you,' Aidan suggested.

'Not yet. I'm not ready yet.' My usual reply.

I developed a routine – a way of being – that helped me to cope. I was able to predict what the day would bring and I was happy with that scenario. No surprises, no being caught out with a situation I couldn't handle, or that would be dangerous for the children.

Aidan started doing the weekly shop and dropping the children to school before work. I knew it was a lot to ask him, but I rationalised it in my mind: the risk of something happening to the children if I drove with them in the car far outweighed the inconvenience to Aidan.

Nevertheless, I could see it was all taking its toll on him. I saw the car come up the drive. Aidan parked up and hauled the shopping bags into the kitchen. He looked exhausted.

'Thanks for doing that,' I said.

'No problem,' he said, but I could see he was tired after a long day on the road. Aidan was still working as a sales rep for the paint company, which meant he was on the road a lot. His office was his car and a small room in our house. He was often very tired in the evenings, from driving all day. His job took him out west a lot too and up to Donegal on longer journeys.

'I'm just going to go and get a bit of paperwork done,' he added, heading towards his office.

'I'll put the shopping away,' I said.

'Thanks,' he replied, and gave me a smile.

As I started to put away the groceries, I felt a surge of frustration come over me. I felt pathetic. Why was I like this? I wished that I could do my fair share, the way I used to, but everything felt different now. It made me feel angry – with myself and with life. I turned on the gas light of the cooker, and instead of putting the saucepan down, I extended my arm and held it over the flame.

'Ahhhhh!' I winced as I felt a searing pain. But I didn't move. I kept my arm still over the flame as it burned my skin. I was watching myself, as if from above, not knowing why I was doing it. But somehow needing to feel, needing to pierce the numbness I was experiencing inside. I started to cry.

When I finally moved my arm, the wound was weeping. I placed it under the cold tap. I caught my reflection in the mirror near the sink. I hardly recognised the woman looking back at me, nursing her self-inflicted wound. Her eyes looked empty, and yet full of pain.

'What happened?' Aidan asked a few hours later, spotting the raw mark on my arm as I rolled up my sleeve to do the dishes.

'What do you mean?' I asked.

'Your arm.'

'Nothing,' I said, rolling my sleeve back down.

'That's definitely not nothing,' he said. 'It looks badly burnt. What happened?'

'I caught it in the cinders as I was stoking the fire,' I said, though I knew he wouldn't believe me.

Later that night, when the children were asleep, Aidan and I lay side by side in bed, neither of us saying a word. I could feel the tension in the air.

'How did it happen, Catherine?' he asked me again.

'I couldn't cope with what was going on in my head,' I said.

'And what happened?' he asked. 'You can tell me.'

I was silent.

'Catherine,' Aidan said, sitting up in the bed, 'you can tell me.'

'I held it over the gas light on the cooker,' I said, though I could hardly believe the words coming from my mouth.

He sat up a little taller. 'Why did you do that to yourself?' he said, trying not to sound angry.

'I can't explain it . . .' I said, and I couldn't. It just happened. I wondered if it was all part of the PTSD – these old wounds resurfacing.

As the weeks and months passed, I felt as though my world was getting darker, like the colour of life had faded. I was afraid of everything. Other things started happening that felt out of my control. At times I would find myself somewhere, in a situation, without fully realising what had brought me there.

Sometimes in the middle of the night, when I couldn't sleep, I would get out of bed and walk out of the house, down to the abandoned stone cottage at the bottom of the field where we stored our turf. I would sit there, in the damp, cold, quiet of that house, alone with my thoughts. Thinking, and yet not thinking. My headache felt a little better in that dark room surrounded by those old stone walls. I had no role to play there in that cottage. It didn't know me. I was nothing but skin and bone and a beating heart. It wanted nothing of me, nor me of it. It gave me a sense of calm.

One evening, I was sitting there in the cottage, soaking in the darkness of the night. My eyes were shut. It was quiet and still, not a breath of wind outside. Then, all of a sudden, I heard a noise. A crunching underfoot. I looked out the window. I could see nothing – it was pitch black. Then I heard the latch of the door open.

'Come back to bed, Catherine.'

It was Aidan. I could just about make out his shape, standing in the doorway.

'You frightened me!' I said.

'Well, you're frightening me with this carry-on,' he replied. 'Come back to bed.'

I didn't move. But neither did he. 'C'mon, Catherine, it's late,' he said.

I knew he couldn't understand what was happening, and I couldn't explain it. Because I didn't understand it either. I wasn't making it happen, it was happening to me. I walked over to Aidan. He put his arm around me. 'You're frozen,' he said, trying to warm me up as we walked towards the house and got back into bed.

As the months wore on I could feel Aidan watching me, trying to evaluate me, from day to day, when I sat down to my tea in the morning or when I went to bed at night. 'Morning. How are you?' he'd ask, though it was a loaded question.

He was watching for signs that I wasn't coping. And so it went on. We established a new kind of dynamic – a cautious one. I kept to the house as much as I could. It was difficult to imagine doing anything normal anymore, especially anything that involved other people. I grew anxious at the thought of socialising. But deep down, I knew I couldn't avoid it forever, much as I wished I could.

Aidan had a work night coming up, an important one – a dinner that spouses were expected to attend. He had been going to all his work nights alone, but I knew I was expected at this one. The date had been in my diary for weeks, and each day it was creeping ever closer. Though Aidan wasn't aware of the extent of my anxiety, I thought about it almost every day in the lead-up to the event – would I *have* to go, could I get out of it, how would Aidan feel if I didn't go to yet another one of his work nights. These questions went through my mind again and again.

The day finally came around. It took all my strength, but I didn't make an issue of it. Aidan came home from work to find me dressed for the party in a blouse and trouser set that I felt comfortable in. He looked surprised. 'Ready to go?' he said, gently.

'Yes,' I said.

We went through the motions, though we both knew there was a lot going on for both of us beneath the surface.

Aidan was worried about how I might behave, in front of all his work colleagues, and I was worried I might have another panic attack or that I'd find the social side of it too difficult. It felt like a façade that I didn't have the energy for. The constant chat. The noise of it all. My head hurt at the thought of it. All the unknown factors. And then there was the drinking.

We arrived at the venue – an old hotel outside of town. We parked up and made our way inside, to the banquet hall. As we walked in, I felt unwell, almost immediately. I looked around at all the glamorous women in their gowns, the men in their suits, all mingling, seemingly effortlessly. It was a salespersons' event. Everyone was beautiful and charismatic. They knew how to chat to people. Their conversation bounced back and forth with ease, and the noise and chaos of it all seemed to excite them. It was their fuel. I knew it wasn't mine. But I was doing my best to appear sociable, for Aidan's sake. I smiled as he introduced me to circles of his colleagues. The inevitable questions followed: what do you do? I found that question hard to answer. I hadn't had a 'job' in a long time. 'I raise children' is what I wanted to say, but it never seemed like the answer people were looking for. 'I manage the farm,' I said, which surprised them, but they seemed satisfied with that.

As the evening wore on, I made several trips to the bathroom. It was a chance to sit in silence for a few minutes. I came back to the table, hoping it would be time to go home.

'I'll get this round!' Aidan said, taking a mental note of what everyone was drinking. 'Another soda water?' he asked me. I didn't take alcohol.

I nodded and tried to subtly catch his eye. He turned to look away from me and went straight to the bar. He knew what I was trying to say to him. 'Enough now, Aidan. Enough.'

It was 2 a.m. and the pints were still flowing. Aidan returned with the drinks. I sat and sipped my soda water, watching the minutes go by. Aidan became more jovial as the night went on. There was no sign of us leaving.

When he stood to go to the bathroom, I followed him out into the lobby and tapped him on the shoulder. 'Can we go home?' I asked.

He looked disappointed. 'Just one more,' he said.

'I can't do it, Aidan. I need to go home,' I said. I put my hand to my head. I could feel a headache coming on.

'I'll get my jacket,' he said reluctantly.

'I'll see you at the car,' I said.

The drive home was quiet. Neither of us had much to say. The roads were dark, not a street light in sight, as we slinked our way through the night, back towards the farm. Aidan started nodding off. I welcomed the calm of the car and the cool night air. I breathed a sigh of relief as I parked outside the house. Home, I thought, at last.

I went to the kitchen to get a pint of water, and placed it on Aidan's bedside table. My head hit the pillow. I closed my eyes, and felt a weight lift off me. I had survived it, the whole night, without a single incident.

The next morning, Aidan was groggy. He woke late.

'Sausages are heating in the oven,' I said, as he came into the kitchen, looking tired. I knew it wasn't going to be a good day. I could sense it. 'I've to check on the cows,' I said, as I headed out the back door to the boot room.

I kept to myself for the day. I needed to tend to the cattle and feed the sheep. There were jobs to be done, and that kept me busy until tea time. At least the cattle didn't talk to me, didn't expect me to be a certain way. I could be myself. We were happy in silence, the cow and me. That's why I loved nature – there were no falsehoods, no pretence. Everything was very raw and real. And practical. We all did what we needed to, to get by.

By evening time Aidan seemed in better form. The worst of the hangover had worn off. But there was an unspoken tension between us. A kind of heavy disappointment. Somehow we weren't what we needed the other to be. And maybe we both wondered if we ever would be again, if we had it in us to be *us* again.

'Are you not eating?' Aidan said, as he saw the table set for one.

'Not hungry,' I said. 'I'm tired. I'm going to bed.'

I went to the bedroom, feeling his loneliness as he sat by himself at the table, and mine as I went to bed alone. I didn't have the energy to talk, to pretend I was anything but exhausted. I was tired all the time. I got into bed and pulled the duvet around me. I heard Aidan open the door.

'Catherine,' he said. 'Catherine?'

I turned to face him.

'We have to do something about this. We can't let it go on.'

'I know,' I said.

There was a long silence.

'It scares me,' I said.

He sat on the bed beside me. 'I know, but we'll do it together, okay? You and me. Promise. We'll make things better.' He placed

72

his hand on my hand. I loved him so much in that moment. I knew that he meant it too. He would be there with me, through anything. I knew that.

The next morning, as I lay in bed, I watched the early-morning light shining through the crack in the curtains, as it danced on the wall of the bedroom. I felt a new sense of determination. I decided I was willing to do whatever it took to get better. I owed it to Aidan to do that. And I owed it to myself. And the kids.

I made an appointment and went back to the doctor who referred me to the psychiatric unit in Galway for assessment. There, a psychiatrist listened to my symptoms and I was put on medication.

When I got home, I looked at the bottles of pills laid out on the bedside table, all the different colours – chemicals to mix in my brain and make me whole again. Was this what I was missing – vital parts of my brain contained in these capsules of blue and green? I just had to hope they would work their magic and bring me back to myself again.

I took them, dutifully, every day. But after a few weeks, I started to question whether they were working. 'I don't know if this is doing anything,' I said to Aidan one night as I took my tablets before bed.

I still felt tired all the time, and down. That's the only way I can describe it. I was constantly deflated. No matter what the day brought or what happiness presented itself, I couldn't see the beauty in things. I couldn't see anything anymore. I was just surviving. And barely at that.

Aidan picked up the Sunday papers that weekend, as he always did. We sat in the kitchen reading them over a cup of tea. I read the main section, then started flicking through the magazine. Something caught my eye – a headline about someone suffering from anxiety and panic attacks. I read the piece. When nothing else would work, it said, she had tried something called electric shock therapy. The woman in the article said it had changed her life completely.

I left the article out on the kitchen table for Aidan to see. For the rest of the day, the words from the interview ran through my mind. It sounded frightening, but after reading that woman's testimony about how well it had worked, I started to wonder whether I should try it – if it was something that was done in Ireland. If there was a chance it could work . . . I just might be willing to give it a go.

I told Aidan I wanted to try it.

'Are you sure about this?' he asked, as he finished reading the article. 'It sounds . . .'

'I know,' I said. 'But to be honest, it can't be worse than this.'

He looked at me when I said that. I knew I had hurt him. It's hard to tell someone who doesn't have anxiety what it's like or how hard it is to live with. It wasn't that I was unhappy with our lives, or with him. It wasn't like that. I knew Aidan would do anything, change anything about our lives, if he thought it would help, but it wasn't about our life together or anything he was or wasn't doing. It was about me. The inside of my brain. It was internal, not external. And I would do anything I could to fix it. To make it stop. To make the darkness stop. I wanted to be able to rear my kids – to be there for them in every way I could for as long as I could. This was holding me back and I wasn't going to let it get the better of me.

I sat opposite the doctor as he explained the procedure. They would put me under general anaesthetic, he explained. Once I was sufficiently sedated, they would attach a clamp to my tongue. This would deliver the electric shock. It worked by recreating the effects of a seizure and thereby altering the chemicals in your brain. At least that's how I understood it.

Aidan was with me in the doctor's office. 'Seizure?' he said, taken aback.

The doctor reassured him that it wasn't dangerous.

'Will it hurt?' I asked.

'You won't feel a thing,' he told me.

'Will I remember it afterwards?'

He told me that I wouldn't. I would be unconscious for the whole thing and, all going well, would wake up as though nothing had happened. The doctor told me that I might feel quite groggy for a while, and there was a chance I would have a headache too. I asked about the success rates. Positive, he said. The outlook was optimistic. For some, it worked wonders.

I decided I would begin the treatment the following week. Aidan drove me to my first appointment. We were both nervous. 'Ready?' he asked, as he fetched the car keys from the table.

I nodded. 'Ready as I'll ever be.'

Aidan was worried, I could see it in his face. I just focused on the fact that this was a way to get better, and how good it would be to feel better, at last.

We arrived early to the hospital. When my time came, they guided me into a small room and told me to sit into what looked like a dentist's chair. They explained the process. When everything was ready, they injected the sedative into my arm, and attached the clamp to my tongue. Then everything went dark.

When I came to, my head felt heavy and I was disorientated. 'Where am I?' I asked the nurse.

'You're in the hospital,' she said. 'You've just had the electrotherapy procedure. How are you feeling?'

'Tired,' I said.

I just wanted to sleep and sleep. But in my own bed. I wanted to get there as soon as possible. When it was time to go home, Aidan brought the car up to the front door. He gave me his arm to lean on as we made our way slowly out of the hospital and into the car park.

'Can I lie out on the back seat?' I asked. I didn't have the energy to sit in the front.

Aidan helped to lower me into the car. When we got home I went straight to bed. The children came to see me and brought me a cup of tea. My heart lifted immediately at the sight of them, all four lined up at the bottom of the bed.

For the next few weeks, I tried to keep a normal routine, so that the children didn't feel anything was out of the ordinary. But I wasn't fully myself, and I think they were starting to notice.

'How was school today?' I asked Alicia one afternoon.

'I told you already, Mam,' she said, looking confused. 'I drew a butterfly, remember?'

I didn't remember.

'That one,' she said, pointing.

And sure enough, there it was – the butterfly drawing taped to the fridge door. I must have put it there. But how had I forgotten that?

The doctors had warned me that my memory might be affected for a few weeks. And that I would get headaches. The headaches were difficult, but nothing that Solpadeine couldn't solve, and even though the memory loss was a bit unnerving at times, I reminded myself that it was only minor.

Aidan was on the road with work as he had some important sales to get across the line. I tried to look after the kids as best I could, but I was more tired than usual. Not quite myself. Somehow, Adrienne seemed to pick up on this. Even though she was only eleven years old, she was naturally maternal and kicked into action to help me organise the others. Alan was nine and full of energy, as was seven-year-old Alicia and four-year-old Aaron.

I went to wake the children one morning as I always did, but when I opened the door to their bedroom I found their beds empty. I followed the trail of teddy bears and pyjama bottoms to the kitchen, where I saw all four of them dressed and sitting at the table eating their Weetabix. Adrienne had made it her business to get her sister and brothers out of bed, dressed and ready for the day. She was beaming with pride as I walked into the kitchen.

'Look at you all dressed and ready!' I said. They were all very excited to have surprised me. 'Thank you,' I whispered to Adrienne, giving her a kiss on the forehead.

I continued with the electrotherapy treatment. I had four procedures in total. It was taking its toll on my body – and I was very tired.

'Do you think it's working?' Aidan asked. I could see the look of hope in his eyes.

'Of course,' I said.

Though I wasn't sure at all. I just needed to believe that it was working, that it could make things better. And he did too, I could see that. What use would it be to doubt it? At least if we believed it might work, we might help the process along. That's the way I looked at it.

And it did seem to be helping a bit, though not as much as I had hoped. I tried to be more positive around Aidan and the kids, but deep down I had all the same feelings, I was just trying to battle it on my own.

When it was later discovered that my womb had relapsed, it was suggested that my hormones could be acting up. They gave me a couple of options – more medication, or a hysterectomy. I weighed it up, and even though I was quite young for a hysterectomy – I was just 34 – it seemed to make the most sense. They could remove the problem, take it out of my body. And we were finished having children; we were very happy with our four. So I decided that's what I should do.

I went into the surgery knowing I would come back changed. Without my womb – the space that had grown my four beautiful children. Their first home.

As the doctor injected the sedative into my arm, I felt myself drift off to sleep. When I woke, I was disorientated. I looked down at my body. There was a layer of tinfoil tightly wrapped around me, with warm air blasting out of a blow-heater in my direction, and yet I was shivering. Aidan was by my side, sweltering with the heat.

A doctor came in and examined me. 'We thought we would have to rush you to theatre again, but we have found the bleeder,' she said. I saw her make the sign of the cross as she turned away.

I was in the ICU for the next two days, where they inserted drips into my arms and kept an eye on my vitals.

'Time to move onto the ward,' the nurse said one afternoon. I felt confused. 'Okay,' I said.

They told me that all had gone very well. 'A success,' she said.

'That's good,' I said. I felt exhausted. I was wheeled out onto the ward, where they would keep an eye on me for a few more days.

The ward was dark and quiet at night. After the rush of intensive care, my mind was attempting to come to terms with what had just happened. As I lay in bed, I put my hand on my stomach, as I had done so many times when I was pregnant, to feel what was growing inside. But this time, as I rested my hand on that same sacred space, I waited to see what emotion might come over me. And then I felt it. Relief. It wasn't what I expected, and I experienced a pang of guilt for feeling that way. As though I should have been mourning a part of me, a part of my womanhood, but instead feeling like a weight had been lifted.

I had been worried that I would become pregnant again, that if I had another child, I wouldn't be able to look after it. At least not the way I thought I should. Especially the way I had been feeling lately. I knew that I wouldn't be able to give it the love it deserved. That, with too many children, my love and attention would be divided, and I would become distant from my children, like my mother had been. I was the fifth child in my family and I knew what that felt like and it's not something I wanted to do to any child.

I had also worried that if I didn't have the hysterectomy, my mental health might deteriorate. I had sworn to myself that I would mind my children and keep them safe, always. And I was prepared to do anything to keep that promise.

I lay there, knowing that my body was changed forever. This was me now: a woman without a womb. From the outside, no more or less than I had been before. But to know there was a cavity there, a nothingness, in a space that had created so much life. I closed my eyes tight and thanked my womb for all that it had given me – those children, who made life worthwhile, who kept me going, no matter what. I thought of that piece of flesh – where was it now, that part of my anatomy, which had been cut out of me. Then I thought of the life it could no longer create.

I thought of women who yearned with all their hearts to become mothers, who checked their pregnancy tests, watching, waiting for a double blue line to emerge, heartbroken when only one appeared. And those who bled in the middle of the night, and cried for a lost child who they had already imagined a life for, who they already knew in their hearts, and in their womb.

It is a sacred space, the womb. But it is also a place that can cause great pain for women – the endless hormones, the suffering. It is little talked about – the madness that comes with pregnancy and birth. They call it 'baby brain' and 'brain fog'; they call it 'hormonal' and 'postnatal'. There are many names for it, but only a woman who has lived it knows what it is really like to have her mind controlled by her womb, that silent part of her anatomy that gives so fruitfully and takes so ruthlessly in return.

It was time to let it go – that part of me, that part of my life. For the sake of my sanity. I could only hope that this would help me to think clearly again, to feel present again. To be me again.

What I didn't realise is that I would soon be letting go of a whole lot more.

CHAPTER THIRTEEN

The Call

◠

I'll never forget that call. It came one quiet Friday afternoon. Out of the blue. I suppose that's how these things happen sometimes.

It was my sister Mary. 'You need to come quick,' she said. 'Mam's taken a bad turn.' My mother had collapsed, she told me.

Aidan took the kids, and I rushed up to my mother's house. I was full of dread for what I was about to see or what might happen next.

She was worse than I imagined. She could barely lift her head from the pillow. The moment I saw her, my tears started falling. I had never cried in front of my family like that before. There was something about her powerlessness that shocked me. A woman who was always so strong, so stoic, suddenly so weak and vulnerable. She had never seemed as though she needed anyone. And now she needed us more than ever, and we were powerless to help her.

That evening she was brought to hospital by ambulance. I went up to the ward with my brother Martin. The whole family gathered around. It was clear what was happening – we were losing her. The team at the hospital were surprised by how quickly she was deteriorating. The last thing she said was, 'Where's Michael?' He was travelling from County Offaly.

I was sitting in the corridor. All of a sudden, the doctors rushed past in a frenzy. There was a lot of moving around inside the room, and then there was silence. At that moment, I felt a gentle breeze passing my face and going eastwards. I don't know how I knew, but I knew it was her. And just like that, my mother was gone.

I never shed another tear for her after that. Maybe because I felt she was going to have a bit of peace at last. All her life she had a tortured soul. Now, at last, she could rest easy. No more nightmares, no more secrets.

I didn't cry at her funeral. I watched her being carried away. It was like we were back to the way we were again. She and I. I just felt angry. In my head I just kept saying, 'What was wrong with me, Mam? What was wrong with me, that we couldn't be friends?' The hurt ran deep and I felt numb, all at the same time. As I watched her being lowered into the ground, I knew there was no going back. No chance to make things right. What was would always be.

'What was wrong with me, Mam? What was wrong with me?'

CHAPTER FOURTEEN

One for the Road

~

We tried to get on with life after the funeral, to pick up where we had left off. But it wasn't easy. Just because you have one problem doesn't mean you can keep everything else at bay. This was something we were starting to learn the hard way. I should have seen it coming. I should have known where we were headed, but sometimes these things creep up slowly and start to become normal somehow, and by the time you fully see it, it's too late.

I continued taking my medication and going for electric shock therapy. It seemed to be working. It was keeping things stable. But as I got better, Aidan got worse. As the years wore on, he was drinking more and more.

It started slowly, in ways you wouldn't pay much heed to. He would binge drink at weddings and family events. By the end of the night, he wouldn't be able to hold himself up and we'd have to take him home. I dreaded going to any kind of event that would serve alcohol, because I knew how it would end. I hated seeing Aidan drunk, because of what I had witnessed in childhood. I had seen the damage alcohol could do – how it could destroy a home and the people in it. For that reason, I never drank, but the reality was that Aidan was drinking and he continued to drink. To everyone else, it just seemed like great craic and that Aidan was a character. Everyone loved him and the drink just made him all the more jovial. It was the after-effects that people didn't see, that no one ever admits to. All the things that come with alcohol – the exhaustion the next day, the depleted energy. This went on for about ten years.

Over time, Aidan started drinking on a more regular basis. It wasn't just for events or family occasions. He was stopping by the pub after work every evening and coming home drunk. Every night was the same. I got used to going to bed alone. I would stay awake to hear him arriving home. I pretended to be asleep, I lay very still as he made his way into the bed. The smell of alcohol on his breath made me feel sick. He would fall asleep immediately and snore loudly. I tossed and turned, and when I couldn't take it anymore, I went downstairs and slept on the couch.

But one night Aidan didn't come home. I waited for the familiar sound of the key in the door, followed by the fumbling downstairs, and the steps up to the bedroom. I waited to feel him sliding into bed beside me. But there was nothing, no sign of him. I turned on the bedside lamp and looked at my watch. It was 3 a.m.

I put on my dressing gown and went downstairs. 'Aidan?' I called. 'Aidan?' No answer. I went from room to room turning on the lights, checking to see if he'd fallen asleep on one of the chairs. He wasn't there. I started to panic.

I ran out into the yard. No car in the driveway. He hadn't come home by car. Unless he had tried to walk home, or he had been given a lift by someone. I heard a noise – a fox rummaging around the yard. I must have startled him. He leaped into the next field.

The sheds, I thought. He might be in the sheds. I ran across the field, opened the door and called for him, 'Aidan?'

'Aidan!' I yelled. I was worried he might have fallen over. I ran back into the house and fetched my coat. I grabbed the torch from the kitchen. I decided I would retrace his steps – all the way to the pub. I ran out the gate and searched the ditches all along the road, yelling his name. I was shaking. I walked quickly, shining the torch into the hedges and the surrounding fields as I went. It was a dark night, pitch black. And then, as I rounded the next corner, I thought I saw something.

I shone my torch in that direction. It was a car – *our* car – at the side of the road by the ditch. I ran as fast as I could, 'Aidan!' I screamed. I reached the car, and saw Aidan slumped over the steering wheel. I opened the door. 'Aidan! Are you okay?' I shook him.

His eyes opened. He looked disorientated. 'Where am I?' he said.

'At the side of the road . . . you didn't come home.'

He rubbed his eyes and tried to make sense of what was happening. 'Are you alright?' he asked me.

'I'm fine,' I said. 'It's you I'm worried about. You're freezing. Let's get you home,' I said.

Aidan moved into the passenger seat and I drove us both home. When we were safely inside the house, I wrapped a blanket around him and handed him a cup of tea. 'I put a good bit of sugar in it,' I said. I was hoping it would help with the shock. I rubbed his back and tried to return the warmth to his body. He looked exhausted. 'Let's get you into bed,' I said. I helped him up the stairs. I didn't want him to fall.

The next morning, Aidan slept in. He came downstairs eventually. 'What happened?' he asked, as he entered the kitchen.

'You didn't come home,' I said. 'I found you parked by the ditch half a mile away.'

Aidan looked shook. I put on the kettle to make him a cup of coffee. He seemed ashamed of what had happened. But frustrated too. He went to take a cup from the press, but lost his grip. The cup fell to the floor and smashed into pieces. 'Fuck!' he said, pounding the cupboard with his fist.

I fetched the dustpan and brush and swept up the bits of porcelain scattered across the floor and threw them in the bin. Aidan's eyes were closed as he leant against the cupboard.

'I'm going to go and do some work on the farm,' I said. I walked out the door. I wanted to leave the kitchen quickly so Aidan wouldn't see that I was upset. It was relief more than anything. Relief that Aidan had made it home. That he was okay. I wouldn't know what to do if anything ever happened to him.

As I walked towards the cattle shed, a heavy feeling came over me. I blamed myself for letting things get so bad. I should have done something years ago, I thought to myself. But I also wondered what I could possibly have done.

I just wished I could feel Aidan again, in the way that I used to. That closeness. I wished that I could bring him back.

He was always the one who was able to make things better. The one who made me and the children laugh. He was the fun dad and the loving husband. But not anymore. That Aidan was slipping away. Day by day, parts of him were disappearing, and I didn't know if I was ever going to see him again. How do you grieve someone who is still alive – who is still there, in front of you, and yet not there?

Everyone's relationship with alcohol is different. Some people drink every day. Aidan was never like that. Aidan's problem was not knowing when to stop. He had a preference for spirits, and one drink would turn into two, and quickly into three.

And it was all part of the culture, which didn't help. When we went to visit family, relatives would say, 'Ah, you'll have a drink . . . what'll you have?' And he wouldn't be able to say no. Whenever he got a taste of alcohol on those occasions, he would always follow it up by going to the pub at night. We would leave as a family but then Aidan would peel off on the way home and spend the night in the pub. The kids seemed to get used to it. That's what broke my heart.

As they got a little bit older, they began to opt out of visiting those relatives. We all dreaded weddings and funerals. Even Christmas became something none of us looked forward to. Any family celebration was wrought with nervous energy – waiting for Dad to get drunk. In the beginning, months could go by when Aidan would be completely sober, but as time passed, the gaps between binges became shorter.

He was never aggressive or violent in any way – he didn't have it in him to be like that. But the drinking was self-destructive. I worried that something would happen to him when he was in that state – that he'd drive the car and have an accident, or fall down the stairs or something like that.

By the time the children were in their twenties, we had weathered a lot as a family and they were starting to speak their minds. One Sunday evening, it all came to a head. Aidan was out at the pub when Alan, our elder son, who had long since moved out of the house, came to pay us a visit for Sunday lunch. I gave him a hug at the door and welcomed him in for a cup of tea. I loved to see the kids coming home. No matter how old they got or how long they were out of the house, it was like a piece of the jigsaw slotting into place when they walked back through the door. I watched Alan as he took off his coat and sat down to the table. He had grown into such a lovely, gentle young man.

'Tea?' I asked.

'Yes, please,' he said. 'Do you need a hand with anything, Mam, while I'm here?'

He was always trying to help us, always wanting to see what he could do to mind us. It's funny how the tables turn – you mind them and then they mind you. But they pretend not to. To make you feel like the parents still.

'Nothing at all,' I said. 'Thanks, though.'

We sat and talked about how his life was going. He was working in merchandising and delivery for Fleetwood paints. Following in his father's footsteps. He was enjoying it, he told me, and it was working out well for him. He also had a joke or two to cheer me up, as he always did. Then he turned to matters of a more serious nature.

'And how are things here, Mam?' he asked.

'Ah, you know yourself, we're ticking along,' I said with a smile.

'Where's Dad today?' asked Alan, though he knew the answer.

'He's just popped up to the pub for a drink,' I said. 'He'll be back soon, I'm sure.'

But he wasn't back soon. Hours passed. Alan waited with me. When a natural break came, instead of getting up to go, he would move the conversation on to something else, prolonging his visit. I could sense he wanted to see his father when he came home. We were in the sitting room, talking by the fire, when the front door opened.

Aidan fumbled in the hallway, then came into the room. 'Alan!' he said jovially, moving towards him for a hug. He was obviously very drunk.

Usually we all continued as though everything was normal, but this time was different. Alan stood up with an expression on his face I had never seen before. He was angry, very angry. 'How did you get home, Dad?' he asked pointedly.

Aidan was taken aback. Suddenly the mood in the room was very serious. 'I drove,' he said.

'You drove?' said Alan, raising his voice. 'How many drinks have you had today, Dad?'

'Ah, I had one or two. What's it to you?' said Aidan, getting defensive.

'One or two?' Alan was yelling now. 'You've never in your life had one or two! Who do you think you're fooling?'

'Who do you think you are, talking to me like this in my own house?'

The yelling intensified. I had never seen Alan so angry. It was like all the years of hurt and pain and disappointment that had been locked away inside him were suddenly coming to the surface. I walked out of the room, listening from the kitchen as the argument got louder and louder.

No one had ever stood up to Aidan before. No one had spelled it out – that what he was doing was dangerous, and stupid. It was going to kill him if he didn't stop. It was escalating into an enormous row. Somehow I knew to stay out of it. They needed to fight it out themselves.

Then I heard the front door bang and a car start in the driveway. I hoped to God it wasn't Aidan. I went to the window. It was Alan's car driving away. I thought about going into the sitting room to check on Aidan. That would have been the humane thing to do. But instead I just looked out the window, at the gap where Alan's car had been.

I didn't have it in me to go and console Aidan – to tell him Alan had overreacted or not to take it to heart. Though I knew that's what he was waiting for me to do. I couldn't, because I didn't believe any of those things. Alan was right, in everything he said, and it was a long time coming.

I was angry too. Angry at all the times we'd watched Aidan

get drunk, all the times I had to explain to the children why Daddy was going to be home late. The times I pretended he was at work, just to give him a sense of dignity.

When it was clear I wasn't coming into the sitting room, Aidan walked into the kitchen. He looked deflated. He had been crying. I expected him to be on the defensive, as he always was.

But this time was different.

'Is he right?' he asked me, quietly. 'Do I have a problem?'

I looked at him. How could he even be asking that question? Surely to God he knew the answer. I nodded. 'He's right,' I said, exasperated.

We talked it through. Something had to change, I told him. Or it would break us all. We agreed that we would find a counsellor, as a starting point. The following morning I looked online and booked an appointment for Aidan.

And sure enough, Aidan followed through. Instead of going to the pub that week, he went to see the counsellor. He was trying. I was proud of him for that. Maybe this time things would be different. I asked him how it had gone. 'Do you feel you clicked with him?'

Aidan didn't say much. 'Yeah, it was fine.'

I decided not to probe, hoping he would find his own way through the process.

But as the months wore on, things slipped back into their old ways, and the counselling didn't seem to be changing his behaviour at all. I chose my moment, one night as we were going to bed. 'How is it going with the counsellor?' I asked.

Aidan's breath smelled of drink.

'Have you been honest with him about the extent of things?'

'Look, I'm tired of all this. I don't have a problem,' he said. 'I'm just sociable. I'm entitled to a few drinks every now and again.'

He said sociable because we both knew I wasn't. It was me

who was the odd one, who couldn't appreciate a drink and a laugh with people. And somehow I was making him out to be the problem. All that was implied in that one cutting word.

The arrogance of it, I thought to myself. When he was drinking us all away – everything we had worked and lived for. This happy life. Disappearing down the drain like a flat Guinness.

I turned over in the bed and pulled the duvet around me. There was no point in talking to him anymore.

The next day I made a decision – I would speak to the counsellor myself, to be sure he knew just how bad things were for Aidan. I felt guilty interfering, but there was no point in Aidan going to a counsellor if it wasn't doing any good.

When Aidan was out one afternoon, I drove to the counsellor's private rooms and knocked on the door.

'Hello?' said a voice from inside. 'Come in . . .'

'Sorry to disturb you,' I said. 'My name is Catherine Corless, I'm Aidan's wife.'

He looked surprised. 'Sit down,' he said.

I sat down. I explained that I just wanted to let him know what was happening with Aidan – so that he wasn't getting the wrong impression. I explained how bad his drinking was and how much it meant to the whole family to help him to give it up, for his own health and safety. I told him about how I found bottles hidden in the house and about his binge drinking.

He seemed shocked at this disclosure. Because of patient confidentiality, he said he couldn't discuss the matter any further.

Just as I was leaving, he said, 'Look, I like Aidan . . .'

'So do I,' I said. 'He's my best friend.'

I couldn't help but feel angry that the counselling wasn't helping more. I wanted other people to see the urgency, for the counsellor to realise just what we had lost in losing Aidan, as he was, and had always been. He didn't know Aidan, the real Aidan, and what an incredible man he was. He didn't know how much we were missing him and what it would mean to the kids to have their dad back again.

But nevertheless, it was Aidan's fight to fight, and I knew I shouldn't be getting involved behind his back. I just wished there was a type of electric shock therapy or surgery that would help him. Some quick fix that would make things better.

I had accepted that anxiety and panic attacks were part of my life. They had become part of who I was. Things became easier once I accepted that fact. I was able to cope when the anxiety was overpowering, because I had come to realise that it would pass and there were more good days than bad. I continued to take my anxiety medication and it was helping. Being outdoors also helped, walking the fields or working in the garden. I had learned to avoid noise, and crowds and social activities. I had coping mechanisms and medication to help keep me stable. I felt lucky in a way because, for me, there was a strategy, a way of keeping my demons at bay.

But for alcoholism, there seemed to be no such thing. It felt like we just had to figure it out ourselves – muddle through somehow and hope that Aidan could stay sober.

The kids were worried too. I got the sense they were talking among themselves about how they could help. Adrienne and Alicia came to the house one day to discuss things with me. They had an idea, they said. They told me about an addiction centre in Dublin, and presented some information on it. It just might work, they said . . . if their dad would ever agree to it.

The centre had an eight-week programme to help people through their addiction. From what I could gather, the approach was that they would work with Aidan to get him to realise and admit that he had a problem. This, for me, was crucial. It was at the very heart of things. Until he admitted there was a problem, nothing was going to work.

For years we had been tip-toeing around, trying to make him realise what was happening, but he was always on the defensive and would blame everyone else. The excuses were endless: that he had to accompany a customer to the pub or that he had to be sociable or couldn't offend a relative by refusing a drink from them.

After some very difficult conversations, Aidan agreed to try the treatment programme, begrudgingly. He was feeling pressured into it, with the whole family involved. It wasn't what he wanted to do, I could see that. I watched him as he packed his bag. He was getting ready to check himself in to the rehabilitation centre for eight weeks. He was silent. He didn't want to speak to me or have anything to do with me that night.

How did we get here? I wondered. I thought of that first night in the Ranch House in Cummer when Aidan took me by the hands and spun me around. When we laughed and were carefree. So much ahead of us then. Now I felt we had so much behind us, and I could no longer see the road ahead. For the first time in my life, I couldn't see where we were going together. Nothing made sense. Through everything we had experienced – the anxiety and panic attacks – I had always felt like we were in it together. Now I felt we were drifting apart and I didn't know how to stop that from happening. We had always been a team. Until now.

Aidan folded his shirts and put them into the suitcase the way he would if we were going on a trip together. The Aidan standing in front of me was sober. It was as though everything was normal. So it seemed wrong that the real Aidan, the sober Aidan, was the one packing to go away. He was the one I wanted to stay.

That's the hardest part – when you think you know someone, and then they seem to be someone else. That was true of both of us. We were different people now than when we were younger.

You know that the real them is still there, deep down, if only you could help them come out again. And you see glimpses of them – snatches of moments during the day that remind you they're there. And then they're gone again.

It was those moments that were keeping me going, knowing that Aidan was in there, and hoping that with some professional help he would walk back through the door in a few weeks' time. That's what we were all clinging to, that hope.

The next morning we drove to the clinic in Dublin. We parked outside the building and stared out the window for a moment, neither of us saying a word.

'Right, I better get going,' said Aidan, taking his bag from the back seat.

'Good luck,' I said.

I watched as he walked up to the door, bag in hand. It was a lonely walk, going into that battle on his own. I wished that I could do it with him, hold his hand through it. But I knew he had to do this alone, that it wouldn't do any good to be there with him, because I had been with him all this time and I hadn't been able to help him. Maybe now, in the hands of professionals, he would get the help he needed.

He turned at the door and gave me a wave. I waved back. I thought of the moment at the bottom of the hill at my aunt's house – that day that he asked me to the dance, when I turned and caught his eye. We were a lifetime away from that now.

That night I woke with a fright when I reached across the bed and Aidan wasn't there. I sat up, and then I remembered – he was in the hospital.

Two months was a long time. The programme was very tough, and Aidan was finding it all very difficult. I visited once a week. I took the train to Dublin, then a bus to the centre. But neither of us had much to say to the other. It was a long way to go to sit in silence. It was strained, awkward. I looked across at him.

When things take a turn, it's incredible how someone you once felt so much warmth from can suddenly turn to stone, can look at you in a whole new way. Without love. It's how we were looking at each other lately. And it was hurting us both so much.

The anger had built up between us. Years of hurt and pain. It should have been a relief, the fact that he was getting help, but somehow it seemed to bring up a lot of unexpressed emotions. And Aidan felt he was going through hell, trapped somewhere he didn't want to be. Because of me.

Eight weeks later, when he walked back through the door, I wanted to ask how he was or what he had gone through, but I was afraid he might blame me, so I didn't ask. It would be up to him to tell me, in his own way, in his own time.

I waited to see if things would improve.

CHAPTER FIFTEEN

Walk the Line

⌒

Aidan was in a bad place after the treatment programme. He was angry all the time. With me. With himself. With everyone and everything.

But somehow, despite how he was feeling, the programme seemed to have worked. He hadn't touched a drink since coming home. Months went by and still no sign of drink in the house, no smell of it on his breath. Cautiously, I began to relax. To breathe again. Finally, we could put this behind us. Or so I thought.

Then I found the thing I feared most. One morning I went to fetch an old pair of shoes from the back of the wardrobe to do some gardening. And there they were, two bottles of whiskey. Hidden behind the old shoe boxes.

The next few months were difficult. Our relationship was suffering. I felt betrayed all over again and I was angrier than I had ever been before. And so was Aidan. On his bad days he could be very mean. Never violent, it wasn't in him to be violent. But he wasn't Aidan. He snapped and growled. On those days I pretended he was someone else. It made it easier somehow. Because he *was* someone else when he was drinking, and even when he wasn't drinking, as time went on there was less and less of his old self there. And without Aidan, there was no 'us' either. Addiction is like that: it doesn't just take away the person, it takes all their relationships too – rots them, slowly, over time.

I stayed out with the animals for as long as I could every day. I found reasons to be away from Aidan. But I was feeling trapped. The house and farm were the only places in the world where I had felt safe. And now, it was the saddest place to be. No kids. No Aidan. Just me and a drunken man I didn't recognise.

The addiction centre had recommended that Aidan go to AA meetings. He had gone to a few, but then decided they weren't for him. 'It's demoralising,' he'd said. 'I can't do that anymore.' I didn't press him on it because I came to realise that putting him under pressure achieved the opposite result.

As an alternative, the treatment programme proposed that he could attend facilitated meetings. They might suit you more, they suggested. A group of people suffering from addiction came together, gathered in a circle and spoke of their difficulties. Like AA meetings, but in a more casual setting.

For some reason, this appealed to Aidan and he agreed to go to his first meeting. I was expected to come too. So we made the trip back to Dublin. I had to stop myself from thinking we were going backwards, finding ourselves in that familiar car park, walking up to the door of the treatment centre again. I had to think positively. Any kind of help is a positive step forward, I told myself.

And it was at one of these meeting that one of the facilitators said something to me that helped enormously. 'This is not your fault,' he said. 'Even if you were an axe-murderer, it would have nothing to do with Aidan's drinking.'

When I heard that, I felt a weight lift from my chest. So much guilt comes with addiction. You feel it's your place to help the other person to stop, and when they don't stop, you blame yourself.

Something about those meetings seemed to spark a change in Aidan. Maybe it was listening to other people's stories, maybe it was telling his own, out loud for others to hear. I don't know what it was exactly, but he seemed different afterwards. But it was short-lived and he was back drinking soon again.

On his good days Aidan made promises – promises that things would get better, promises that he would be sober from now on – but I had learned from the family day meetings in the addiction centre that anyone who has an alcohol problem will agree to anything or will promise anything you ask them to promise. It's a defence, just to get you off their back.

It was one thing making promises to me, but when he made a promise to our daughter Alicia, I worried he would let her down. And on the most important day of her life.

One evening, he came home early from the pub.

I was surprised to see him coming through the door. 'Is everything okay?' I asked, as he sat down in the kitchen. 'Did something happen?'

He looked shook. 'It's Alicia,' he said. 'She wanted to talk to me about the wedding . . .' He paused. 'She wants me to walk her down the aisle, but only if I'm sober, she says.' He had his head in his hands. 'How did things come to this?' he said. 'How did it get to be this bad?'

'It'll be okay,' I said. For a moment, I caught a glimpse of the old Aidan. I wanted to hug him and tell him never to leave again. I could see how much all this was hurting him.

He loved Alicia, like he loved all the children: with all his heart. I knew it would have taken all her courage to say that to her father, to ask him to do that for her. She adored him. He was her hero. And she must have known it would hurt him to hear those words.

'What did you say to her?' I asked.

'I promised her I would.'

We were both silent. We felt the weight of that promise. It would have been easy for me to say that he would be able to do it, but the wedding was months away yet, and the truth was, neither of us knew whether or not to believe him. We couldn't trust him anymore. He couldn't trust himself.

Aidan asked me to help him. I said that I would, but told him things were going to have to change. Our lives would need to be very different, if he was going to succeed in giving up the drink. No more pubs after work, no more socialising.

It was a hard conversation, but deep down Aidan knew what had to be done. It felt different, somehow, to all the conversations we'd had before about giving up alcohol. This time Aidan really wanted it. Because Alicia wanted it. He would do anything for his kids.

'You'll have to come straight home after work,' I said.

He agreed. The next day he came straight home, and the day after that, and the one after that. It was strange at first, to see him there in the evening. We hadn't had dinner together in a long time. We did it for a week, which turned into two weeks. I could see it was hard for him.

The kids called a lot, mostly to ask how Dad was. I think they were all anxious – holding out hope that things would come right this time. Aidan was always the strong one, the dependable one. I'm sure they worried about how I was coping with it all.

Alicia rang. 'How's Dad, Mum?'

I knew what she was asking me. 'He's . . . he's trying' was all I could say. Though I believed he was on the right track, I couldn't trust that he wouldn't go back to the drink again. I wasn't prepared to be part of a broken promise. Not this one.

I tried to keep a mental distance from it all, but as the months passed I saw more and more of the Aidan I knew shining through. In the little things he did – thoughtful things he would never have done when he was drinking.

Then the day came. The day we had all been waiting for. Alicia was getting ready in her old bedroom. I was making a big breakfast fry for all the family. I went upstairs to check on her. I opened the bedroom door, and there she was. No longer the little girl whom I used to tuck into bed at night. Now she was a woman. A beautiful woman in a beautiful white dress.

She smiled at me. 'Is . . . Dad with you?' she asked, nervously.

'He'll be up in a minute.'

'How . . . is he?'

'He's really good. He's looking forward to walking you down the aisle.'

She smiled. I could see the relief in her eyes.

The congregation gathered in our local village church. The music began to play. I turned to see the big wooden doors open, and the silhouette of Aidan and Alicia appear against the spring light outside. Aidan took Alicia arm in arm and walked her proudly down the aisle. As their arms linked, I saw the strength in both of them – holding one another up. No one in the crowd, apart from the family, knew just how significant that moment was. How much it meant to all of us to see them both there standing side by side.

Alan came bounding over to Aidan after the ceremony. He put his arm on his shoulder. 'I'm proud of you, Dad,' he said. 'You did it.'

'I was nervous,' said Aidan.

'It took guts to be nervous. Drink would've been easy.'

After the ceremony, Alicia walked over and hugged Aidan. There were tears in her eyes. 'Thanks for walking me down the aisle, Dad.' They both smiled, knowingly, as Aidan held his daughter's hand.

I could see how much it meant to Aidan, to know he was back to being the children's father again. It was his favourite thing to be.

CHAPTER SIXTEEN

The Letter

⌒

Our lives returned to some kind of normality after Alicia's wedding. It was like we had finally rounded the corner, and found ourselves again. Or at least a new version of ourselves. I still kept to my routine – I woke early every day and did my jobs around the house. I tended to the animals and kept things simple. I didn't leave the farm.

I felt like the colour was slowly coming back into the world. I had my Aidan back. I could talk to him again, laugh with him. It made me realise how much I had missed him. How much I needed him.

Aidan was feeling much more himself again. But we always kept an eye on things, stayed vigilant, to make sure we didn't slip back into the old ways. We counted the sober days, quietly in our heads, as the weeks turned to months. It was around that time that we started to relax a bit – to feel like sobriety was the new pattern. The new normal. And it was, because Aidan never touched a drink again.

I had my Aidan back. And just in time, as neither of us knew then just what the future had in store for us and how much we would depend on one another in the years to come.

It all started one morning when we received a letter in the post. The postman pulled up outside the house as he usually did. He waved at me through the window as he placed the post on the welcome mat. I waved back to say thank you. The daily ritual. I looked forward to him coming every day. It was a quiet interaction, but an interaction all the same. I went to the door and collected the pile of envelopes. They were all addressed to Aidan.

That night as I was preparing dinner, Aidan opened the post at the kitchen table.

'Hmmm . . .' he said, 'that's odd.'

'Everything alright?' I asked, as I drained the potatoes.

'It's from a woman in America,' he said, reading through one of the letters he had received. 'Looking for her Irish ancestors.' He put it down dismissively.

'Can I see?' I asked.

He handed me the letter. I sat down and read through it. It was from a woman in California who was hoping to trace her family in Ireland. She was a Corless and was writing to all the Corless families in Galway.

The next day, the letter played on my mind. I kept thinking about what it would be like to have a look for your family. For many Americans there seems to be a search for family – tracing their emigrant past for a sense of belonging, to know where they are from. It is something I imagine most people might ignore – a letter in the post from a stranger. And perhaps that would have been the sensible thing to do. But every so often things stay with me, for whatever reason, and they tumble about my head for days, sometimes weeks. This was one of those things.

A few days later I went up the yard to muck out the cow shed and bring in the bales of straw. I was still thinking about the letter. I thought about my home, the farm. I knew where I was from, where my roots were, and all that that meant – the good and the bad of it, the complexity of it. And that complexity was part of me – it shaped me. I imagined what it would be like to feel untethered – floating almost, from place to place, looking for that sense of home. That sense of belonging.

'Have you thought any more about that lady's letter?' I asked Aidan as we sat at the dinner table that evening.

He looked bemused. 'What letter?'

'The lady from America . . .'

'Oh, that . . .' he said.

I could tell he hadn't thought any more about it.

'Would you mind if I looked into it?' I said.

He nodded enthusiastically through mouthfuls.

The next day I got to work. I knew that, coincidentally, my own grandmother on my father's side had been a Corless. I wondered if my extended family might be able to help. I rang around to distant cousins, and started taking notes as they each gave me different bits of information that might be useful.

Then, on advice from one of the family, I decided to call to the house of an elderly relative, my third cousin who lived in the same townland that the American lady believed her ancestors to be from. He welcomed me into his cottage and we sat over a cup of tea by the fire in the kitchen. I thanked him for meeting me, and told him about the woman from America and showed him her letter.

'Ah,' he said, removing his cap and scratching his head. 'I think I can work that one out.'

In a strange twist of fate, it turned out that the woman was related to me. It transpired that a great-grandaunt of mine, Kate Corless, had emigrated to Cincinnati, Ohio in the 1870s and this American woman was a descendant of hers. Kate had married an O'Flaherty man, and their family had done well there. They helped to build many of the bridges and buildings in Cincinnati and had made a good life for themselves.

I took some photos of the house, and then walked to the ruins of the old Corless homestead nearby and took some photos with the intention of printing them and posting them all to the lady in America.

Talking to my cousin made me curious about my own family history. I started putting together the bits of information I had been given from my cousins. Then I started asking questions, taking notes. Slowly I began to piece together our family tree. With every bit of research I did, the picture was becoming clearer.

I wrote to the lady in America with great excitement and included the family tree in the letter along with the photos, so that she might be able to make sense of it all. I also put in a note, saying, 'I hope this tree helps you to find your roots.'

Several weeks later she replied, saying how much it meant to her to finally know where she was from.

It gave me a great sense of purpose, knowing that I could source information that would be helpful to other people. When I put my mind to it, I seemed to be able to find things out and piece them together – something I'd never done much of before. I liked the process of seeing a picture emerge, through different parts of the puzzle.

I was delighted I could help the lady in America. To think that it might have brought some happiness to her, to fill in the missing pieces of her life.

That evening, I sat by the stove in the kitchen and laid the family tree out on the table to study it once more. As I looked at it I knew, deep in my heart, that there was something I was trying to ignore, something that was bothering me, something that was unfinished.

There was still a missing piece in my life, a missing part of the tree: my mother's side of the family. The only thing I knew about my mother was that she was born in 1912 and was from Keady in County Armagh. That's as much as I could piece together, because she had never told us anything about herself. I had never met my maternal grandparents and she had never spoken of them. Her life before the farm in Tuam had always been a mystery.

And now there was no one left to ask. My father had passed away some years after my mother. He died at the age of 95, and had worked the farm right into his final years. His love of nature and the outdoors had kept him going all those years. And though he never said much, his presence felt like a link to the past in some way – a connection to my mother through him. When he died, the whole chapter of my childhood officially came to an end – that house and farm and everything it represented now just a memory. And so much was still left unspoken.

I let out a long sigh.

Aidan was making a cup of tea. 'Everything okay?' he asked. 'Ah,' I said, 'it's just Mam . . .'

He didn't need me to elaborate. He knew what that meant.

I felt I was missing a part of myself when I thought of my mother. She left nothing of herself behind. No stories of her childhood, no sense of where she had come from or who our people were. Whenever I had asked her questions as a child she had a way of diverting the conversation to avoid answering. She would tell me to leave well enough alone, or suddenly remember with some urgency some chore I had to go and do. And somehow the years passed and these same rituals continued into adulthood. I learned not to ask and she continued not to tell. It is only when someone is gone that you really feel the void of those unanswered questions. When there is no chance of ever hearing their answer.

I thought of the day Meena had appeared on the doorstep – the cousin we never knew we had. 'Tell them nothing about me,' my mother had said.

What was it she didn't want us to know? What could possibly be in her past that was so secretive? I decided that I would investigate. Many years had passed since my mother had died and yet I still felt that something was unresolved. I really needed to know who she was. I wanted to try and piece together that part of my mother's story, that part of myself.

And what I came to discover helped me to understand my mother, and other people, in a way I never had before.

CHAPTER SEVENTEEN

In Search of My Mother

⌒

It was time to find out about my mother's past. I needed to know who she really was, and what she had been hiding all these years.

But where to begin? All I knew was where my mother was born. I tried to think of any other information that would be helpful. In retrospect, I reckoned Meena must have come to Tuam to tell my mother something. I thought back to the sequence of events around that time. Perhaps she had come to deliver a message, one that must have been important. It was a lot of trouble for Meena to go to, to seek her out and trace her the way she did, as my mother had not been in touch with any of her family for decades, as far as we could tell. She told us she'd lost touch with them all because her brothers were dead and she didn't know the next generation.

A few weeks after Meena's visit, my mother had packed a bag and told us she needed to take a trip up north. It was very unlike her to go anywhere. She had never done anything like that in all the time I had known her. Meena appeared again. She pulled up in a little green Mini and parked outside the house. My mother got into the car with her suitcase and they drove away. They returned a few days later.

She never explained why she left. What had brought her back to the place she had grown up – somewhere she never spoke of or visited? None of us knew and she wouldn't talk about it. That was her way.

But now I needed to know. I contacted Meena again to ask if she had any more information that might be helpful. She told me she had known her grandmother, Bridgette, who was my mother's mother. And from what she could make out, Bridgette had married a Protestant after my mother was born. It made me wonder what had happened to my grandfather – my mother's father. Had he died? She never spoke a word of him, so I had always presumed he had died. I thanked Meena for her help.

With this new information, I contacted the births, deaths and marriages office in Armagh to request a copy of my mother's birth certificate. I felt guilty for doing it. As if I was prying on her. I knew she wouldn't have wanted me to do it. But I couldn't face living the rest of my life wondering why she was the way she was.

A few weeks later, her birth cert arrived. And there it was: my mother's name, her date of birth, and her mother's name: Bridgette O'Hare.

And then it all made sense in an instant. There was no father's name on the birth cert. I knew what that meant. My mother was born out of wedlock. She would have been considered illegitimate. This was the big secret she had been hiding all her life.

For as long as I could remember, I had carried a pain inside of me that I couldn't reach, because I didn't have a connection with my mother. I couldn't turn back time. She was gone now. And even if I could, I knew nothing would be different. She would still be that same distant person she had been all her life. In a way, now that my mother was gone, there was no one to guard her secrets. Maybe now, we would finally be able to break down those barriers and connect as mother and daughter.

'Why don't we just go there?' Aidan suggested. 'See what we find out.'

He was talking about Keady. It was a good idea. At least it would feel like a proactive thing to do. So with that, Aidan and I decided to pack up the car and head to Armagh. Perhaps we would find people who had known the family and would be able to tell us more about them. We booked ourselves into a B&B in Keady for a few days. We arrived late in the evening and settled in for the night after a hot meal in the local pub.

The next morning we woke early and went to the library in Armagh. I searched through all the local genealogy books, looking for any trace of my mother's name. I found nothing in the library. The next stop was the Cardinal Ó Fiaich Memorial Library in Armagh town which held a lot of genealogical records. I was holding out hope that I may find something or someone to help me there. When we arrived I met with one of the librarians.

'I'm trying to trace my mother's heritage,' I told him.

I felt like an American tourist. He was very kind about it and very helpful. He told me about a few people who were local to Keady and knew a lot about the history of the place and the people who lived there. He gave me their numbers and suggested that I give them a call.

That evening I rang one of the numbers. A man answered. His name was Joe Jordan. He sounded elderly. I told him what I was hoping to do. He would love to help out, he told me. He wasn't sure I'd find the answers I was looking for, but he would do his best, he said. He could show us around the local sites, schools and cemeteries and maybe something would transpire that would be of help. I thanked him for his kindness and we arranged to meet on the main street the following morning.

Joe was smiling as he walked towards us. As soon as he spoke, I recognised him as the person I had talked with on the phone. He was a very friendly man in his seventies. I noticed the familiar 'och' and 'aye' in his greeting, a reminder of my mother's Keady accent. I briefed him on what I knew about my mother, but with so little to go on, he could only speculate on where she may have gone to school and where she may have been fostered, but he was very happy to show us around.

He took us in his car and we drove all around Keady and up to Foley, the townland where my mother was born. As I looked out the window I tried to imagine my mother walking those same roads, on her way to school or out to the farm. I tried to picture her life and what it might have been like. But as I looked out at the vast sea of green – the fields upon fields that led to the horizon – I felt that familiar sense of disappointment that I had come to associate with my mother, not knowing if she really did have any attachment to this place. I still felt as though she was missing. I was closer, but I still hadn't found her. Not by a long shot.

It is a difficult thing to explain to someone – how it is possible to be searching for someone you have known all your life. How you could co-exist, and yet never fully know one another, even as mother and child. For those who have not experienced it, it must be very hard to imagine, for the bond between mother and child is often the strongest bond of all. But when it is missing, its absence is felt so deeply. It's something you can never get past. It holds you hostage, in my experience, for your whole life: that sense of not belonging, to anyone or anywhere. For me, that is the hardest thing.

I mentioned to Joe that my mother often talked of the time she spent with a family called the Connollys. From the bits of research I had done, I knew that there had been an Edward and

Margaret Connolly with a son James, and that Edward had been a retired RIC sergeant, and that they lived in Ballymartrim.

'Connollys, you say? Ballymartrim?'

'Yes, do you know them?'

'There were Connollys a long time up in Tullysaran, quite near Ballymartrim. I'll bring you there,' he said.

We drove for another few miles, and arrived at the place he was talking about. 'Around here they lived,' he said, 'before they moved to Dublin.'

I looked around me, trying to soak in everything I was seeing – the lanes and crossroads, the farms and houses. This was the closest I had come to knowing anything of my mother's life before she lived in Tuam. It did me good to see it. I felt a lot closer to her all of a sudden.

Joe told us that there was a reunion of sorts happening in the area in a few weeks' time. It was a historical gathering – bringing together past pupils of the various local schools. 'You never know, someone there might know something of your mother,' he said.

We decided we would come back for the reunion. We thanked Joe for all his help.

'I don't think I was much help to you, unfortunately,' he said.

'You really were,' I told him, 'more than you know.'

That afternoon, I rang the local parish priest. I asked if he might have a copy of my mother's baptism cert that he could give me, as I was in the locality. He said he would have to post it out, that it could take a couple of days to get it all together. I gave him my address and thanked him for his help.

We decided to head back home then. I felt we had come as far as we could, on this occasion, and took comfort in knowing we would be back in a few weeks' time for the reunion.

We were only home a few days when the phone rang. It was the priest from Keady. He wanted to follow up, he explained, because, try as he might, he couldn't seem to find a Kathleen born to a Bridgette O'Hare.

I felt suddenly deflated. Perhaps my mother wasn't from Keady after all.

'Are you sure that was your grandmother's name?' he asked me.

'Positive,' I said.

'There is a Kathleen here . . . born on the same day as your mother, but to a Bridgette Curran.'

'Curran?' I said. I had never heard that name before in relation to my mother.

'Could it be the Kathleen you are looking for?' he asked. 'Beside Kathleen's name in the ledger it says: "married to Patrick Farrell, Tuam".'

'Yes, that's her!' I said. 'Patrick Farrell was my father.'

My mother must have contacted the priest for a letter of freedom when she was getting married – as proof that she had not been married before. I took a moment to try to piece it all together. This proved that my mother had been baptised in that church. She had been there as a baby, with her mother. But why was her mother down as Bridgette Curran?

It might have simply been a mistake by the priest at the time, when he was recording the local baptisms. Or could it be that Curran was the surname of my mother's biological father? Maybe my grandmother had pretended to be a married woman with the surname of the father of the baby, for the sake of the baptismal cert. I thanked the priest for his help and he promised to send on copies of the documents to my address so that I would have them for reference.

After the phone call, I got to work searching for a Bridgette Curran, as well as a Bridgette O'Hare. I couldn't find a single record of either of them. I started to wonder whether Bridgette may have been illegitimate too. As far as I knew, my mother had no aunts or uncles, so it led me to believe that my grandmother was an only child.

Meena had told me that Bridgette had three sons after giving birth to my mother. It wasn't clear if the boys were full brothers or half-brothers. I was able to find their baptism certs, though there were no birth certificates for any of them. On the baptism cert it said that Bridgette O'Hare was the mother and Samuel Trimball was the father. He must have been the Protestant Meena had told me about.

Whether Bridgette and Samuel were married or not is another thing. I went in search of their marriage cert through the births, deaths and marriages office. I was hoping that if I could get their marriage certificate, it would give a father's name for Bridgette, which would help to give some context for who she was, but there was no marriage certificate to be found. I had reached a dead end.

Whether they were married or not or whether Trimball fathered all those boys or not I may never know. All I know is what I've been told – that he left her when the children were young and took off with another woman.

Though Meena had said that Bridgette had given birth to my mother before she met Samuel Trimball, I wanted to know for certain that he was not my grandfather. Meena seemed to think he had been in America for a long time before returning to Ireland and meeting Bridgette.

So I searched through the shipping records, and I found a record of him leaving Ireland and not returning until many years later. It meant he would have been in America when my mother was conceived, so it was clear he was not my grandfather.

My mother had often talked of the Connollys. In fact they were the only 'family' she'd ever spoken of. She had worked for them, she told us, and they'd been very good to her. Old Mrs Connolly in particular.

I decided to reach out to Eileen Connolly, the granddaughter of Edward and Margaret Connolly. My mother had mentioned her several times and I knew they had kept in touch. I wrote her a letter and told her I was hoping to find out more about my mother's past and was wondering if she might be able to help – if she could remember anything about my mother's childhood.

Eileen wrote back, and was very helpful. She said that, from what she had been told through the years, my mother had gone to work for the Connollys at the age of eight or nine and had stayed with them until she was sixteen. Eileen remembered a story about my mother working at her grandparents' farm.

She told me that when Kathleen arrived there, on the farm just outside Keady, she began working in the fields with the men. But when old Mrs Connolly saw her coming in from the fields soaked to the bone and covered in mud, she said it was no way for a young girl to be living. She wouldn't have her working in the fields like that a moment longer, she said. And so my mother was brought indoors, to work in the kitchen, and to help around the house. It was the first bit of kindness ever shown to her. How confused and lost she must have felt, being fostered all those years: moved from family to family, just miles from where her own mother lived, forced to work hard and without a family of her own.

Meena had also said that she'd been told that my mother had been in and out of orphanages for the first few years of her life. I didn't think this was true, but I wanted to be certain. I set about checking all the records of the local orphanages, hoping to find some trace. But there was none. No Kathleen O'Hare in any of them.

My mother had told me that James Connolly (only child of Edward and Margaret) was a customs and excise officer and when the family needed to move to Dublin for his work, they asked

Kathleen if she would go with them. She jumped at the chance, and so became a kind of housekeeper for them. She grew very close to the Connollys and she stayed in touch with them for the rest of her life. I felt reassured, knowing she had found a family of some description eventually, who cared for her and valued her.

The date came around very quickly. It was time to travel back to Armagh for the school reunion. This time we stayed in a local hotel. The reunion was held in Tullysaran Community Centre, near Manooney national school. As we drove up to the community centre, I saw the cars parked outside. Through the windows, I could see people standing around, talking with one another. That familiar wave of anxiety came over me. I dreaded having to mingle, but felt reassured that Aidan would be by my side and would help me break the ice, as he always did.

The set-up inside was lovely. They had gone to a lot of trouble to display all the photographs of past pupils down through the ages. There was an introduction by Joe Jordan, who explained what the event was all about and encouraged us all to talk to one another, to reminisce and ask questions if we needed any help with anything.

We walked around the room. Aidan chatted to people as we went. I was walking along, looking at the various photographs of past pupils, studying the years very closely, searching for any sign of my mother's name. Then something caught my eye. In one of the class photos, from 1924, there was a young girl, about twelve years of age, who looked just like my mother. There was something about the way she was standing, how she held her shoulders, that was so familiar. Her head was tilted to the side, looking away from everyone, ever so slightly. It was the kind of thing she would do. I looked a little closer.

'Aidan, I think that's her. I think that's Mam,' I said, pointing to the girl in the photograph.

Aidan looked closely at the picture, then after a few moments said, 'You know, that really could be. It looks very like her.'

I searched the caption, looking for her name, but it wasn't there. Some of the other students were named, but not this particular girl. Joe happened to be passing at that moment. Aidan explained to him that we were trying to find out whether that might in fact be Kathleen in the photograph.

'Have you checked the roll book?' he asked.

My ears pricked up. 'The roll book?'

'Yes . . . it's just over there – it's the school roll book from the 1900s. It should include the class you're looking at in the photograph.'

He pointed to an old leather book which lay open on the coffee table in the middle of the room. I thanked him for his help and eagerly made a beeline for the book. I flicked through the pages, looking for the correct year. When I found what I thought was the year, and the class, I used my index finger to carefully scroll down through the names on the page. And then I found it.

'Aidan, look at this,' I said, beckoning him over.

There it was, written in scribbled black ink: 'Kathleen O'Hare (orphan)'.

'Orphan?' said Aidan.

'I know,' I said. It seemed terrible to think they would brand her like that, even in the roll book, particularly as she wasn't technically an orphan.

I called Joe over again to thank him for pointing us in the right direction. I showed him the name on the page and explained that I didn't believe my mother was an orphan as she had known her mother in adulthood – a woman named Bridgette. He told me that sometimes the protocol was to write 'orphan' when the child was illegitimate. It differentiated them from the other children, he explained.

How awful, I thought. What difference was it to the teacher whether my mother was born out of wedlock or not. Surely it would have no bearing on her ability to learn.

Seeing those three words – Kathleen O'Hare (orphan) – and looking at the little girl in the photo, I finally felt like I had a piece of my mother's childhood in my mind and in my heart. I could picture that little girl, sitting in her classroom. I took a photograph of the class photo. I wanted to show my family back home. I looked at the details written beside her name. They had her age wrong. She would have been 12 in 1924. They had her a bit younger. But she was a small woman, and so as a child may have appeared younger than her age. It was probably a mistake. I was sure it was my mother. I just knew it.

We thanked the organisers of the event for including us and told them how much it meant to have been able to prove that my mother had attended one of the local schools in the area. They were very kind and said they would help me with my search in any way they could, which was very kind of them. But I doubted we would ever find out much more. She was a very elusive woman, my mother, like her own mother.

The next morning, before we left, I wanted to visit the school in Tullysaran that I now knew my mother had gone to. The school itself had since closed down, but I still wanted to see it. When we got there, we walked around the grounds. I took some photos, and prised a small piece of the flaking plaster from the wall and put it in my pocket. A small memento from my mother's mysterious childhood.

As we drove back to Galway, I looked out the window at the fields. My mind was full of memories of my mother as I tried to piece together the story of her life. I thought back to when I was a child. My mother would often wake in the middle of the night, moaning. She suffered from terrible nightmares. The sound would wake us all, with a fright. It made me wonder what had happened to her – all those years that she was passed from family to family, before she found the Connollys. What kind of abuse must she have endured.

I looked at the photograph of her, which I had saved on my phone. That little girl of twelve. What kind of harsh world had she known since she was a baby? I wanted to take her out of the photo and hug her and care for her. It was strange looking at the photo, knowing what became of that little girl – the life she went on to lead. A good life, by all accounts – a loving husband, five healthy children and a farm and house to run. But there was an emptiness in her, a distance that could not be reached, even by those closest to her. Those years of neglect had robbed her of her ability to love fully and to connect with other people – two of the most important parts of life.

And then it dawned on me. My mother was that red-haired girl. The one I had played the trick on in school. Once upon a time, that had been my mother. The 'orphan' in the class. No wonder she was so upset to see what cruelty the red-haired girl had to endure. I wished I could tell her how sorry I was.

When we got home I had the photograph printed. I put it in a safe place, in the file I kept with all the information I had gathered on my mother. I treasured that photograph – this little part of Kathleen O'Hare, the child who was abandoned, was lost, and now, at last, was found.

CHAPTER EIGHTEEN

Ask Why

~

Children are only children for so long. Eventually, as every mother learns, you have to let them go.

Aaron had been the last to leave. I helped him pack up his things, all the parts of his childhood disappearing into boxes. He was going to college. He had secured a place in a teacher training college. He was delighted, and we were very proud of him.

And then, they were all gone. Even years later, I could never get used to the children not being there. The house still felt quiet without them. The busyness of family life seemed to be over as quickly as it had begun. One moment they were babies, the next they were heading out into the world, getting married and having babies of their own.

And here we were. Back to the two of us. The years passed, and we kept ourselves busy – Aidan with his work, and me with the farm and garden. But it was in the quiet of those evenings, in 2005, that I decided I needed to do something else with my time.

I was 51 years old, and a strong feeling was coming over me lately, a curiosity, if you like, a sense that I still had more to give.

I still wonder what drew me to the ad. One Thursday morning I opened the local *Tuam Herald* newspaper and there it was, in the 'Kilkerrin Notes': an advertisement for a local history class. It was an evening class starting in two weeks' time. 'Do you want to learn how to research?' it said. 'Would you like to learn where to find answers?' It was exactly what I wanted to know. Looking into my mother's past and that of the American lady had given me a taste for research, and I loved it. But I wanted to be better at it. I scribbled down the phone number. The next morning I rang and booked a place on the course.

I was nervous the first time I attended the class. I hadn't been in that kind of learning environment since I was a child at school. But it was just once a week on a Monday evening for three hours, in the community hall in Kilkerrin. It was local, even though it was affiliated with the Maynooth University, and the class size was small. It was manageable, I told myself.

Very soon I was immersed in the material. I was lapping everything up. I didn't have time to feel anxious. I was listening to everything the lecturer was saying. Our first assignment was to write a chapter for a book that our tutor would be publishing at the end of the course year. We had to pick a townland of the Kilkerrin area and write about 4,000 words on the landlord of that area.

'Look around you,' our teacher said. 'History is all around you.'

When the class was over, I got into my car and headed home. The drive felt very different from usual. As I looked out the window, my eye was drawn to the borders of the farms as I passed. They all looked about the same size. I thought about land division and wondered about the history of land in Tuam. Who owned what and when. Land ran deep in the blood in Ireland. It was a part of people.

The topic felt close to home for our own land growing up had once been part of a landed estate. I knew every corner of our land. When I was a child sometimes I would play a game. I would close my eyes as I walked, to test my knowledge of the terrain. I could anticipate every bump in the earth, every stile and upturned stone. I knew it as well as I knew my own body. It was a part of me. I loved exploring, and whenever I was out walking I would survey the farms as I passed, trying to work out the borders.

So I got to work, researching and writing about landlords in the Kilkerrin area. I went to the library in Tuam. I spilled over the books for days on end, reading about the land in the surrounding areas and how it had been affected by the Land Commission. Through the history of the land I could make out a history of Ireland. I spent the next few weeks working hard on the essay. Finally, I submitted it.

We continued to learn from our tutor Gabriel O'Connor, who was an excellent teacher and had a passion for research and local history which was infectious. Then, when the Kilkerrin book was published at the end of the year, which included my chapter, I was approached by the editor of the *Journal of the Old Tuam Society* (*JOTS*), who said he was impressed by my work, and asked if I would consider writing an essay for their annual. I was chuffed to be asked, and I readily agreed.

Over the following years, I went on to write three more essays on landlords around the general Tuam area. I found the research fascinating, discovering how people lived in the past, and how laws and government policies influenced their lives. I got a lot of information from local people. I enjoyed interviewing them, asking questions about their lives and those of their ancestors. And I loved being busy, having a sense of purpose as I tried to discover more and more information about the past.

In 2010 the editor contacted me again, looking for another

essay. Perhaps on a different topic if I wished. I was to come back to him with a proposal.

I woke early the next morning, the question playing on my mind: what would I write about? I had breakfast and headed out for a walk.

'History is all around you,' I reminded myself. I walked around, trying to see the town through a new lens: seeing what had been before, rather than what was there now. What other history could be in Tuam, I wondered.

Absentmindedly I found myself walking the familiar route to my old school. I stopped where the mother and baby home once stood. In its place was a housing estate, built in the 1970s, with a children's playground in the middle. If you didn't know that there had been a children's home there once upon a time, you would never have guessed it. I wondered how many people living in the housing estate knew about the home. It didn't seem right, somehow, to erase history like that, to build something new in its place, as though it never existed.

In the corner of the playground was a little black gate. I walked through it and was amazed to find a small garden, well tended to. It was like stepping into a secret garden, in the middle of the harsh, cold tarmacadam playground. How had I never seen this before? There was a patch of grass and a few flowerbeds, and in the corner was a grotto. I went to take a look at it. There was something about it that wasn't like other grottos. When I looked carefully, I noticed that it was made out of an old white bath tub, cut in half, to form the border around the statue of Mary. I wondered if this was a tribute to the old mother and baby home.

I walked to the other side of the playground, where part of the outer wall of the home still stood. I remembered back to when I was a child, looking up at the shards of glass on top, as they glistened in the sun.

I thought of the red-haired girl from school, the one we'd played the trick on, who was the same age as me. We had been living parallel lives on either side of the wall. Where was she now, I wondered. What had her life been like in that place? And what had happened to her in the end?

That's what I'll do my piece on, I decided: the mother and baby home. If only to know what might have become of that red-haired home baby.

CHAPTER NINETEEN

Stolen Childhoods

⌒

A few days later, I was reading the *Tuam Herald* by the range in the kitchen when something caught my eye. I nearly didn't see it as I was turning the pages absentmindedly. The headline was 'Stolen Childhoods'. It was a letter to the editor.

In it the author, who described himself as 'Martin', wrote that he was a former resident of the Tuam mother and baby home. As far as he could make out, he had been placed in the home in 1947 at the age of two, but he knew very little about his life there. He was reaching out to anyone who might know something about St Mary's, as the Tuam home was officially called, and who might be able to help him learn more about his early years there.

At the age of five, he explained, he was fostered out to a very uncaring family. He wrote about enduring many years of hardship and misery, until eventually he was able to free himself from the situation. He fled to England, and never returned to his homeland.

Now, decades later, he was reaching out to anyone in Tuam who might have information to help him piece together the fragments of his story – with the hope of finding out who his biological parents might have been.

I wrote an email to the editor, asking if I could contact this man. He kindly forwarded my request to 'Martin' with my contact details so that he could get in touch with me. A few days later I received a letter from a man named Michael Hession. He had used a pseudonym when writing to the paper, he explained. In his letter to me, he told me a little more about his life.

There was a warmth and honesty to his words. I wrote back and asked questions: what could he remember of the home? What had his life afterwards been like? What was it like to be fostered out at such a young age?

A conversation struck up between us – two strangers who had never met as we began writing back and forth. I explained that I was doing some research into the mother and baby home. He was keen to help me in any way he could.

I loved receiving Michael's letters. When the post arrived, I looked out for his handwriting on the envelope and the English stamp. His letters read like diary entries. I felt he wanted to tell someone about the life he had led, to get it all down on paper. Some of the letters were humorous, others were heartbreaking. Michael had a way of seeing the good in things, even when life was particularly hard on him.

As I got to know Michael, from afar, I began to realise that this was far more than an academic project. What had once been about research was now about something much more personal. It was about Michael, and all the children who had been at the home with him. From his letters, I could start to imagine what life was like for the children there, and for their mothers too. I could see the effect the home had had on him. How he carried the pain all through his life and the heartbreak of being separated from his mother. He had grown up in the world alone, without family, desperately trying to make his own way.

I asked him if I could include him in my essay. He would be honoured, he said. But on one condition – that I use his real name: Michael Hession. He felt he had been denied an identity for far too long. His foster mother had called him 'Sonny' all his life. He had never been acknowledged as his own person. And now, that's what he really wanted.

I decided it was time to get to work, researching the home. I was moved by Michael's letters and felt I needed to know more about what had gone on in the mother and baby home. I couldn't have known, then, just what lay ahead.

CHAPTER TWENTY

Research

‿

I drove to the library in the centre of town to do some research. I told the lady at the information desk what I was looking for, and she pointed me in the direction of the historical archives. I picked several books from the shelves and thumbed through them, searching the index for mention of the Tuam mother and baby home, or 'St Mary's' as it was formally called. I found nothing about the home. I looked again. It must be a mistake, I thought.

I asked the librarian, who was very helpful, but we couldn't seem to find anything that mentioned the home, except for a small excerpt of an essay written by a university student many years previously as part of a thesis. There was a short mention in the essay about the mothers who had given birth in the home. It talked about how they had to give up their babies after their year's stay there. Give up their babies? I read the piece again, to make sure I had understood correctly. I had always thought that the home was an orphanage for children who had lost their parents.

Ask why. It's what our lecturer had always taught us. Why

were the mothers giving them away after a year? I needed to find out more. But where? I scoured the shelves of the library, with the help of the librarian, searching for any other mention of the Tuam mother and baby home. But, to our surprise, there was nothing there. It seemed bizarre considering what a feature it had been in the locality, and for so long.

I tried to think about what I had been taught in my course. If there was nothing in writing, maybe I could find out more information locally, from oral accounts. I decided to try and find out what people in the locality knew about the mother and baby home. I went back to the Dublin road housing estate, which now stood on the home's former site, to see if anyone remembered it or had any information on it.

I knocked on the first door I came to. A woman answered. I explained that I was doing some research about the old mother and baby home, and wondered if she knew anything about it. She looked confused.

'It used to be just over there,' I said, pointing to the place beyond the playground. She was sorry, she said, she didn't know anything about it.

I knocked on the next door. This time a man answered. He knew nothing either, he said.

I went from door to door until I had asked nearly everyone in the estate. I was about to give up when someone suggested I speak to a woman named Bridie, who lived across the street. 'She's been here a long time,' I was told. 'She might be able to help.'

Weary from all the negative responses, I decided I would try just one more house before going home. I walked across the road and knocked on the door.

'Are you Bridie?' I asked.

'I am,' she said.

I explained that I was writing an essay for the local journal and wanted to know more about the home and what went on there.

'Sorry,' she said, 'I don't really know much about that.'

My heart sank – another dead end. I thanked her and was just about to leave when she called me back.

'There is someone who might be able to help,' said Bridie. 'A man named John Mannion. He's the graveyard caretaker.' She gave me his details. 'He knows all about it,' she said. 'He'll tell you about what those two boys saw.'

'What do you mean?' I asked.

'Ah, John'll tell you all about it,' she said. And with that she closed the door.

I rang John the following day and we arranged to meet. I had set out to write a simple essay – something historical about a local institution – but it wasn't until I met John and he told me about Frannie and Barry, two local boys, and what they saw that I started to wonder if something much darker was at play, something much bigger and more important than I could ever have imagined. I could scarcely believe the story he told me.

CHAPTER TWENTY-ONE

Frannie and Barry

⁓

The year was 1975, John Mannion said. It was a rainy afternoon in October in Tuam, some time near Halloween – a
time when children delight in stories of ghosts and ghouls. But
little did those boys know of the fright they were about to get,
and the real-life horror story they would become part of.

Frannie and Barry were just twelve and ten years of age.
Frannie's father waited at the top of the town, outside The Thatch
pub. He watched as his son ran down the road, towards home.
When he turned his back, the boys took a detour and headed for
the apple trees near the deserted building that once was the mother
and baby home, in the heart of Tuam. They were collecting
apples, stuffing them into their pockets, when they heard a noise
– the man who owned the trees had spotted them in his garden
and was coming out of his house, shaking his walking stick in
their direction. They had been caught! They quickly clambered
over the wall and found themselves in the grounds of the old
Mother and Baby home. Frannie landed with a thud into a kind
of hollow in the ground. The sound made him curious.

'Barry!' he called, as he pulled back the weeds to reveal a concrete slab which was cracked across the middle. 'Look at this!'

Barry scrambled over the wall. They got down on their knees and pulled at the broken slab until finally they managed to prise it open and peer inside. Below them was a deep, dark hole. They squinted as their eyes adjusted to the darkness. Inside the hole, they saw what looked to be a hollow tank, and at the bottom of the tank lay a pile of skulls and bones. Frannie, in a moment of mischief, bumped Barry, the younger boy. Barry lost his grip and fell into the hole. He let out a scream, and immediately began to cry.

Frannie panicked. He leaned over as far as he could. 'Put out your hand!' he yelled to Barry. He grabbed Barry's arm. 'Hold on tight!'

He pulled with all his strength and hoisted Barry out of the hole, back into the open air. They tumbled backwards, scrambled to their feet and ran away as fast as they could, Barry still crying from the shock. As they ran, they began to laugh, perhaps out of nervousness,, until they reached a safe distance from the scene. Could that have been real, they wondered. What had they seen?

They ran all the way home to tell their parents what had happened. They were told, in no uncertain terms, never to go back to that spot again.

The authorities were informed. The guards said it was famine bones. The priest came and said a prayer. And then the area was covered up. The Bon Secours sisters were also contacted – they had moved to a private hospital in the town – but they said they knew nothing about it.

The boys were told to forget what had happened, to move on.

They grew up. Frannie joined the defence forces and travelled the world, and Barry moved to England. They were told they must have been mistaken, that they had embellished the story over the years, as children tend to do. But they knew what they had seen. And the questions have stayed with them all their lives.

What if they weren't famine bones?

I could hardly believe what John was telling me: these boys had discovered some kind of tomb, by the sounds of it. Whom did those bones belong to and what were they doing there? Who put them there and why?

Why? The question burned in my mind.

CHAPTER TWENTY-TWO

Names

❧

I had a terrible feeling that those bones were connected to the home. But I wanted to be proven wrong. I needed to find out about the people who had lived in the home. If there was nothing to be found about them in books, perhaps the best route was to look for official records held by state authorities.

I rang the births, deaths and marriages office in Galway and asked to book the research room. But to my surprise they said it was no longer available to the public. When I questioned it, they explained that their records were stored in shelves in a small back room and it was becoming too difficult for them to allow the public in to research.

The public office of births, deaths, and marriages in Galway was under the auspices of the Western Health Board, now known as HSE West. These records were public – so, in theory, anyone should be able to access them.

'Is there any way you might be able to help me?' I asked. I was speaking to Anne, the archivist. I told her I needed information about the Tuam mother and baby home.

She asked me what I wanted to find out.

'I need to know how many children died at the home,' I said.

Anne said she would set aside some time to try and locate the information for me, and that if she found the records, I could buy them from the archive. 'But it might take a few weeks – is that okay?'

I told her it was no problem, and thanked her for her help. And sure enough, a few weeks later, Anne called. 'I just wanted to confirm something,' she said. 'Are you *sure* you're happy to buy all these records?'

I was confused by the question. 'How many could there be?' I asked.

Anne cleared her throat. 'Two hundred . . . so far,' she said.

'Two hundred? Are you saying two hundred children died at the home?' An image of the red-haired girl flashed through my mind.

'That's what I've collected so far,' Anne told me. 'I have a feeling this is only the beginning – there may be a lot more.' She explained that the records would cost five euro each. And with 200 records already, that was a thousand euro so far.

I was silent for a moment. It was a lot of money. And it could potentially be thousands more. I didn't have that kind of money, I explained.

'Well,' she said, 'maybe I can do something for you . . .' She suggested a scaled-down version – instead of buying the records outright, she could put the information on a spreadsheet for me. It would cost a good deal less.

We agreed to this and she promised to send me the information as soon as possible. I was very grateful to her.

A few days later I went to the computer to check my email. And sure enough – there it was – a message from Anne. There was a spreadsheet attached. I printed it off and laid it out on the table. All the names of the children were printed, alongside their date of birth, and the date and age they were when they died.

I read through the list. Two hundred little people, I thought. Two hundred lives. Patrick, Mary, Matthew. Five months, four months, three months.

I thought of what my children were like at that age. At five months old a baby starts to play peekaboo. I remembered Adrienne hiding behind her teddy bear and laughing wholeheartedly as she re-emerged. At five months old they're nearly ready to start eating solids – their first taste of food. It should have been a time of great excitement and exploration for Patrick. And at four months old, Mary was probably just learning how to roll over. At three months old, Matthew would have known how to smile. He would have been starting to laugh. That beautiful baby laugh. I thought of all the times he might have laughed in his lifetime. All that he might have become, if he had been given a chance. All that potential gone from the world. But why?

I felt angry at the thought of it. How had so many children died in the care of the nuns? Then my thoughts turned to the story of Frannie and Barry and of the hollow they had found with bones inside it. A terrifying correlation was starting to form in my head. Were these the bones of the children who died in the home? Was that hollow some kind of crypt? If that was the case, why was it not marked in some way? My head started to ache. I put down the paper, and rubbed my eyes to relieve the tension.

'Time to get some rest,' Aidan said, coming into the kitchen. He could see my anxiety coming on.

I thought back to when Adrienne was a baby. I used to go to her cot at night and listen to her breathing. I was so afraid she might stop, afraid that something might happen to her. I watched her so closely.

I poured a glass of water and made my way to bed. But that night, no matter how hard I tried, I couldn't get to sleep. The names of the children were racing through my mind. When I closed my eyes I imagined rows and rows of cots lined up in a big, cold, draughty room. I could hear the babies wailing, crying out for their mothers. And then there was a baby that wasn't crying. As I got closer I could see that the baby wasn't moving. I looked to see if his chest was rising, listened for the sound of breathing. Nothing. I imagined his listless, cold, dead body being lifted from the cot. The worst image imaginable. A dead baby. Every person's worst nightmare. And here they were – 200 of them in one house. A house of horrors. How could this be?

CHAPTER TWENTY-THREE

Maps

～

I couldn't let it go. I needed to fully understand what had happened here. A list of dead children, and bones discovered on the grounds. It was all starting to seem very strange. And why were these children dying? Was it a lack of medication, perhaps? An epidemic of some kind? Were children across the country dying in equal numbers during those years? I needed to find out.

A woman attached to the Adoption Authority of Ireland gave me the name of a person in HSE West to contact. I wrote them an email asking for archival information about the Tuam home. I received a prompt reply, saying that they did not have any records except for the registers of the Tuam home which contained private information on mothers and babies.

Frustrated, I emailed again. This time I reiterated that I would not expect to be given private information, that I just wanted general information on who was involved in running the home. Finally, a reply came. This time they stated that they did not have any records whatsoever. Somehow that didn't seem right. How could there be no records of an institution of that magnitude? I got the impression they didn't want me to contact them again. And if I did, I would be met with the same vague reply.

I was hitting a brick wall with every attempt to find information. As the Tuam library didn't seem to have any records of the home, I wondered where else I could look. That's when I thought of the university. I made some calls and discovered that I could use the library in NUI Galway. I would get the bus into the city the following day to see if there was any more information about the home there. Perhaps it had been entrusted to a larger library.

I knew I couldn't leave these questions unanswered. I had to resolve the issue in my own mind. I needed to get to the bottom of what had happened. The names of the children kept going through my mind. I had a strong feeling that something sinister was going on. I just wasn't sure what it was.

I walked through the university campus, watching the students milling around, coming and going from lectures, talking with friends, coffees in hand. Talking about the world and all its politics, no doubt. It made me wonder what it would have been like to have been a student at university. Perhaps in another life, I thought, as I reached the library. It felt very grand, with its high ceilings. When I walked up to the desk I saw the librarian filing something in the back room. She signalled to me and said softly, 'With you in a moment.' Suddenly I felt anxious. I felt like an imposter. Why was I here? What would I tell the librarian I was doing? I wasn't a student. I wasn't an academic. I was just an ordinary housewife. What business did I have being here in the university? I turned to go.

But just at that moment, the librarian appeared. 'Sorry about that. What can I do for you?'

I couldn't leave now. 'Hi,' I said. 'I'm hoping to do some research, please.'

She was very helpful. I felt immediately at ease. She asked me what I was looking for. I told her I wanted to research some old buildings around Tuam – namely the mother and baby home.

She walked me over to a separate room and pointed me in the direction of the microfiche machine. 'Here you go!' she said. She must have noticed the confused look on my face. 'Will I show you how it works?' she asked. She sat with me and talked me through how to research particular items and how to use the machine. 'If you want to give it a go, I'll be right over here if you need anything.'

I was grateful for her kindness. I hadn't imagined I would need to use anything other than books.

'Oh!' she said, as she went to leave, 'the map section might also be useful to you, if it's buildings you're interested in. I'll show you where that is.'

She guided me towards the map section of the library. She explained how the categorising system worked. The maps were hanging in a large filing cabinet. They were given specific numbers for different areas of County Galway, with several maps for the Tuam area. There were also other maps pointing out heritage monuments, such as 'cilleens', which were areas where unbaptised children were buried, as they were not allowed to be buried in consecrated ground. Other maps were marked by townland, or geographical feature.

I thanked her, and got to work. I leafed through the maps, searching for one pertaining to Tuam. I found the correct file, then tried to hone in on the home in particular. Then I spotted it – it was a map dated 1925, which indicated it had been revised from a previous version of the map from 1892. The map showed the layout of the workhouse, which is what the building originally functioned as, before it became known as the home. I then found a map of the same area from 2007, which showed the existing housing estate and playground.

I looked at the map from 1925, then I looked at the other one from 2007. Just then, something caught my eye – a small but distinct difference between the two. On the earlier map, at the back of the home, in very small writing, was written: 'sewage tank'. At first I didn't think much about it, but then I looked again at the location of the tank. I turned the map and tried to visualise myself at the site. If I wasn't mistaken, the sewage tank looked to be in the exact spot where Frannie and Barry had discovered the bones. It seemed to be the same place, but I couldn't be sure. I made a copy of the maps on the photocopier.

I decided I would come back another day to use the microfiche machine. I wanted to go and check if I had the correct orientation in my head. I needed to visit the site in person. I left the library and got the bus back home. The following morning, I drove to the Dublin road housing estate and parked beside the playground. I tucked the map under my arm and walked towards the old stone wall on the far side of the enclosure. I opened up the map and studied the contours as I stood in the spot where Frannie and Barry had fallen all those years ago. As I turned the map, it became clear: the very spot I was standing on was marked 'sewage tank'.

What did this mean? It made sense that the ground would be hollow if there was a tank there. That must have been why the boys fell through it. But did this mean that the skeletons they found were buried in the sewage tank? The idea made me feel nauseous. I quickly stepped back several paces. The thoughts of standing on top of the bodies made me recoil. Or worse still, the idea that the ground might give way and I might also fall through and find myself among them in the sewage tank.

I thought of the list of names of children who had died in the home. Was this what had happened to them? Patrick, Mary, Matthew. It couldn't be, I thought. The guards had said they were famine bones, from the time of the workhouse. Strange, though. If they were famine bones, would they not have been discovered when putting in the sewage tank? It would seem only logical that the sewage tank had to come first, and therefore the bones had to date after the workhouse time.

I looked around at the surrounding houses. Their back windows looked out onto the tarmacadam playground. I thought back to when I used to walk here, as a child, before there were any houses, just open fields, a road and the high walls of the mother and baby home. How much can change in a short space of time, I thought.

Suddenly the heavens opened and the rain fell heavily. I ran to the shelter of my car. I sat there, looking out at the site, through the constant rhythm of windscreen wipers swishing back and forth, as the rain fell in sheets upon the old grey playground that nobody used.

Was it possible that the children from the home might be buried there, in the ground beneath this playground? I thought of the nightmare that kept me awake at night – the image of those babies being taken, lifeless, from their cots. But what had happened to them then? Was it conceivable that their dead bodies were hidden in the sewage tank? I was starting to feel anxious again. The thought was overwhelming. I needed to talk to Aidan, to think it all through with him. I put the map safely in the glove box and made my way home.

I talked it through with Aidan that night. I had become fixated on the babies. We talked of little else these days, it seemed. I decided I needed to do some more research, to see if I could get to the bottom of this new development.

I went back to the library in Tuam to use their microfilm machine. Someone had recommended I look through the old *Tuam Herald* archives. I typed in 'Tuam' first of all, to see what would come up. There were reams and reams of newspaper articles, mainly from the *Tuam Herald*, the oldest newspaper in County Galway., It had been in circulation since 1837. If there was anywhere I could find information about the home, it would be there. I typed in 'mother and baby home' and a list of articles came up. But it was an advertisement that stopped me in my tracks. Entitled 'Tenders for Coffins', it was dated 1939 and read:

Tender for coffins for Children's Home, plain and
mounted, in three sizes, must be 1' thick, made of
seasoned white deal, clean and free from knots and slits,
pitched and stained in large, medium, small sizes.
Mounting must be similar make, but mounted with
Electro Brassed Grips, Breast and Crucifix.

There was something harrowing about a coffin for a child. A cot for a child was more fitting, but a coffin . . . The thought sent a shiver down my spine. I scrolled through the list of articles. The advertisements looking for coffins appeared sporadically, indicating that deaths were a regular occurrence in the home. I needed to investigate further.

I scanned the articles, hundreds of them. As I flicked through them, one in particular caught my attention. It was about the sewage system in the workhouse. It talked about problems with the sewage overflowing. According to the article, this problem seemed to occur during the time of the workhouse, from 1910 to 1918 or thereabouts. Then I found another article about the home becoming connected to the main sewage network, which happened around 1936 or 1937. So this meant that the existing sewage system would have become defunct at this time, and the tank no longer used for that purpose.

Could it be, therefore, that it was then used as a burial chamber?

The thought was terrifying. I decided it was time to approach the only people who could know for sure. There were so many questions in all this – so many 'what-if's. I knew what I had to do next.

CHAPTER TWENTY-FOUR

The Nuns

I wrote directly to the Bon Secours sisters. They had to have the answers we were looking for, and maybe, just maybe, with all the time that had passed, they would be willing to talk about what had happened – whatever the truth might be. I had to assume the best of them.

In a handwritten letter, I explained that I was undertaking a local history project and was looking for information about the Tuam mother and baby home and I was hoping that the Bon Secours sisters who ran the home might be able to help me with my research. I posted the letter and waited for a reply.

Every day for three or four weeks I watched as the postman came and went, but no news came from the Bon Secours. Then one day a letter arrived; I didn't recognise the writing on the envelope. I hastily opened it, and sure enough, at the top of the page was a religious emblem with the words 'Sisters of Bon Secours – Good Help to those in Need since 1824' written beneath it. It was now 2012. It was hard to believe they had been operating for so long.

I read through the letter very quickly, excited at the prospect of a reply.

Dear Ms Corless

Thank you for your letter of the 7th of January.

The project sounds as if it will be very interesting.

Unfortunately, as you may be aware, the Home operated by our Order closed in November 1961 and the Children were transferred to other homes. At the time, all the Records for the Homes were handed over to the Western Health Board and/or to Galway County Council. We therefore, unfortunately, do not have any records in relation to the Home in our possession.

I have, however, been able to locate reference to the Home in a publication titled 'Milestones on a Faith Journey' with an account by Bishop James Fergus on the Bon Secours sisters and the Home and I am attaching a copy of that to this letter. It gives a good historical account of what was originally the Workhouse and then its transformation into the Home. You will see there is a photograph of the home with some of the Sisters standing in front of it which might be of interest to you. I have done my best to copy it as well as I can so that you can see the photograph.

I also have come across what appears to be an abbreviated version of Bishop Fergus' article and I am also enclosing a copy of that as it might be of some further help to you.

I regret that I am unable to assist you any further but wish you all the best with your project.

Yours sincerely,
Sr Marie Ryan
Country Leader

I looked at the photograph that accompanied the letter. The correspondence was friendly in tone, but not overly helpful. The article by the bishop painted a picture contrary to the one that was emerging from other sources. I couldn't help but think of it as religious propaganda, but I tried to keep an open mind.

CHAPTER TWENTY-FIVE

The Workhouse

❧

I had come to appreciate how important historical records were, as I was trying to piece together this mystery. But I was also aware that they were often written by people in positions of authority. Testimonies from the mother and baby home were scarce and I was struggling to find them recorded in any history books, so I went about trying to find other people, like Michael, who had been in the home, to talk to them about their experience.

To hear in their own words what they had gone through was a great privilege and one I was not going to take lightly. I felt I owed it to the people who had come forward to tell their stories that I work hard, so that perhaps some good might come from all this.

I had spent the best part of two years researching – reading through articles and records and speaking to anyone who might have information about the home. I gathered first-hand accounts where I could find them and tried to get as many different sources as I could. A picture of the home and how it had operated through time was starting to emerge.

The first step had been to investigate how St Mary's mother and baby home had come to be. What I discovered was that the building had originally been used as a workhouse. It was built in 1841 under the Irish Poor Laws and was intended to house up to 800 people. It would be a place for the poor and destitute to find accommodation and a form of employment. The Tuam workhouse opened its doors officially in 1846 during the Great Famine. The building was divided up into large dormitory wings, including an 'idiots' ward' and an infirmary, with more sheds added on later and a fever hospital built close by, to house fever victims when illness was rampant and medicine was scarce. From what I could make out, the workhouse continued to operate for 60 years after the famine ended because of the extreme poverty in Ireland.

But this was just the beginning of the story of that foreboding building. A place that seemed cursed to be forever full of sadness and pain.

British troops took command of the building in 1920, with the 'inmates' evacuated a year later and sent to a workhouse in Loughrea. In 1923, during the civil war, eight anti-treaty IRA volunteers were lined up against the sacristy wall of the Tuam workhouse chapel and executed, one by one. It was the only wall of the building left standing after the workhouse was knocked down in the early 1970s. Today it stands as a monument to those eight executed men, another dark feature of this eerie playground. There is a commemorative plaque in the centre, dedicated to their memory, which was erected by the nuns who later took over the running of the mother and baby home at that same site. The plaque makes special mention of Sister Hortense, thanking her for the dedication.

The building officially belonged to Galway County Council. In 1921 the Galway Board of Health ordered the closure of all workhouses and union hospitals in the county, apart from the hospital wing of the Glenamaddy workhouse as this continued to provide care for destitute and orphaned children, under the auspices of the Bon Secours sisters, a nursing congregation who had originally come from Dublin to take charge of this hospital wing.

The bishop at the time, Bishop Fergus, decreed that this was a great compliment to the sisters and their work and so they were permitted to continue to operate in Glenamaddy. I read the pamphlet written by Bishop James Fergus which the nuns had sent me. He had been sent to Glenamaddy as a curate in 1921, and in the pamphlet he gives a glowing account of the sisters' nursing skills.

It soon transpired that the Glenamaddy workhouse was no longer fit for purpose. It was in dire need of re-roofing and refurbishment. As the years passed, nothing was done to rectify the problem, and it soon became clear that a new premises was needed. The former workhouses at Mountbellew and Portumna were suggested, but the sisters had set their sights on the old Tuam workhouse, and sought to be transferred there.

It was important for me to get a sense of what the workhouses were intended for and how this differed from the home the nuns were proposing to run. What I discovered was that, up to this period in Ireland's history, the workhouses catered for the destitute, the old and infirm, orphans and unmarried mothers, but that now, after the Anglo-Irish treaty, things were about to change. The Irish Free State decided to place the administration of such institutions on a county basis and to separate the treatment of the sick entirely from poor relief. So the workhouse system closed down, and the inhabitants were divided into different institutions. County homes were established for the sick and elderly, those with mental illnesses went to former workhouse buildings which became known as psychiatric hospitals for the 'insane' or depressed, and mother and baby homes were established for unmarried mothers and their children. Meanwhile, Magdalene laundries were a separate system again. It seemed that if mothers in the home gave birth to a second child out of wedlock, they were sent to the Magdalene laundry. There they would spend years paying for their 'sins'. It was an ingenious system from the nuns' perspective as they received free labour for years on end.

And so, in 1925, St Mary's mother and baby home became a reality. The *Tuam Herald*, under the heading 'Conversion of Workhouse into Children's Home', reported that the cost of the transfer was £5,000. The article mentions the disputes that erupted over this enormous sum of money. Some members of the Tuam Town Commissioners believed it was far too much and argued that the people of Tuam were also against the idea. And they were not the only ones, apparently, as the archbishop, Thomas Gilmartin, also seemed bitterly opposed to the relocation of the home to Tuam.

It was interesting to note, though, that in Bishop Fergus's pamphlet, he recorded that 'one or two Tuam Town Commissioners voiced some opposition to the transfer' but he did not include the archbishop in this opposition.

After much deliberation, it was finally agreed by all involved that the best solution was to move the children's home to Tuam. There was a small delay in the transfer, as the building was still operating as a military barracks run by the Irish Free State.

Once the military had completely vacated, it was time for the new inhabitants of St Mary's to arrive. According to Bishop Fergus, the first people to make the transfer to Tuam were Mother Euphremia and Sister Hortense and some of the older children under their care. They found their new surroundings in an awful state, with weeds everywhere and long grass entangled in barbed wire. In some of the rooms, floorboards had been torn up to make firewood. Otherwise, the buildings were in fairly good repair and must have been at least marginally better than the Glenamaddy workhouse the children had come from.

Gradually the remaining nuns, mothers and children arrived, and the work of clearing and cleaning began in earnest. They laid out paths and started painting. They worked very hard, and within a few years the grounds were tilled from wall to wall and were producing crops and flowers. The regular staff was increased to four with the arrival of Sister Gabriel. The first mother superior was Sister Elphage, and she was succeeded by Sister Priscilla Barry, who spent the rest of her life in Tuam. Bishop Fergus also mentions three women who stayed with the sisters all their lives: Bina Rabbitte, Annie Kelly and Mary Wade.

Dr Thomas B. Costello was announced as medical officer for the home and the Rev. Peter J. Kelly, a grandnephew of the former archbishop of Tuam, Dr John McEvilly, was made chaplain. The building continued to belong to Galway County Council which was responsible for repairs and maintenance. A capitation grant was paid to the nuns for the cost of upkeep of the mothers and babies, and for the salaries of doctors. A maternity unit seems to have been added later.

I was starting to develop a clear picture of how this home came to be the way it was: who was involved and what kind of place they created. I was finally ready to write my essay. From the evidence I had gathered, I knew that what I was about to write was not going to go down well with the religious, or the authorities such as the council. But I needed to expose what I had found. I was determined to publish what I believed to be the truth, no matter what the repercussions would be.

CHAPTER TWENTY-SIX

The Home

I called the essay 'The Home'.

I began at the end, with the closing of St Mary's in 1961. But even though the home was now shut forever, this did not bring an end to the pain and suffering of the women and children who had passed through its doors.

I set out my intention for the essay: to outline the history of this institution and give voice to some harrowing personal accounts of children who spent time there. I explained that it had been difficult to find many people locally who were willing to talk about the home, and concluded that either the memory of those I spoke with had dimmed over the years, or perhaps the stigma of unmarried mothers still existed.

One of the descriptions I found of the children's home was in a book called *Irish Journey* by the travel writer Halliday Sutherland. He painted a rather naive picture, in my view, having heard the harrowing stories from the home's former residents. He described it as a long, two-storeyed building on its own grounds.

These were well kept and had many flowerbeds. The Home is run by the Sisters of Bon Secours of Paris and the Reverend Mother showed me around. Each of the Sisters is a fully trained nurse and midwife. Some are also trained children's nurses. An unmarried girl may come here to have her baby. She agrees to stay in the Home for one year. During this time she looks after her baby and assists the nuns in domestic work. She is unpaid. At the end of the year she may leave. She may take her baby with her or leave the baby at the Home in the hope that it will be adopted. The nuns keep the child until the age of seven, when it is sent to an Industrial School.

There were 51 confinements in 1954 and the nuns now looked after 120 children. For each child or mother in the Home, the County Council pays £1 per week . . . Children of five and over attend the local school . . . The whole building was fresh and clean . . . I walked along the path and was mobbed by over a score of the younger children. They said nothing but each struggled to shake my hand . . . Then I realised that to these children I was a potential adopter who might take some boy or girl away to a real home. It was pathetic . . . At the Dogs Home in Battersea, every dog barks at the visitor in the hope that it will be taken away.

Mr Sutherland then left the home for his next appointment – tea at the archbishop's palace where Dr Joseph Walsh gave him a friendly reception. His description of the home seemed to lack any kind of compassion. Had he sought permission to speak to the mothers who were confined there, he may have come away with a very different account, as all the evidence was clear that mothers were not permitted to take their babies with them when they left, nor were the children sent to industrial schools. It was a report full of inaccuracies.

A former resident of the home, who would have been a child when Halliday Sutherland visited, was the late John Cunningham, former editor of the *Connaught Tribune*. In his article 'Emotional Minefield of the Rights of Mothers and Adopted Children from the Ireland of Yesterday' published in 1998, he wrote about the searing and emotional partings of mothers and babies. John spoke to a woman in her sixties, who spent most of her life in the home and gave this account of what it was like there:

> What were the young women to do? Many weren't wanted at home, they were ostracised by society . . . in those days a young woman could not become pregnant and stay at home. It was as simple as that. I saw the devastation when they were parted from their children . . . they nursed the child and looked after it for a year and then they went one way and the child stayed to be adopted, or to be boarded out a few years later. I don't know if many of them recovered from the heartbreaking parting. For instance, I was boarded out myself. That was the way Ireland was at the time . . . But I will never forget the parting of some of the mothers and their children. It was heart-rending.

John added that, in order to understand the complexity of these partings, we must look at the situation the unmarried mother was in. She would not have been able to face her family with a baby without a father, he explained. To them, she was a 'fallen woman', a disgrace to the family. Pregnancy outside of marriage was against Catholic teaching and brought shame upon the family. Many women were forced to leave home and would have been penniless and without any support. Their only hope was to head for England and start a new life there. Indeed, many unmarried pregnant girls would have gone to England to have their babies, rather than face the mother and baby homes, John wrote, which is backed up by evidence elsewhere.

Halliday Sutherland in his chapter on the Magdalene Home gives a table of figures that he acquired from a charity called Crusade of Rescue in the Diocese of Westminster, which was set up to help single women.

For the years 1950 to 1953, the number of women who had come from Ireland to seek the charity's help was 485, and, of those, 51 were from County Galway. The social worker Ruth J.A. Kelly also states in her research that many charitable services in England were unable to cope with the large numbers arriving from Ireland, quoting an English social worker who said, 'The fear of these girls has to be seen to be believed . . . what sort of society do you have in Ireland that puts the girls into this state?'

This led me to wonder – where were the fathers of these children? There was no mention of them in any of the material. Neither the church nor the state, nor indeed society at large, seemed to lay any significant blame, shame or responsibility on their shoulders; instead, it was the women who were banished and punished for 'their' crime.

I discovered that the only effort to make the father responsible was the passing of the 1930 Illegitimate Children (Affiliation Orders) Act, which was a weak attempt to facilitate unmarried mothers in suing the fathers of their babies. The passing of this law allowed the poor law guardians to initiate proceedings against the father if the child was supported on the poor rate, but obtaining a decree involved cross-examination of the mother and corroboration of her evidence, which, for many, would not be conceivable.

An alternative legal route was for a woman's employer or parents to bring a civil action for 'seduction', claiming loss of services as a result of the woman's pregnancy. Costs in such cases could be high and awards low. The woman herself could prosecute, but doing so was an ordeal in a society where pregnancy brought disgrace, and the legal process was intimidating. Cases were not easy to prove, and corroboration was still required. If the man defaulted in his payments, the penalty was a return to court, which was a slow and costly process. This made it impossible for women to get any kind of financial assistance from the father of their child. The system gave no supports to unmarried mothers and thus created a vacuum whereby the mother and baby homes were the only option available to many women in this situation.

It angered me to think of this – the way the system so often treats women in this way, making it impossible for them to have justice, let alone equality.

CHAPTER TWENTY-SEVEN

A Home from Home

~

Fostering was a major part of this story, and an experience I had not fully understood until now.

Imagine finally being freed from the institution you had been incarcerated in your whole life, as a child, having survived there, somehow, without the comfort of your mother. Then told you are to go to a foster family – people who will care for you. You are taken away, somewhere new and alien, to live with strangers, only to find that they are cruel and that life is just as harsh, if not harsher in their care. This is the picture that was emerging about the fostering system that was used in Ireland at that time.

This was something the interviewees I had spoken with had talked of at great length and was a much bigger part of the story than I had previously anticipated. The system at that time seemed to be that children were boarded out to foster parents once they reached the age of four or five. The foster parents received an allowance for clothing and food for the child and in many instances it seems the child was put to work in the foster parents' home and on their farm. Many of the children were fostered out only to provide unpaid labour for the foster family.

Advertisements were placed regularly in the *Tuam Herald* looking for foster parents. Applications were made on a special form and were lodged with the secretary of the county home in Loughrea. The council then sent out a form to be signed by the parish priest and the home assistance officer. In some instances this system worked well, but more often than not it was greatly abused.

And this is where Michael Hession's story came in. I set to work writing about Michael's experience of being fostered, using his full name as he had wished. Michael Hession was one of the many children fostered out from the Tuam mother and baby home in the 1950s, I explained. And he was one of the unlucky ones, being sent to an uncaring family who treated him like a slave.

Michael could remember the day he left the home. He was made to wait in a hallway with long windows draped in heavy amber curtains. Then he was taken outside and put into a car. He didn't know where he was going. The car drove for miles, out into the countryside, before stopping to deposit him at a thatched house, where he was to spend the next twelve years of his life.

In piecing together the story of his life, Michael had gathered some official reports, given to him when he applied, through the Freedom of Information Act, to the Western Health Board for his personal records. Among those records was a copy of the form of contract that was signed by Michael's foster mother, where she agreed to all the conditions in the indenture to protect, feed and clothe him. The sum of £1.50 per month was to be her allowance for his care, and a clothing allowance of £5 a year was to be allocated.

But Michael did not benefit from this allowance, for it was never spent on him. In later life, he would call this new home 'the Abyss', as that was what it felt like at the time, though he didn't have the words to describe it when he was there. He wrote that he often wondered how the nuns managed the selection of the children for fostering: 'We could have been raffled, take your pick or lucky dip . . . or maybe auctioned off.'

When I read Michael's letter, I thought this must be an exaggeration, that it couldn't possibly be the case. But many of the reports I discovered subsequently in the *Tuam Herald* about the Board of Health meetings at the time echoed Michael's point. One was headed 'Boarded Out Children for Cheap Labour in North Galway':

> The present system of fostering out children is not too efficient and an effort was not always made to find the home that most suited the child or the child that most suited the home. The allowance given to foster parents was not always spent on the child's welfare.

In another article, entitled 'Councillors Hear of Complaints in Inspector's Report', the *Herald* reports:

> Greater care should be taken in the selection of foster homes . . . it would be well to explain verbally to the foster parent the conditions under which the child has been boarded out, e.g., the obligations of the foster parent to send him to school regularly, to facilitate inspectors, to allow inspections of all parts of the foster home, and to expend the full amount of the clothing allowance . . . These conditions are embodied in the boarding out contract, but few foster parents ever read this document and in general they seem to be quite unaware of its contents.

Michael's letters were harrowing to read. He was used by adults and never given any care or love. They stole his childhood, as he put it, and he carried that pain with him for the rest of his life. His foster family denied him adequate food and clothing, and expected him to do the work of a man, from the age of five – digging and clearing drains, rebuilding big stone walls, repairing double ditches and barbed wire fencing, and cutting acres of thistles, while often keeping him from going to school, against his will, to look after their farms, six miles apart.

One of Michael's clearest childhood memories was the day he got a puncture in the tyre of his bike when he was out working on one of the farms. Tired and cold, he dreaded the thoughts of walking six miles home, so he called to a house nearby to ask for a pump. He knocked on the door, and a kind woman answered. She brought him in to the fire and gave him tea and scones.

After that day, the severe hunger he was feeling drove him to deflate his bicycle tyre again and again. He went back to that same house, to ask for the pump each time, knowing that he would get another hot cup of tea and a little kindness. No doubt the old woman knew why he was coming. She must have felt for him – cold, wet and dirty from working all day on the land, with no one to care for him.

Later in life, Michael was also able to obtain his health records from the Western Health Board, which related to the years he was at national school. These included days of absence, and general reports of his ability at school. He proved to be a bright student despite missing many days on account of his foster mother keeping him at home to labour on the farm.

A treasured possession of Michael's was a copy of a letter sent by the principal of the technical school to the Children's Officer, County Buildings, Galway, asking: 'What is to be done with Michael Hession of . . . boarded out to . . . I was speaking to him some evenings ago and he is very upset that he is missing classes at the Tech. He deserves a chance.'

Unfortunately, Michael's story was by no means an isolated case. An inspector's report presented to Galway County Council in 1956 revealed:

. . . a very undesirable and unpleasant state of things . . . the callous treatment meted out to some of these unfortunate children, as instanced in the report, bears comparison with that imposed in the better class prison camps in totalitarian countries during the war. Neglect seems to be quite the common thing in some cases, and in the others, it borders on cruelty. Farm animals, or a certain valuable species of dog, are better treated than humans, and there is an urgent need to review this whole system of boarding out children who by accident of birth have neither home nor family.

Those words echoed in my mind: 'by accident of birth'. That's what this was all about. Those children, through no fault of their own, were born into this situation. Not that they themselves were accidents, but rather that none of us is responsible for the way in which we enter the world, or to whom and to what circumstance. It is all accidental, random, and, to a certain degree, the rest of our lives are predetermined by these factors.

I wanted to give several examples of real human stories in my essay, because no matter where I looked, I could not find these stories written into any kind of history. And I felt they needed to be heard. They deserved to be heard.

'Paddy' was a man I had met. I sat and had tea with him in his house, and he told me the story of his life. It was a great honour that he was willing to share his thoughts with me. I was meticulous about recording what he said, so we could commit his story to history.

His experience in a foster home was very similar to Michael's. He asked me not to mention his real name, so Paddy is a pseudonym. He too was born in the home, in 1946. His mother, who lived quite a distance from Tuam, was sent there by her family for fear that anyone in the community would discover that she was pregnant. It is difficult to completely appreciate the stigma that existed in Ireland at the time towards unmarried mothers and their children. But there must have been an entrenched fear on the part of the family, to go to such lengths to hide the pregnancy from the community.

Like most of the children who were born in the home, Paddy had very few memories of the institution itself because he was fostered out when he was just a boy. However, he does remember his foster home, and it still pained him to speak of his time there. When I went to Paddy's home, I found it remarkable that it was his wife who spoke so emotionally, such was the impact on her of her beloved's ill-treatment as a child.

It is interesting that, in Paddy's case, his mother paid for his keep in the home right up until he was 16. As Paddy was to discover in later years, his mother worked at two jobs in England, presumably to ensure her son's welfare in the home in the hope that he would have the best options open to him. According to Paddy, the nuns did not inform her that her son had been fostered out, but still graciously received and kept each instalment that she sent them.

Paddy's foster family went on to have eight children, and it was his job to help look after them, as well as doing the farm work and managing the bog. All he remembers from an early age is work, work, and more work. He also remembers an inspector calling to the house. When the inspector was due, Paddy was washed down and dressed in clothes and shoes he had never seen before. But after the inspector's departure, the good clothes disappeared and he was put back into his everyday rags. Paddy never owned a pair of shoes as a child, winter or summer.

I stopped for a moment and tried to fully take in that information. I tried to imagine a little boy farming in the depths of winter, with no shoes on his feet. I thought of my own children – the lengths we went to, as parents do, to make sure they were always warm and dry. It pained me to think of the sting of a cold Irish winter on a young boy's bare feet.

Paddy couldn't remember going hungry, but he will always remember being the last to be served a meal at the table. He was a foundling, an outsider, illegitimate. He would never be equal to the others and he was not allowed to forget it.

This harsh, cruel treatment seemed to be commonplace. Another man I spoke with talked of the times he was locked in a chicken coop when the family who were 'looking after him' went to the local fair for the day. To think that so many people had experienced this abuse as children in Ireland was heartbreaking.

Another former resident requested that I just call her 'Elizabeth'. She was living in New York, but grew up a world away from that big city. Elizabeth was just four years old when she left the home in August 1941 and was placed with a foster family. She says that they were miserable years. A memory which has never left her was of an incident that happened when she was a young girl. She was sitting on a three-legged stool in the kitchen when suddenly her foster mother whipped the stool out from under her and hit her husband over the head with it. She was in shock as she watched the blood pouring down his face.

She also spoke of the painful memory of being locked in a shed overnight as punishment. Her one little bit of consolation was that her birth mother was in a position to visit her at the foster home, and on one occasion when she found the little girl filthy and infested with lice, she immediately contacted the authorities, who then filed a report. A manager's order (MO), dated June 1943, states that 'Elizabeth' should be handed over to her mother. From what I have gathered, Elizabeth was then taken to her grand-mother's house by her mother for a short while, but her grandfather refused to accept her; she was not welcome there. And so she was brought to the Ballinasloe industrial school which was run by the Sisters of Mercy, and remained there until she was 15, at which point she was sent to work in a shop in Dublin, with board and keep. What a cruel place the world could be for some people, I thought as I pieced together the journey that Elizabeth had been on. No doubt when she walks down a busy Manhattan street no one would guess that she had such a story to tell.

Though it seemed to be uncommon, some of the fostering experiences were positive. 'Kevin' from Mayo was born in the Tuam home in March 1942, and at the age of three was placed with a childless couple who looked after him and cared for him throughout his life. He found a loving home; he was one of the lucky ones. He requested anonymity as his story is ongoing and he has siblings to consider.

After working in England in later years, Kevin returned to Mayo and began to wonder about his real identity. He was able to locate his records from the Western Health Board in Galway, and from his birth certificate he found his mother's name and former address. He used this information to try to track her down, but when he arrived at the address his mother was nowhere to be found. He was greeted by an uncle, who made him welcome but unfortunately was not able to tell him where his mother went after she left the home in Tuam. She simply disappeared, he told him. No one in the family knew what had happened to her. But what he could tell him was that she had also given birth to a girl, a few years before Kevin was born. With this information, Kevin was able to track down his sister. He had gone looking for a mother, but instead had found a sister.

Kevin got on with his life, married and had a family, but always held out hope that he might find his mother some day. In later years, his daughter also took on the task of trying to locate her and even sought the help of the Salvation Army in England, but without success.

I was so moved by their story that I offered to help them, if I could. I had picked up a few useful researching tips and was happy to put my skills to the test. After many months, much in-depth researching, and frequent cross-checking with Kevin's daughter, we narrowed the possibilities down to two families. I took a chance on one surname and phoned a family in the English midlands. After exchanging some brief details, I realised that, yes, I was on the right track! Kevin's mother had married twice (the name changes being the biggest obstacle in tracing her), and had, in all, seven more children. The heartbreaking news was that she had passed away only four years earlier. I relayed the news to Kevin and his family, who, although being sad at her passing, were really overjoyed to at least have the answers they had been searching for, and a grave to visit. They organised a reunion with all the extended family – Kevin's brothers and sisters whom he had never met. It gave me great joy to hear that Kevin finally had a sense of who his family were and that he was reunited with his siblings.

So these were the stories of those who were fostered, or 'boarded out'. The next topic to broach in the essay was that of adoption. This was a grey area and one that concerned me. It wasn't until the early 1950s that adoption became legal in Ireland. From my research, I could see that the vast majority of applications came from the US, and it was nearly always babies that were sought. A report in the *Tuam Herald* of that era gave an insight into the process.

Within the last 18 months six children from the Children's Home in Tuam have been adopted by families in the U.S. The Home Assistance Dept. of Galway Co. Co. are at present investigating applications for 14 more adoptions for U.S.A.

Inquiries revealed that Miss Áine Walsh Staff Officer of the Home Ass. Dept. and her staff have a really tricky job to perform in the adoption of children by Americans. The applications generally come from clergymen in the States on behalf of childless couples. This is the start of a very tedious and intricate process. The Co. Co. staff then get down to the routine of getting all available information on the applicants. Through Church and State Authorities background, religion, reputation and finance are inquired into, before the Galway Authorities are satisfied that a child from the Home will be bettered by adoption . . . Photographs of children are sent across the Atlantic, but in some cases wealthy couples have come to Tuam and made choices first hand. The Home Assistance Dept. arranges for emigration. Passports and Visas are obtained, travel tickets are procured, the child is clothed and arrangements are made for the safe conduct to the American Port of debarkation . . . In all cases, Catholic children go to Catholic homes, and other denominations are adopted only into foster homes of their own creed.

This was all that I could gather in terms of adoption from the home. So it seemed that some children were being sent to America. But what of the others – the ones who weren't fostered or adopted? What happened to them?

CHAPTER TWENTY-EIGHT

The Others

❧

'Tenders for Coffins'. These harrowing words advertised by the children's home appeared sporadically in the local newspaper, which indicated that deaths were commonplace there.

I needed to investigate further. I spent months researching and found that a staggering number of children had lost their lives in the home. While the figures are shocking, it should also be remembered that Ireland had at this time a very high infant mortality rate, when poverty was rampant and routine vaccinations for commonplace diseases such as measles and tuberculosis, as well as other advances in medical care, were still some decades off. However, it seemed that a child in a home was much more likely to die than a 'legitimate' child growing up in a family environment.

The death records showed that for the years 1925/26, 57 children, aged between one month and three years (plus two aged six and eight years), died in the Tuam home. Of this number, 21 died of measles; other causes were convulsions, gastroenteritis, bronchitis, tuberculosis, meningitis, and pneumonia. Another outbreak of measles in November and December 1936 took the lives of 22 children, all under three years of age. For the years 1930 to 1960 (when the last death was recorded), I took a random list of children from each decade who had died, as there were too many deaths to look at them individually. Other causes of death were as follows: pertussis (otherwise known as whooping cough), anaemia, influenza, nephritis (kidney inflammation), laryngitis, congenital heart disease, enteritis, epilepsy, spina bifida, chicken pox, general oedema (dropsy), coeliac disease, birth injury, sudden circulatory failure, and fits. In later years, measles had become less of an epidemic. Most of these children were under three years old.

The conditions would not have been good in the home, with all the children living together in that crowded, damp setting. Disease was rife. But was it more than that, I wondered. Were these children being neglected?

And what of the ones who died – where were all these children buried? The county council archivist suggested that perhaps the Bon Secours sisters kept their own register of deaths and burials. Following her advice, I wrote to the Bon Secours archivist in Cork, but she informed me once again that they did not have any records on the home; that when they left Tuam, all records were forwarded to Galway County Council, who later handed them to the Western Health Board in Galway.

So I contacted the Western Health Board, who told me they had no knowledge of the register. Perhaps none was ever kept, or it was lost over time. Maybe some of the children were claimed by relatives, to be buried in cemeteries outside the Tuam area, it was suggested. But that idea didn't seem plausible to me. With so-called illegitimate children far outnumbering orphaned children in the home, and knowing that relatives would not acknowledge them in life, I found it quite unlikely that they would claim them in death.

So I posed the question: is it possible that a large number of those little children were buried in that plot at the rear of the former home? And if so, why is it not acknowledged as a proper cemetery? The Ordnance Survey now indicate all 'cilleens' (cemeteries for unbaptised babies) on their current maps. This little cemetery is not acknowledged in any shape or form, and would have been forgotten about only for the kindness of the local couple who tend to it so well. What remains now, I suggested, is to erect a specific memorial in this cemetery indicating that here lie the 'home babies'.

Today there is no sign that the mother and baby home once existed, except for a small part of the old boundary wall. 'Children's Home To Be Closed after 33 Years' was the headline on the front page of the *Tuam Herald* on 4 February 1961. Galway County Council, which was the controlling authority, had come to an agreement with the Department of Local Government and Public Health that the institution should be closed.

The renovation of the building had been under consideration for some time, but was eventually rejected by the department on economic grounds. The occupants were to be sent to similar institutions, such as the Sacred Heart home in Castlepollard, County Westmeath; St. Patrick's in Cabra, Dublin; and Sean Ross Abbey, Roscrea, County Tipperary. By the summer of 1961 the home was totally vacated.

The Tuam town commissioners discussed what to do with the building. It was proposed that a new clinic be situated there, but an objection was made that this was unsuitable, because of its dilapidated state, and because the clinic needed to be centrally located for ease of access.

And so the home that hundreds of children had passed through over the decades was destined to crumble and decay behind the high stone walls that surrounded it. When the sisters and the children left, this dark, formidable building stood empty and silent for many years. Its grounds sprouted brambles, nettles and weeds, and its only visitors were a few local boys who scaled the high wall looking for adventure in its wilderness.

It was on one of those escapades that the two boys came upon the hole in the ground, where they discovered several small skulls. I recorded the story of Frannie and Barry in the essay, explaining that it was presumed that the area had been used to bury famine victims. So nothing further had been done, and over a decade later the building was demolished and a housing estate was built on the seven acres where it had stood.

I decided to pose the question – to put it out there into the world. Were those bodies that the boys found really the remains of famine victims? Was that the most plausible explanation, or was there something much darker at play? Could it be that the children from the home were buried in the grounds, in the patch of earth which now bordered the playground in the middle of the housing estate?

It was very unlike me to do something so public. I was starting to doubt myself. What if it wasn't true? I didn't have enough evidence to prove it. But there was enough to ask the question. And I felt I had to do that.

I cannot fully explain it, but I could feel a kind of force, something deep inside, that was urging me on, pushing me to pursue this, no matter what. I just knew in my bones that there was a dark and disturbing case to be answered and I couldn't put my mind at ease until I knew the truth.

CHAPTER TWENTY-NINE

Suffer Us Children

I hadn't heard from Michael in weeks. The envelopes with his distinctive handwriting had suddenly stopped appearing on our doorstep. He must be busy, I thought, though it was very unlike him not to write, especially as the last correspondence had come from me.

I decided I would write again, to let him know that the essay was nearly completed and that it would soon be published. I was excited to tell him that his story would finally be acknowledged – that people would know of the injustices that had been done to him and all the children like him who lived in the mother and baby homes.

A few days later, I received a letter I really wasn't expecting. I saw the same British stamp on the envelope, but the handwriting was different to Michael's. I opened it up and couldn't believe what I was reading.

It was from a lady who said she was a dear friend of Michael's. She wanted to let me know that Michael had passed away after a long illness and that he had died peacefully. She told me that he often spoke of me and of his excitement that I was writing an essay which would include his story.

I put the letter down and sat there, not knowing what to do or what to think. Michael had never mentioned he was ill. And though we had never met, I felt I had come to know him. We had become friends over the two years that we had been corresponding. I looked forward to his letters, and loved writing to him. To think that he was gone forever, and that we would never have the chance to meet in person. He had lived such a difficult life. And now, for his life to be taken from him at a time when he should have finally enjoyed some peace in his old age seemed so cruel.

I went to the drawer where I kept his letters. I took them out and read them again. It was emotional reading his words, knowing that he had now passed away. In a sense I felt like the undeserving keeper of his story, knowing that these precious letters, like diary entries, told the story of his life.

When Aidan came in from the farm, I gave him the news. He too was shocked. Somehow Michael, this person we had never met, had become a big part of our lives, probably more than he ever really knew. It was Michael's letters and the stories of his childhood that spurred me on if I ever became tired of researching. I felt I needed to do this – to get to the bottom of it all, for Michael. So that at last he might have a tiny piece of the justice he so deserved.

I searched for the poem Michael had written in one of his letters. I read it over and over again, then went for a walk in the woods, to think about Michael and the life he had led. The words of his poem echoed in my mind: 'Suffer us children that carry this cross / Suffer us children that Ireland forgot'.

And it had forgotten them. Even to this day. I could only hope that Michael had finally found the peace that had eluded him all his life.

'Suffer us children that carry this cross / Suffer us children that Ireland forgot'.

CHAPTER THIRTY

Deaf Ears

I added Michael's poem to the essay. It seemed a fitting tribute to the person who had inspired so much of the research. When I was finally finished, I read the essay over and over again. I gave it to Aidan to proofread – to see if he might spot anything that I hadn't seen – any mistakes I might have made or anything I might have overlooked. I revised it many times, until finally I felt I couldn't look at it anymore. The words were starting to lose their meaning, I had read them so often. It was just 15 pages, but I was agonising over the detail. I clicked 'Send', then breathed a sigh of relief. It was gone to the editor.

'Sent!' I said to Aidan triumphantly.

He congratulated me and reminded me how much work had gone into the research. 'But, mind,' he said, 'don't be disappointed now if they don't publish it, for some reason.' Aidan was concerned that the accusations in the piece and questioning whether there may be human remains buried in a sewage tank might all be a bit too risky for the journal to publish. After all, it wasn't quite the essay they had been expecting.

He was right. I had to be prepared for that. But for now, I just needed to go for a walk and get some air. I was tired of looking at the computer screen. I walked out the door and whistled to our dog Shadow to follow. He ran ahead of me and up into the fields looking for rabbits. As a collie-newfoundland mix, he was in need of plenty of exercise. I always got a kick out of people's reactions when they saw us out and about together. He's so big he looks more like a bear than a dog. He came bounding back to me to check in before running off again. I felt he knew I had a lot on my mind. We call him Shadow because he is always with us, wherever we go.

It was blustery and the rain was spitting down. I walked out towards the woods and I breathed in the crisp country air. I pulled down the hood of my raincoat and faced up to the sky, to feel the rain on my skin washing away the staleness of having been inside. I let out a sigh and continued my walk. The ground was wet beneath my feet as I navigated the rain-drenched soil in my wellies.

The words of the essay were going through my mind. I almost knew it by heart and without meaning to was reciting it in my head. I hoped I had included all the information that was needed. I was always nervous when sending an essay in to the *Journal of the Old Tuam Society*. I couldn't help but feel like a bit of a fraud. Even though I had spent the best part of two years researching it, I still doubted myself. I had begun my research in 2010, and it was now the autumn of 2012. The society was made up of very learned people – historians who knew a great deal about the topics I was covering. I often felt like I might be found out: who was I? I had not studied history in university and did not profess to be an expert, by any stretch of the imagination.

I waited for a reply. A few days later the editor wrote, thanking me for the piece and confirming that the journal would be published soon and that they would be in touch about the launch.

It all came around very quickly. The annual was published in December. One cold wintry evening, Aidan and I got ready and headed into the Synod Hall, part of St Mary's Protestant church in Tuam for the launch. I was a little nervous because for every launch they took one of the essays from the journal and made it the focus of the night, and this time they had chosen mine. They had invited a guest speaker, a retired teacher, who spoke of his memories of the 'home children' in his classroom and his distinct memory of the sound of their hobnail boots click-clacking on the paths leading to the school. After the presentation, each of the contributors was given a complimentary copy of the journal to take home.

That night I sat beside the range in the kitchen, opened the journal and read my piece, as though I was an outsider reading it for the first time. Aidan sat next to me and read the essay for what must have been the hundredth time. We both agreed that it was comprehensive. I stated the facts, and ended the piece asking the question: is it possible that a large number of those little children were buried in that small plot at the rear of the former home? And if so, why is it not acknowledged as a proper cemetery?

And so it was done: the question was being asked, as plain as day. I worried about how the church might react – if they would be defensive or, worse yet, angry. Whatever the reaction, it was published now and there was no going back. I would have to deal with the consequences, whatever they may be.

And so I waited . . . and waited. I waited for the phone to ring, for someone to get in touch – the church, the local media, someone in a position of authority. But no one did. I had somehow naively believed that once I wrote the article for the *JOTS*, our local media, the church, the powers-that-be might have taken up my research and declared some shock at my discovery. And then it would be taken out of my hands – people who could do something about it would take over from here. Or so I thought.

The weeks and months passed, and not a trickle of concern from anywhere for the home babies. Not even from the church. I had imagined that our archbishop, Michael Neary, would contact the Bon Secours sisters and take the whole matter under his wing. I had played the whole thing out in my mind – how it would go, what they might say. But none of that was coming to pass.

At first I felt a sadness, but it was turning into anger the more time went on. 'It's just not right,' I said to Aidan one night as I pored over the documents again. 'How is there not war over this? Hundreds of dead children!'

'I know,' Aidan said, 'I know.'

I couldn't comprehend how this was being allowed to happen. How people were happy to ignore this horrific crime that had been committed on these poor innocent children. I thought of my own children as babies. I thought of all the children I had minded over the years. There was nothing more precious than a child. And yet these adults had taken advantage of their innocence, had robbed them of their childhoods and had neglected them to the point of death. And even then, they had not shown them a modicum of decency. And for what? Why? Because they were born out of wedlock. It made me furious to think of it.

I was angry too, about poor Michael, dying without any sense of justice, still believing that no one in the world cared about what had gone on in St Mary's. And now, for the first time, I could see that perhaps he was right in that assumption. No one cared.

I was annoyed at myself too. I had not done what I set out to do. What had it all been for? All the research, all the digging.

The silence had been broken but it had fallen on deaf ears.

CHAPTER THIRTY-ONE

Unfinished Business

In a way, I had no choice but to return to normal life after the essay was completed. I had given up my trips to the library and was back to tending the animals and working the farm.

But a feeling deep inside kept coming back to me, knowing that the question still remained unanswered: what happened to those children in the home?

One night I woke with a fright. I had been dreaming I was walking out the gate of my parents' house when all of a sudden the ground opened up beside me. There was a girl trapped in the hole and she was screaming for me to help her.

It was just a dream, I told myself, as I looked around at the darkness of the bedroom. I took a deep breath. But the sounds of the girl's screams still echoed in my mind.

'I can't let it go,' I said to Aidan the next morning as we walked out towards the cattle shed.

'Let what go?'

'The babies . . . I can't let them go,' I said.

He looked at me, surprised. He must have wondered why this

of all things had captured my attention in a way nothing else in life ever had. How I had it in me to do things for the babies that I sometimes didn't have in me to do for my own family. I had been able to go and talk to people and put myself out there in ways I had been avoiding for many years. I couldn't explain it. It was as though for the first time in my life I felt a real need to do something. Because it was becoming apparent that no one else would.

As a child, I had felt powerless and alone in the world. I felt like I had no voice. Even my own mother didn't want to hear from me. I had made a promise to myself long ago that my children would grow up in a house where they felt heard and understood and, most of all, safe and protected. And we had managed to do that for them. I had vowed that I wouldn't let anyone else mind them, that I would be there for them, no matter what. I knew how important that was for children. Because I knew what the opposite felt like – what fear and loneliness could do to a person. I couldn't stand to think of any child growing up in that way. And now these children who had been subjected to so much fear and injustice in their lives, it seemed no one wanted to hear from them either. They had no voice. I knew I had to be a voice for them.

I had given it time – waited to see what would be done once the story was out there – and so far, nothing had happened. Not a thing. I had to do something.

I needed to know the full story. It was going to take more time than I had devoted to the essay research. It seemed like it deserved more than that. I decided to go back to the births, deaths and marriages archivist to see if I could find out more.

I rang her and asked if it would be possible to continue to record the number of deaths in the home. Originally she had given me just a sample of them, we had stopped at 200. I now wished to know how many there were in total.

She said she would look into it and come back to me. A few weeks later she rang. I'll never forget what she said. '798 children were recorded as having died,' she told me.

When I realised that number – nearly 800 children – I felt numb. This was four times what I had originally anticipated. Nearly a thousand children dying in that home. Something really was not right.

I rang my daughter Adrienne. She was sitting on the back step outside her house in Enniscorthy with her six-month-old baby. The line went silent after I told her the news.

'Are you still there, Adrienne?' I asked.

'It's just so sad,' she said, 'those babies.' Her voice was starting to crack. I could tell she was upset.

She was so horrified to think that so many were left to die, as she held her baby a little tighter, a little closer. To think what it must have been like for those mothers to say goodbye to their children, and for the children to be institutionalised in that way, and then to die without their families close by. I told Adrienne I would ring again the next day, when we'd both had time to digest the news.

That night, I felt an anger surge inside me. To think that this was the same church that was telling us how to live our lives and how to be good and truthful. I suddenly felt angry at everyone. I was angry at the people who wouldn't help, at the empty letters I received instead of the information I required. Why did no one care that so many children had died? I couldn't understand it. I knew in my heart I had to do something about it, but I just didn't know what.

CHAPTER THIRTY-TWO

Searching

I arranged to meet John Mannion, the graveyard caretaker, again. A lot had happened in the two years since we had last met. I had something I wanted to ask him.

We arranged to meet inside the cemetery gates, just opposite the housing estate. It was a cold autumn day. I pulled my coat tighter as I waited for him to arrive. I looked around at all the graves – names and inscriptions, every headstone a symbol for a life lived and lost. It makes you wonder what it's all about sometimes, when you see the end there in front of you – where we are all headed. It's a strange thing, life. Everything else we do has a goal – something we are moving towards – but to think that ultimately we are all moving towards death . . . it's a stark and sobering thought.

I saw John's van arrive and pull up just inside the gates. I walked over to say hello, and I told him about the research I had been conducting – what I had discovered since we had last spoken. I told him that 798 children had died in the home. And then I asked him the question I longed to know the answer to: 'Where do you think those children are buried?'

He looked at me for a moment, as though weighing me up. 'Well, I know where they're not buried,' he said.

Before I could ask any more questions he handed me a large leather-bound book. 'The burial records,' he said, 'for the cemetery. None of those children are in it – you can see for yourself.'

I took the book, surprised by the weight of it in my hands. He opened the door of his van so we could shelter from the wind. We clambered into the front seats. I opened the book and looked through the pages . . . names and dates, for every person buried in the parish for generations: their age and date of death, and their name – the person they were for every moment they were alive.

I thought about what John had said. *None of those children are in it . . .*

I took out the printed records of the children who had died in the home and one by one cross-referenced their names with the alphabetical index at the front of the book. When I didn't find a child's name I crossed it out with a pencil and moved on to the next one. It was time-consuming, to say the least. John sat with me the whole time. I had nearly gone through the entire list, crossing out each name, when, to my surprise – a match! One of the children's names was in the book. And then I found a second match. So I now knew what had happened to two of the children, but 796 were still unaccounted for.

When I reached the end of the list I sat up. '796 children are missing,' I said to John.

He nodded. We knew what this meant.

I thanked him for his help and we both agreed that something needed to be done. I got back into my car and drove through the graveyard and out past the housing estate across the road. I just couldn't understand why the children weren't buried in that graveyard. It was only a few hundred metres from the home.

I later discovered that the two children buried there were orphans. So if these children were orphans and were buried in the graveyard, that led me to wonder if the children who weren't orphans were in fact buried with their families – grandparents or relatives in the homelands they had originally come from.

Though I was sceptical of the idea – after all, why would they accept them in death but not in life? – I needed to investigate to see if it could be possible. Perhaps there was some legal obligation, in which case they would be buried with their kin, so it was worth looking into. I figured that the majority of the women in the Tuam home would have come from Galway and Mayo, and therefore if the children were buried in their 'homeplace', that's where those records should be, though it is difficult to speak of homeplace in relation to these children, as they had never known a home in their lives.

I contacted Galway County Council and they put me in touch with their archivist. They were in the process of putting all the records of cemeteries online and so the records were not immediately accessible, she explained. I told her that I was looking to see if any of the names on the death records I had matched their records – to see if any of the children who died at the home had been buried elsewhere in the county.

There were no matches, the archivist told me, after she had completed the search.

I moved on to Mayo County Council. I asked for the names of the local cemetery caretakers, like John Mannion, who would have the books with all the burials recorded. Within a few weeks I heard back from those caretakers, and each had the same answer – none of the children were recorded as buried in their cemeteries.

So, no record of the children's burials anywhere, it seemed. It was very odd. Why were there such meticulous records of the babies' births and deaths, but no record, anywhere, of a single burial? As I sat at the kitchen table looking at the list of names I found myself whispering, 'Where are you? Where could you be?' Though deep down I felt I knew where they were. I just wanted so badly to be proven wrong.

And then a thought came to me – a strange but somewhat plausible one. What if all these children *didn't* actually die? If they had died, they had to be buried somewhere. They couldn't have vanished into thin air. So maybe, just maybe, some of them weren't buried at all, because they weren't dead. Could it be possible that their death records were falsified?

From the records, we could see that children from Tuam were being adopted legally by Americans in the 1950s. So these children would be accounted for, but what about before the 1950s? The Tuam home had operated from the 1920s and many of these children had disappeared long before the 1950s. What if they had been *illegally* adopted – sent to families in America.

I thought long and hard about this. If a child had been adopted by a family outside of Ireland illegally, then there was little chance of finding a record of that agreement. But surely there would have to be a record of the children arriving in another country. If they crossed international borders, someone somewhere would need to record it. Immigration, presumably. I broke it down: because we're an island, there would have been only two ways they could have left – by sea or by air.

I decided to check the shipping records first, to see if any of the children on my list were recorded as travelling by sea. I had joined a website called Ancestry.com. It was a bit costly at 130 euro for 6 months, but it had detailed shipping records to the US, along with census details for the UK and the US, and indexes for deaths and marriages up to the present for Ireland and the UK.

I searched through the shipping records to the main ports in

America and Canada into which Irish ships would have come for the years 1900 to 1930. The records gave the name, age, and home address of most passengers, as well as who they were going to stay with on arrival in North America. Some of the records even gave a description of the person, for example 'fair skin, brown hair, blue eyes', and their height. After a thorough search, however, I discovered that none of the children were listed as having travelled to America or Canada.

I then checked the flight records on the same website, but nothing came up there either. The flight records were not as detailed, and so were a little less reliable.

Another dead end. I had exhausted almost every avenue. At this point, one had to assume that these children had died and were buried somewhere in Ireland. But where?

CHAPTER THIRTY-THREE

Plaques and Tapes

⌒

I hated to think of the babies with no headstone, no proof that
they existed, that they mattered in the world. I felt I needed
to organise some way to commemorate them, to mark their
existence. But I wasn't sure where to begin. John Mannion
suggested I get in touch with a woman named Teresa Kelly. She
knew a lot of people locally and was very active in the community.

I met with Teresa the following week at the home site beside
the playground. I brought the list of names with me. We talked
it over and decided that we should form a committee – to get
local people involved in deciding what we could do to commemorate the children who died at the Tuam home.

Teresa seemed to know everyone in Tuam and very quickly she
had formed a committee made up of ten people from the local
community. At the first meeting, it was my job to explain how I
came to have this list of names and why I felt there might be a
chance that the babies were buried on the site of the old mother
and baby home. I was nervous speaking in public, but I tried to

focus on the outcome – if something could be done for the babies, that would be a huge step forward. When I was finished speaking, I looked around the table. I wondered if anyone else felt as moved by the plight of the babies as I did.

We decided to adjourn for the evening so that everyone could reflect on what they had heard, and we agreed a date for the next meeting. I wasn't sure what exactly I wanted to come out of this new committee, but it felt good to have some people on board – I didn't feel as alone with the whole thing. I felt a new sense of purpose: there was a team now, and between us all we should be able to get to the bottom of what had happened in Tuam.

The next meeting came around a few weeks later. Teresa opened, thanking everyone for coming. A discussion began as people talked about the home and what it must have been like. They told anecdotes they had heard about it. And then the question, the elephant in the room: what to do about the children who had died there.

There was silence for a moment. Then someone suggested that a commemorative plaque might be a nice idea. Everyone agreed, nodding in unison. This was a fitting thing to do. We could fundraise, suggested another. This too seemed to go down well with the group.

And so it was decided – a fundraising effort would commence to erect a number of plaques with all 796 of the children's names on them.

'A nice, positive tribute,' said one of the members.

'Yes . . .' I said, nodding slowly. I could hardly keep up with how quickly it was all decided. But I couldn't work out how I felt about it all – I knew something wasn't sitting well. I didn't let on, though, as I knew everyone was doing their best. Yes, plaques would be lovely, I agreed.

And so the conversation focused on the types of activities that would be organised to fundraise. It felt as though the women around the table were accustomed to this kind of thing – organising fundraisers and community events. I was so disconnected from the community. Perhaps this is how things are supposed to work, I thought. They all seemed to think so. I felt like I was missing something.

It was only when I was back in my car driving home that I really had a chance to digest it all. A number of plaques with the names on them? Somehow this wasn't what I had been expecting. For months I had agonised over the disappearance of these children – I longed to know where they were and what had happened to them in their short lives. With the formation of the committee, I felt I would finally have a team of people with a similar lust for the truth. But plaques? It seemed so simple, so final, so accepting. I felt we needed to do more.

I couldn't wait to speak with Aidan about my frustration. He was always a good gauge of whether I was being unreasonable. He was usually able to put me straight – he had a good read of how things worked in communities, of what mattered and how to go about doing things with other people. I never really understood all that. It seemed to come naturally to others – working in synchronicity. I found people difficult to understand, mostly; they were generally quite sentimental and not overly practical, in my experience.

'What good will plaques do?' I said, as Aidan and I sat by the fire.

'Well, it's a nice way to commemorate the children,' he said. 'They deserve that, at the very least.'

I stared into the flames as they danced up and down. I could feel the warmth of the fire on my legs, with Shadow curled up at my feet. I was trying to understand how the committee could be satisfied with simply erecting plaques. It didn't get me any further in my quest to find out what had happened. But on the other hand, without plaques there was no acknowledgement of the children at all, so perhaps I should see these commemorative symbols as a good first step – a modicum of decency to remember the lives of the children who died.

I decided the only thing to do was to get behind it. Wholeheartedly. Erecting plaques didn't have to be the only thing we did, it could just be a start, a move in the right direction.

At the next committee meeting there were further discussions about fundraising opportunities. Galway County Council had agreed to contribute to the plaques, and when the Bon Secours sisters had been approached to see if they would do likewise, they had asked how much Galway County Council was putting forward. Two thousand euro, the committee had informed them. So they had said they would match that. The cost of the five bronze plaques with all the names of those who died in the Tuam home would come to 6,500 euro, so we had to find an extra 2,500 euro somehow. Some ideas were put forward, and roles and jobs were allocated.

During the coffee break, several of the members struck up their own conversations. They all seemed to know one another. And it was in the middle of all this that I overheard one of the ladies telling another that she had a friend who had a tape recording of a woman who used to work at the home.

A tape, I thought. A primary source. It was almost too good to be true. 'A tape recording?' I asked, interrupting their conversation.

'Yes, I believe so. A number of tapes,' she said, swinging around to see who had asked. She seemed somewhat surprised by my interest.

'Of a woman who actually worked in the home?'

'Umm . . . yes,' she said. 'I think I remember her saying something about that, a long time ago.'

'Do you think she would still have them?' I asked.

'She might . . .' she said, casually.

I decided I would wait until the end of the meeting to follow up with her. After more talk of the plaques, and questions raised and debated, the meeting was adjourned. Everyone packed away their pens and notepads. Someone started a conversation with me. I politely replied, but kept one eye on the woman I needed to speak with, to make sure I could catch her before she left.

'Excuse me a moment,' I said, making a dash for the door, as I saw the other lady leaving. She was nearly in the car park by the time I caught up with her. I called after her.

She turned.

'About those tapes . . .' I said. I asked her if she would be able to put me in touch with the lady who had them.

She told me she would do her best, adding, however, that the lady was quite religious and might be protective of them. But she would see what she could do.

CHAPTER THIRTY-FOUR

Julia Carter Devaney

〜

'Any luck with the tapes?' I asked by text message, giving a gentle nudge a few days later. That evening my phone beeped. It was her. She apologised for the delay in replying to me. She had heard back from her friend Margaret, who said she would be happy to meet with me and discuss it in person. She included Margaret's details in the message and wished me luck.

I thanked her and dialled Margaret's number. Not a moment to lose. One step closer, I thought. For the first time in a long time, I felt like I was on the cusp of something – a first-hand account from a person who was actually in the home, who might be able to tell us what happened to the babies.

Margaret was obliging. She said I could come and visit her at her home and she would play the tapes for me. That's if she could find them. They had been put away long ago, into some box or other for safekeeping. She would try to root them out, she said.

I asked about the woman on the tapes. Who was she?

'Julia is her name,' she said.

I asked if there was any way I might be able to meet with Julia.

'No, she passed away a long time ago,' she told me, adding that the tapes had been recorded by a woman called Rebecca Barbara, known as Rabbi, a retired shopkeeper, who had also passed away.

My heart sank. I had hoped that Julia might still have been alive. At least then I could ask her in person. Now all my hopes lay in the tapes and what they contained. Some clue as to what had gone on behind those high stone walls. A message from beyond the grave.

I knocked on Margaret's door. She welcomed me in, but seemed slightly cautious, unsure of what my business was with the tapes. She had found them, she said, but she hadn't listened to them in years. She took out a box with eight cassette tapes in it. She blew the dust from one of them and placed it carefully in her stereo. We both listened, quietly, as the tape clicked and the reels began to spin. A voice started to speak, a woman's voice.

'That's her,' Margaret said, nodding.

I strained to hear. The voice was faint and warped. I listened harder, hoping that the words would start to become clearer. Though I could hear it was a woman's voice, I couldn't decipher a word she was saying.

'The tapes must be worn down by time,' Margaret said, noticing my disappointed expression.

'Let's try another one,' I said, still hopeful.

We tried another, and another after that. They were all the same.

I wasn't prepared to give up on Julia. Not yet. I asked Margaret if I could borrow the tapes, just for a week. I promised I'd bring them back exactly as they were.

She seemed reluctant.

I couldn't blame her, I suppose. I was, after all, a stranger. I explained that I wanted to see if I could get the audio enhanced.

I wouldn't harm the tapes, I promised. I would ensure that whatever work was done would be done to a copy of the audio.

She agreed to let me borrow them, but on the condition that if I managed to do it successfully, that I would bring her a copy of the reworked tapes. 'Put them to good use,' she told me as I left.

'I will,' I promised. Though having seen the religious iconography around her house, I wondered if she would approve of the good use I was going to put them to. I thanked her and said my goodbyes.

I rushed home and placed the box of tapes carefully on the kitchen table. When Aidan arrived in I told him the news. He did some research and suggested the name of an audio specialist in Galway, or a 'CD wizard', as he called him.

I got in touch the very next day. It was worth a try, I thought. He sounded confident over the phone and told me where to bring the tapes. Aidan was travelling that way and said he'd drop them in for me. I handed them over to him, nervously. It was a whole world I didn't understand – the world of tech. I had no idea if this plan would work.

I re-emphasised to Aidan just how important it was that nothing happened to these tapes. He said he understood. But part of me still worried that I would do irreparable damage to them. And then not only would I have broken my promise to Margaret, but Julia's account would be lost forever.

I hesitated before handing over the box. 'Are you *sure* it won't damage the originals?' I asked.

'I'll make sure of it,' he said. He promised not to give the tapes to the company if he had any doubts when he arrived there.

When he returned that evening, I asked him how it had gone. He told me they were very professional and that the technician assured him he would take every precaution. He would try to enhance the audio as best he could, but that there was no guarantee it would work, particularly if the original was very old.

I decided to trust him. There was nothing else for it. It was either that, or live with a garbled version of Julia's account which no one could hear. I had to know if the truth was hidden in those tapes. It was worth the risk.

I tried to put it out of my mind until the following week, when they were due to be picked up.

CHAPTER THIRTY-FIVE

On the Other Side
of the Wall

~

Before I knew it, it was time for Aidan to return to the 'CD wizard'. I was nervous until I heard his car coming up the driveway.

'It worked!' he told me, coming through the door with a grin.

'Oh, thank goodness,' I said. 'Can you hear it all?'

'Every word,' he said.

He smiled as he saw the sense of relief on my face. I inserted the first disc in the CD player and pressed 'Play'. We waited. For a moment there was just silence. And then the voice, as if from beyond the grave.

A big open space and big grey stone walls. Each side of it was a three-storey building with a two-storey building in between, beautiful built walls – like the cathedral, cut stone, cold-looking but beautifully built. The women had to have an admission ticket from the doctor to get in, there was no such thing as being signed in. But once they were there they would have to wait a year to look after their baby. One girl escaped, went out, but she was brought back again that night by the guards. The gates were never locked as there were always bread vans and milk carts coming in . . .

I sat rooted to the spot. I couldn't believe I was hearing a first-hand account from someone who was actually working in the home as an adult. Julia was especially fascinating because she had been in the home from when she was a baby. She had grown up in the care of the Bon Secours and went on to be an unpaid servant to the home in adulthood. I was so transfixed by what I was hearing that I forgot the job at hand. I pressed 'Pause' and went to fetch a pen and paper. I needed to record Julia's testimony, to get it down in writing once and for all, in case anything should happen to the audio. I started from the beginning again, stopping and starting the player. I began furiously scribbling down her every word. I was elated, glued to what she was saying. Finally, I had broken into the home I had passed every day on my way to school. Finally, I was getting to see what went on behind those high stone walls.

Over the next few weeks I became completely engrossed in the world of Julia Carter Devaney – listening to her account of life in the Tuam home, of the 40 years she spent there. The more I listened, the more I grew to admire and respect this beautiful, selfless woman.

She had accepted her lot, taken all the harshness in her stride. Instead of being bitter or angry, she devoted herself to her beloved garden, which she said was her sanity. She chose to appreciate the few bright spots in her life – the odd bit of kindness – but over and over again she spoke of the darkness of the home and her heartbreak for the mothers and their babies. She spoke of the suffering of the children and her feeling of helplessness to bring about any kind of change.

As I listened, I began to understand the day-to-day running of the home – what time they rose, what they had for breakfast, and how the women and children were treated. Julia described a cold and loveless place, surrounded, ironically, by beautiful gardens – filled with flowers and vegetable beds as the women were put to work. There was plenty of labour to keep the place looking well, even though the conditions were tough for those who lived there.

All the while, I was waiting to see if any clue would emerge, some nugget of information that would shed light on what had happened to the children there, the ones who didn't survive. I was starting to lose hope that there would be any mention of the children who had died in the home, as I neared the end of the first CD. And then it came – the sentence that stopped me in my tracks.

'Twas nearly the closing of the home. Children died of measles, there were no antibiotics. Dr Costelloe was a very old doctor. Scores of the children died under a year and whooping cough was epidemic, they used to die like flies. Sure they had a little graveyard of their own up there, it's still there, it's walled in now. I don't remember seeing any stillbirths. If the child died under a year there were always enquiries. There wasn't as much about it if the child was over a year. Under a year old, the inspectors would put it down to neglect. They would look upon it as natural if the child was over a year because the child would be more open to diseases.

I stopped the CD and pressed 'Rewind'. I played the excerpt again. Had I heard her correctly?

'Sure they had a little graveyard of their own up there, it's still there, it's walled in now.'

I replayed that sentence again and again. To be sure I had heard it correctly. I called Aidan in.

'Aidan! You have to hear this,' I said.

I played him the piece.

'It's true then,' he said. 'They're buried there . . . Does she say anything else?' he asked.

We pressed 'Play' again and listened intently as Julia went on to talk about other aspects of home life.

'Maybe she'll come back to it,' he said.

She went on to speak of the record-keeping in the home. My ears pricked.

The nuns used to keep these big, big huge books for the county council, and the ambulance would come and collect them to keep account of all the mothers and children, the admissions and discharges, everything about them: their ages, where they came from, and the name of the so-called father, the 'punitive'. They'd go back into the council buildings, I think it was every month they'd be checked and returned again. The advertisement for the children to be fostered would be in the papers. The nuns never followed up on the children once they left.

The interviewer, known as Rabbi, asked the question that was in the forefront of my mind.

Was it right for the nuns to rear children and to discard them as casually as they did, like you'd rear chickens? I'm asking you, is it right? Did they have the moral obligation that they did not fulfil, as religious? These are the people that would tell you very quickly that they were here representing Christ.

And Julia's repsonse:

Well, they weren't Christ-like, that's sure. There was no justice for the children – not at all! They were left to fend for themselves. At five years of age they walked up that front path with a nurse to the ambulance with all their worldly possessions, with a pair of heavy booteens and socks and a new coat and a change of clothes and that was their worldly possessions going out into the world and we'd never see or hear of them again. I used to feel so sorry for the little child when the mother went out into the world. They were like chickens in a coop, all reared in a batch. I don't know how they adjusted at all to the world. Oh it was an awful place altogether to be for any child. I'd say it left a mark on them for life.

She went on to talk about one of her friends in the home, another woman who was working for the nuns, Peg, who was thrown into the Ballinasloe asylum because she was feeling down when the original mother superior left the home. She went to bed on Sunday and they had her in the asylum on Monday, according to Julia, who missed her friend dearly but was afraid to write to her for fear of being thrown into the asylum herself. Only years later, when Julia had left the home and was a married woman, did she have the courage to finally visit her friend.

We continued listening to the recording, hoping something more might be said about the graveyard, but she didn't mention it again.

I delivered the original box of tapes back to Margaret, along with the new CDs.

'It's a pity,' she said, as I handed them over at the door. 'There were more of the tapes . . . they've gone missing.'

I'll never know if the truth lies in those missing tapes, if Julia Carter Devaney ever did say what happened to those babies. But she did say there was a graveyard there. That was a key piece of information, which spurred me on. One step closer to the truth. What went on in that home, over almost four decades, from 1925? And what happened to all those children who are unaccounted for? The truth was locked away the day the home was closed once and for all. And Julia, it seems, played a key role in its closing.

She spoke of what it was like to finally shut the door of that terrible institution in 1961.

> On the night the home closed, myself, Johnny Cunningham and Nurse Burke walked out that gate for good and we were the last to leave. Storm Debbie was raging that night and the slates were flying off the roof. Johnny Cunningham pulled the door after us and said, 'This is the end of an era.' And it was.

At the end of the recording, Julia reflected on life in the home and how it must have affected the children who lived there.

> The poorest downcast family were better off than being in the home; there's love in the family home even though there's poverty. The home children were like chickens in a coop: bedlam, screeching, shouting in the toddlers' room. They never learned to speak properly, 'twas like they had a language all of their own, babbling sounds!
> I have terrible regrets for the children, I feel a sense of

shame that I did not create a war, but, then again, what could I have done? It was a rotten ould place to rear children, marching them around the room to keep them out of trouble.

I had grown to deeply respect Julia. Such a caring, wonderful woman, who lived for so long in that place – the only home she knew for most of her life, until one of the groundsmen asked her to marry him. He was elderly and his wife had died three years previously. He was in need of the company, and could offer her a good home, he told her. She laughed it off at first, but eventually she agreed to go to the pictures with him, and he bought her a bag of sweets, and she felt he was a kind man, and so she said yes, and she married him and went to live with him. He did the cooking, as she'd never been taught how to do anything in the kitchen, and they lived happily together.

It was some consolation to think that Julia had had a semblance of a normal life before she died.

But I couldn't shake that sentence about Julia's regrets. I felt angry thinking of what she had witnessed, and how powerless she was to do anything. That's what it came down to: the powerlessness of women. This was a country that beat women down. By God, how I wanted to create that war for Julia, to fight that fight, now that she was no longer able.

CHAPTER THIRTY-SIX

A Missing Person

❦

'I want to report a missing person,' said Anna Corrigan, when she walked off the street into her local garda station.

The garda took out his pen and paper. 'How long have they been missing?'

'Since 1951,' she said, much to the garda's surprise, and perhaps amusement. 'My brother is the missing person.'

This is the story Anna told me after we got to know one another quite by chance. My daughter Alicia had recommended that I use Google a bit more, to help me with my research so I started to google 'Tuam home' to see what would come up. I spent many hours scrolling through the results, in the hope of finding something useful.

One of the links was to a message board, and within that a discussion about the Tuam mother and baby home. One of the posts was by a woman who believed her brothers had been in the home, and she was searching for answers about what had happened to them. She was looking for anyone who might have information that could help her. There was an email address at the end of the message.

I decided to write her an email, to see if I could be of any assistance and to find out what she might know about the home. We might be able to help one another, I suggested.

I received a reply the following day. Her name was Anna Corrigan. She told me her story. It was a matter for the police, she said, and she had recently reported it.

Born in 1956, Anna had grown up as an only child, or so she thought. It was only many years later, after her parents died, that something a family member said made her curious about her mother's past.

She started to investigate, and soon discovered that her mother, Bridget Dolan, had given birth to two baby boys long before Anna was born, and before she met Anna's father. And so, being pregnant and unmarried, Bridget was placed in the Tuam mother and baby home, where she had her babies: one in 1946 and the other in 1950. The first, a little boy she named John Desmond and then a few years later, another boy, she named William Joseph.

After she gave birth to John Desmond in 1946, Bridget was kept in the home for a year, as was the routine, and then told to leave. In later years, she would claim that, at that point, John Desmond was a healthy, well-adjusted little boy. However, according to the Tuam home register, John Desmond is recorded as having died within a few months.

Then a few years later Bridget 'fell pregnant' again. And again she was admitted to the Tuam mother and baby home, where she gave birth to William Joseph. She stayed with him for a year, before they too were separated.

According to the register, William is also recorded as having died. However, try as she might, Anna could not find a death certificate for him.

Apparently, Bridget had been adamant that William was

adopted. That he didn't die. She had told someone this near the end of her life when she disclosed her secret.

And so Anna told me she was looking for William. She believed he might still be alive – probably living abroad if he had been illegally adopted.

I tried to imagine William. He would be 63 now, living with a different name probably, in a different family who may or may not have told him he was adopted. He may never know the truth of where he came from or that he has a sister searching for him in Ireland.

I replied to Anna and told her what I had discovered about the babies: that there were 798 who died at the home and that I believed 796 of them were buried in what used to be a sewage tank. It must have been very hard for her to hear that, that one of those babies may be her brother, or indeed that both her brothers may be buried there.

As I typed the email, I took out the list of names. My finger traced through them, one by one, and then I saw it: John Desmond Dolan. For the first time I knew the story behind one of the babies' names. I could picture his mother in my mind. I knew that he had a sister – Anna. And a brother – William. Neither of whom he had ever met. My heart ached to think of so much tragedy in one family. I could only imagine how Anna must have felt.

As we continued our correspondence over the weeks and months, Anna mentioned that there was a big story in *The Irish Mail on Sunday* about an angels' plot that was found at another mother and baby home – one that had 200 babies in it. She said she could put me in touch with the journalist who had worked on the story – a woman named Alison O'Reilly. Anna explained that she didn't feel comfortable going public with her own story, but wondered whether I might be interested in speaking with the journalist. No doubt it would be of interest to the paper, she said. We both wanted the Tuam story to come to light, to see some justice done for the babies at long last.

I agreed, and asked Anna to pass on my details to Alison.

The following day Alison phoned, introduced herself and asked about my research. I gave her some details over the phone and she said she would be very interested in speaking with me in person. She would come to my home in Tuam, she said, where I could show her my research and we could discuss it further. That would be important to the paper, she said, to see the evidence first-hand. I agreed, and we set a date for her to visit.

'Are you sure you want to do this?' Aidan asked me that night as we cleared away the plates after dinner.

'Do what?'

'Talk to the media,' he said. 'You know what you're up against with the church, don't you?'

I hesitated. 'I do,' I said.

'It's going to ruffle a lot of feathers,' Aidan said.

'I have to do it,' I told him. 'Not doing it is worse.' In my mind it was black and white.

I could see that Aidan was concerned. I could be naïve sometimes. He tended to know about how these kinds of things played out and how people were likely to react.

I found it hard to sleep that night, wondering if I might attract a lot of the wrong kind of attention. If people might be upset about it. But then, people should be upset that the babies are buried in a sewage tank, I thought. That's what's upsetting. If we don't look for the truth, how will we ever know what went on? That's what decided it for me. There was no way I could live the rest of my life wondering what had happened to those children and be content to let it go. If you could do that, what else would you be willing to let go? What other atrocity could you walk away from?

No, it had to be done. If the media was able to help me to publicise the message, then that's what needed to happen.

In the lead-up to Alison's arrival I found myself reading through the research again and again. I felt a sense of doubt. I had already published my findings, and no one had taken any notice. So who was to say that anyone would find it credible if it was published again? I cringed at the thought of it. But it was a bit too late to be thinking about all that now.

Shadow barked as the car pulled up outside. I looked out the kitchen window and saw Alison coming up the garden path. I invited her into the kitchen and poured a cup of tea. I was suddenly very aware of the sacred heart above the door frame – a legacy from Josie and Paddy's time.

I had grown up in an Ireland where you didn't question the Catholic Church, and suddenly I felt I was about to do something very public that would make a lot of people uncomfortable. There were some people in Tuam, and in other parts of the country, who were still living in that kind of Ireland, who would not welcome this questioning of the powers that be.

I went through my findings with Alison. I laid all the documents out on the kitchen table. I talked her through my research. She was very attentive, taking plenty of notes. I told her what I had discovered – the lists of the babies' names, those who had died in St Mary's mother and baby home, as it was officially called. I told her about the lack of any burial record, though I welcomed any information anyone might have in that respect. I was very open to being wrong, I explained, and I really hoped I was wrong. For the children's sake.

And then I told her what I surmised from all that I had learnt: the harrowing thought that the children might be buried in a defunct sewage tank, beside the playground in the middle of the housing estate. Alison's eyes widened in horror. She noted it down and asked some more questions.

I showed her the maps and the tracing I had done – the area where I believed the children were buried, and the part of the map that was labelled 'sewage tank'. I told her about my attempts to contact the Bon Secours and showed her their replies. I had everything laid out on the table. We talked for hours.

It was getting late. Alison thanked me for my time and said she had better be getting back to Dublin. She would be in touch once she had spoken to her editors.

As I stood in the doorway and watched her drive away, a feeling of apprehension suddenly came over me. There was something definitive about that moment. I had spoken to a journalist on the record. Now there was no going back.

CHAPTER THIRTY-SEVEN

Breaking the Silence

⌒

I woke early that Sunday morning. It was 25 May 2014. I went downstairs to the kitchen. The eight o'clock news came on the radio. I was pouring a cup of tea, half-listening, half in my own thoughts.

The RTÉ news was followed by 'What it Says in the Papers', where they went through the front pages of each of the main national newspapers.

'And on the front page of the *Irish Mail on Sunday*,' said the broadcaster, '"A Mass Grave of 800 Babies: 'Illegitimate' Children who Died in Institution for Unmarried Mothers Run by Nuns Were Buried in Unmarked Plot".' Then they mentioned my name.

I nearly dropped my cup of tea. I went to call Aidan, but suddenly he appeared around the corner.

'Did you hear that?' he said. He was in his dressing gown and looked as though he'd nearly fallen down the stairs, he'd moved so fast. He had been listening to the radio in the bedroom.

'I did!' I said. 'I heard it.'

We looked at one another in disbelief. Then listened intently to see if more would follow. When the piece ended, we hugged one another – a sense of relief came over my whole body.

'It's out now,' I said. 'It's finally out.'

Aidan looked at me, his eyes welling up with tears. We were both emotional. The story was finally being heard. We'd been trying for so long to tell people that this mattered, and finally, someone had listened. All my life I had seen people in positions of power getting away with things while the voiceless suffered in silence. I couldn't bear to think of those children being silenced, even in death.

Finally, their story would be heard, though we couldn't have known at that moment just what lay ahead.

CHAPTER THIRTY-EIGHT

The Phone Call

⌒

Alicia rang around midday.

'Mam, you're not going to believe what's happening,' she said. 'The number of comments on Facebook. It's unreal!'

'What do you mean?' I asked, nervously. I couldn't understand the whole Facebook thing.

'It's gone viral!' she said.

She rang again an hour later.

'There are people sending messages from all over the world, Mam. They're coming in from America – from everywhere, you're not going to believe it!'

This is really building momentum, I thought to myself. The story had finally struck a chord. Finally something was going to be done about this.

The next morning, Monday, the phone rang at exactly nine o'clock. I rummaged around my handbag, looking for my mobile, thinking it might be Alicia again. I found the phone: 'unknown number' flashed across the screen.

I cleared my throat, preparing myself in case it was a journalist following up on the story. 'Hello,' I said.

'Is this Catherine Corless?' It was a woman's voice. She sounded old. And her tone was different. Not like any of the other journalists I had encountered.

'It is,' I said.

'This is Sister Marie Ryan.'

'Sister?' I said.

'Yes . . .' She explained that she was the leader of the Bon Secours nuns. 'What's all this about?' she said, getting straight to the point.

She told me they had been inundated with press and their elderly sisters were very distressed.

I had to think fast. A kind of courage came over me all of a sudden. 'Did you not know about this grave?' I could feel my muscles stiffen as I said the words. It wasn't proven yet, but I knew it *must* be there. This was my chance to question the nuns – the very source. The only people who might have the answers. 'Not so much a grave,' I said, correcting myself. I wasn't going to mollycoddle it. 'It's more than likely they are buried in that tank.'

It was the first they'd heard of it, she retorted quickly, saying they were long gone out of Tuam.

'Surely to goodness you have records,' I said. 'Your congregation would know about it . . . the elderly sisters.'

She told me that the elderly sisters weren't in any condition to talk to the press.

'Well,' I said, 'I'm only exposing what I found. Everything points to the babies being there; we can't find them anywhere. If you think that's not true, can you give us an alternative, because I have tried,' I said.

She re-emphasised that they knew nothing about a graveyard or burials.

I felt that familiar sense of frustration rising in me.

And then she said something I wasn't expecting. 'Could we meet up with you and some of the committee?'

'Yes, of course,' I said. 'We can have a chat any time you like. Would you come to Tuam?' I asked, hoping I could bring them to the site, to try and force some kind of compassion from them.

She said she didn't feel that would be appropriate.

Typical, I thought.

'Can we meet halfway?' she said. 'Can we meet in Galway?'

'We can meet anywhere you want . . .' I told her.

She named a hotel in the suburbs of Galway. We would meet the following week. I hung up and stared at my phone for a moment. I felt strangely elated, a sense of satisfaction, for the babies, knowing that the nuns were irked by the story going public. For decades this dark secret had been buried. Now we were scratching the surface and they didn't seem happy about it.

CHAPTER THIRTY-NINE

Good Cop, Bad Cop

The week went quickly. I arranged for two members of the committee to join Aidan and me at the meeting with the Bon Secours nuns. They would travel separately and meet us in the hotel car park.

I was gathering my things on the morning of the meeting, getting ready for the journey to Galway.

'Ready to go?' shouted Aidan from the front door.

'Coming!' I said. I quickly made my way to the car. Aidan was waiting, with the engine on.

I laughed when I saw him, dressed in his best suit – a pristine white shirt and a very impressive-looking tie. He'd brought along his work briefcase – the one he kept his Fleetwood paint colour cards in.

'You're looking well,' I said, as I clambered into the car. Aidan always liked to dress up when we were going out.

The closer we got, the more nervous I felt. Half an hour later we arrived at the car park of the Clayton Hotel, between Oranmore and Galway, and met the other committee members.

I took a deep breath as I pushed open the hotel door. I was determined not to waste this opportunity to get answers. The mystery of the babies had consumed me for so long, and finally I was going to be able to ask the nuns what had happened. But at the same time, I was nervous. I was worried that it was going to be confrontational. Aidan squeezed my arm and gave me a reassuring smile.

Things could go one of two ways, I thought to myself. The ball was rolling now and the story was publicised. Either the nuns would be exposed and the truth about the babies would finally come to light, or I would be exposed, as the amateur historian that I was. I still didn't have all the facts. I hadn't yet proven that the babies were there. Would I ever be able to truly prove they were there? Through the media, I could be made out to be a charlatan. And the nuns would be able to do that. They were a powerful force to reckon with. Who was I, at the end of the day? I was starting to doubt myself.

We walked into the lobby. I saw two women, one older and one younger, and knew immediately they were nuns – the way they shuffled across the floor as they moved, and the way they were dressed, in conservative clothing of muted pallets. I had no doubt it was them.

At that moment they looked up and spotted us too. They must have recognised me from the photograph in the paper.

Aidan giggled. 'They think you've brought your solicitor along,' he said.

I looked at him and smiled. He had the cut of a solicitor, with the suit and the briefcase. Little did they know it was full of colour cards. I was so glad to have him there by my side.

We ventured towards the nuns as they found a seating area. We said our hellos, made our introductions and sat opposite them. They were both thin and held themselves very straight.

Their faces were stern. They were dressed in white shirts with navy buttoned cardigans and below-the-knee pleated skirts. They were exactly as I would have expected them to be.

We all smiled at one another, awkwardly, and discussed the ordering of tea, all the time waiting to get down to business. The waiter took our order. When he left, there was a protracted silence, until the younger nun chimed in with pleasantries, asking about our journey down and how we were. It felt false, but we went along with it.

The other nun said nothing. She was the one I had spoken to on the phone.

I wondered what they hoped to achieve from this meeting.

Finally, the older nun spoke, and the same questions came again: Why are you doing this? What's this about? How do you know this? Why are we being targeted? She said it was causing damage to the order and it was upsetting their elderly sisters, that it was upsetting everybody. I just let her talk. I said nothing. She paused and looked at me, seemingly unnerved by my silence.

'From my research,' I said finally, 'I have to consider all the women that went through that home. *They're* upset. The survivors are upset. *They're* damaged, because of the way the home was run.'

I could see her bristling. But I knew I had to say how I felt; I may never get another chance to say it to their faces. 'I know you weren't there personally,' I continued, 'but it's your congregation. Your motto is to give love and care to this type of person. And neither was given to the mothers and survivors. I've met a lot of them.'

The atmosphere was just as it had been on the phone call. Tense. Defensive. I talked about some of the survivors I had met and the stories I had heard, of what they went through living in the mother and baby home in Tuam. They listened quietly. They stared blankly. They said nothing.

When I finished, they asked me how I had found all this out in the first place – where did I get the records? I thought there might have been words of compassion or empathy for the people whose stories I was recounting, but it was as though they hadn't even heard it. It seemed like they just wanted to get to the bottom of how I had started all this, and who had let the secret slip.

I told them about my research, through the county council files, and the maps I had found in the library. I watched for even a flicker of shock on their faces as I spoke about babies being buried in a sewage tank.

Nothing.

I asked if they had any records that could help us to solve this mystery and put things to rest, once and for all. To get some justice for the survivors, and peace for those who had died.

They said they knew nothing, that everything was with the Western Health Board. They had given all their files to the county council, they said, and these had subsequently been passed on to the Western Health Board.

For the whole conversation they didn't budge an inch from what they had said previously. I felt there wasn't an ounce of compassion. I couldn't understand it. How could you not be moved by the stories of the Tuam babies? As a woman, as a person – did it not move them in any way? I wondered.

They knew nothing, they repeated. And we left it there. We said our terse goodbyes. Polite, but awkward, the whole encounter.

Aidan and I got back into the car. I felt a heaviness come over me. I had the chance to ask the questions. Why were there no answers? Perhaps I hadn't asked the right questions. We left just as we had arrived. Full of questions with no answers.

'They really played good cop, bad cop, didn't they?' Aidan said of the two nuns. I had never heard that expression before. He explained what it meant.

I agreed. That was their tactic. 'It'll never change,' I said. 'The nuns will never change. Nothing ever changes.'

Aidan nodded.

'*Bon secours*,' I said, 'good help.' I shook my head in disbelief. Nothing, I felt, could be further from the truth.

Back at home, the phone rang. It was another journalist hoping to arrange an interview. Of course, I said, no problem. The phone rang again. Another interview request.

And so it continued.

I decided then and there that I would say yes to every single interview. I'd talk to anyone who would listen. I was more determined than ever. I wouldn't stop talking until the whole country, the whole world, knew what had happened. I didn't care anymore what they'd make of me, or if I'd fall flat on my face. This was bigger than that. It was worth the risk. It needed to be done, no matter what way it went.

CHAPTER FORTY

Story Goes International

⁓

S uddenly, the story blew up. It was being reported all over the world.

It was the seventh of June 2014. The London *Independent* ran with the headline: 'Ireland mass graves: Unearthing One of the Darkest Chapters in Irish History'.

The Guardian reported: 'The Catholic church in Ireland is facing fresh accusations of child neglect after a researcher found records for hundreds of children she believes are buried in unmarked graves at the site of a former home for unwed mothers.'

Germany's *Der Spiegel* wrote about '*Kinder-Massengrab in Irland: Das dunkle Geheimnis der Schwestern von Bon Secours*' (Mass Children's Grave in Ireland: The Dark Secret of the Bon Secours Sisters).

The story ran in Spain, Italy and France too.

Then across the Atlantic, *The Washington Post* carried the headline: 'Bodies of 800 babies, long-dead, found in septic tank at former Irish home for unwed mothers'. It quickly became the most read story on the paper's website.

The New York Times even ran the story: 'Ireland: Orphanage's Mass Grave', reporting that 'a researcher says that 796 children may have been buried in a mass grave beside a former orphanage for the children of unmarried women. The researcher, Catherine Corless, says her discovery of death records for the Catholic nun-run home in Tuam, County Galway, suggests that a former septic tank is the final resting place for most, if not all, of the children'.

Newspapers around the world were reporting on the Tuam babies scandal. It even got as far as Australia, with *The Sydney Morning Herald* writing about 'Irish Orphans' Remains Found in Mass Grave'.

Stories were emerging everywhere, from survivors who wanted to speak out about their time in the Tuam home. I read a piece in *The Washington Post* about a man named John Pascal Rodgers. He told a story his mother had relayed to him, when they were reunited many years later. It was of the day his mother found out that she was going to be separated from him by the nuns, perhaps forever. She snuck into his room and cut a lock of his hair – a memento to keep of her beloved little boy. She was then sent to 'the Magdalene Asylum'. She was just 17 years of age. She remained there, locked behind closed doors, for 15 years, until she had the courage to escape, according to John. Meanwhile, she always wondered what had become of the little boy she had left behind in the Tuam mother and baby home.

In the interview, John spoke of his time growing up in the home. He remembered, clearly, standing alone, beside the ten-foot-high walls, not wanting to become friends with any of the other children, because every time he made a friend, they'd disappear, one after the other. He would cry for his lost friend, then befriend another little boy, and then he would disappear too. After a while, he stopped wanting to make friends, for fear of losing them. He stopped trusting people as he always felt abandoned. The interviewer must have asked where he thought the children were disappearing.

'If he was a healthy little boy, he was probably just bought for a price and shipped off to America or Australia,' he said. 'Most went to America.' And of the ones who were not healthy? 'There were children who were extremely ill,' he said. 'And they would disappear, too. But that was all kept from view. I wouldn't have known about those underground vaults and passageways,' he said. 'They were accessible only to the nuns.'

His words were so powerful. They were another hint at what had been happening at the home. I continued reading all the reports, all the interviews and survivor stories. It was great to see everything coming out into the open, at last.

A few days later, I was in the kitchen when I heard a knock at the door. From the window I saw a garda car parked in the driveway. My heart started to beat a little faster as I quickly tried to calculate where each of our children was at that moment. Or where I thought they were. I answered the door.

'Is this the Corless household?' asked the guard on the doorstep.

'It is,' I said, nervously.

He must have noticed the worried look on my face. He dropped his serious demeanour to show me that he was not there to bring bad news. I welcomed him in.

He asked if I could check for a name on the list of children who had died in the Tuam home.

'Of course,' I said, and I went to fetch my list, which I kept on my desk beside the range in the kitchen.

He asked me to check for a John Desmond Dolan in the 1940s. I knew immediately what this was about. He was investigating the disappearance of Anna's brothers. I pointed to John Desmond's name on the list. The guard nodded, thanked me and took off again, obviously satisfied with this information. What he didn't seem to realise was that it was Anna's other brother William Joseph that he should have enquired about. There was no death record for William.

I watched him drive away, and I wondered what the authorities were going to do now that they knew about all these missing children. 796 of them, to be exact.

CHAPTER FORTY-ONE

Beyond the Parish Pump

❧

The story had been out for more than a week, and still the government had not made an official statement.

Pressure was mounting as groups representing different mother and baby home survivors called on the government to act.

Susan Lohan, co-founder of the Adoption Rights Alliance, an organisation that campaigns for greater access to adoption records in Ireland, told RTÉ that she believed a national inquiry was necessary, to take in all mother and baby homes across the country, as there may also be mass graves in other homes.

Opposition TDs called for a full independent inquiry, saying the government needed to act.

I was following the news closely, to see what developments would come. Online news site thejournal.ie reported that, despite telling them that the Minister for Children, Charlie Flanagan, expected the issue to be discussed at the ministerial meeting on 3 June, when they checked in later that day, a spokesperson for the minister admitted that they had not in fact discussed the issue specifically. However, it seemed that the minister had been in touch with the Department of Justice and with the Taoiseach, Enda Kenny, on the matter and that it was being considered at senior levels within the Fine Gael/Labour coalition.

'The matter is being taken very, very seriously. The full facts need to be established,' said the spokesperson, according to the report in thejournal.ie

What was taking them so long, I wondered. Surely they should come out on the issue. The entire world was talking about it, and yet still the Irish government remained silent.

Survivors began contacting me, and soon they were arriving at the house to tell me their stories, and to meet with one another.

As they sat around the kitchen table, they opened up to one another about their experiences. Many of them had never spoken to anyone about being from a mother and baby home. Aidan and I put out the tea and freshly baked bread. Then we made ourselves scarce. It was their time to connect with other people who had been through the same pain and trauma. For some, it seemed to help. They said the world suddenly felt a little less lonely.

Many of the survivors asked me if I had come across any photographs of the home. The only one I had been able to find was an old black and white image of the façade which the Old Tuam Historical Society had, but it wasn't a great photo, and didn't give much of an insight into what the home looked like.

The survivors themselves had very little memory of the home, as most had been fostered out to families from a young age. I decided to do something that might help them to visualise what the home was like. I had already made a model of the town of Tuam as it would have looked around the turn of the twentieth century (which is now in the county council offices in Tuam), so I decided I would follow the same process to make a model of the home.

I used an OS map of Tuam from 1892, on which I found the ground layout of the workhouse (which was the same building as the mother and baby home), and I magnified it up to scale, so that I would have an accurate footprint of the building.

I travelled to Portumna and took photographs of the old workhouse there, which is now a museum, as its layout was very similar to that of the Tuam workhouse. I studied maps to ensure I had the proportions right.

Then, when it was all planned out, I got to work. A friend of ours, Christy, who excels in carpentry, kindly cut the plywood for me that I had measured out, which created the frame of the home. Then I set about creating the building around it, moulding it out of self-hardening model clay, and decorating and refining it with sandpaper, matchsticks, moss, and acrylic paint.

As I worked on the model, I thought back to the day I had prised open the gate of the home on my way to school. I tried to remember what I had seen, to remind myself what the building looked like.

When the model was complete, I placed it on the kitchen table. Looking at it somehow made it all the more real – the memory of that place, behind the old stone walls, a reminder that it really had existed, and it wasn't so long ago.

CHAPTER FORTY-TWO

A Call to Action

~~~

F inally, after days of silence, there was a statement of some
significance from a member of government. Minister of state
Ciarán Cannon called for 'an urgent inquiry, including a garda
investigation, into the circumstances surrounding the unexplained
deaths of a large number of children at a Tuam mother and baby
home . . .'

He said he had spoken with the Minister for Justice and
Equality, Frances Fitzgerald, and the Minister for Children and
Youth Affairs, Charlie Flanagan, and had recommended a
cross-departmental approach. 'Doing nothing is simply not an
option for us in government when presented with details of this
nature,' Ciarán Cannon said.

The newspapers and radio stations featured the survivors promi-
nently. They were finally being heard, telling their stories from every
corner of Ireland. They had suffered in silence for far too long.
Now the world was finally willing to listen, so what would the Irish
government do about it? This was the question on people's minds.

On 8 June 2014, I turned on my computer to look for any

further developments. And, to my surprise, there was the headline: 'Archbishop Diarmuid Martin Calls for Inquiry after Tuam Baby Scandal'.

The article in the *Irish Independent* said that justice minister Frances Fitzgerald was appointing two senior gardaí, who would immediately begin work examining the site and investigating the claims that 796 babies were buried in a sewage tank.

Meanwhile, Diarmuid Martin, archbishop of Dublin, was adamant that only an independent inquiry led by a senior judicial figure could provide the answers needed. 'The only way we will come out of this particular period of our history is when the truth comes out,' he said. 'With the [Judge Yvonne] Murphy Commission on child sex abuse in [the archdiocese of] Dublin, that was my policy – provide as much information as possible into a properly constructed commission,' he continued.

The archbishop made the point that Tuam may not be an isolated case. 'The indications are that if something happened in Tuam, it probably happened in other mother and baby homes around the country . . . That is why I believe that we need a full-bodied investigation. There is no point in investigating just what happened in Tuam and then next year finding out more.'

I was impressed by his conviction that more needed to be done to investigate what went on in mother and baby homes around the country. The article further quoted the archbishop as saying, 'We have to look at the whole culture of mother and baby homes. There is talk about medical experiments there, we need to look at the question of adoption . . . there are very complicated and very sensitive issues . . . I would say it is very important that any commission set up has full judicial powers. Otherwise you are going to get yourself entangled in a whole series of problems of data protection and so on.' The article was quoting an interview he had conducted with RTÉ.

Things seemed like they were moving in the right direction. I just didn't realise how fast they were progressing. Two days later, on 10 June, it was announced that there would be a statutory Commission of Investigation to inquire into mother and baby homes.

Minister for Children Charlie Flanagan told RTÉ's News at One that the commission would have full statutory powers and would "not be interfered with by government".

It was just over two weeks since Alison O'Reilly's story was published in the *Irish Mail on Sunday*.

When I heard the news, a sense of relief came over me. I felt we had done all we could. It was now in the hands of the government. They would get to the bottom of it in a way I never could, and would ensure that justice was finally served to the babies in the sewage tank and to all who survived the mother and baby homes.

'Well, that's that,' I said to Aidan as we sat down to our dinner that evening. 'Thank goodness that's happening now.'

'Hmmm,' said Aidan in a non-committal way.

'What?' I asked. I couldn't believe what he was implying. We had finally reached a happy conclusion, as far as I was concerned. 'What's in that head of yours now?' I asked him.

'Well, we'll have to see what comes of it,' he said. 'These things notoriously take a long time to get up and running and they don't always turn out as you might expect.'

I was disappointed that Aidan felt that way. He tended to be a good gauge of how things were progressing. I had faith that our democratically elected government would come through and do the right thing, now that they were aware of the issue. I was ready to celebrate, but I took Aidan's cautious attitude on board and decided to wait and see what would happen next. It turned out I didn't have to wait long.

CHAPTER FORTY-THREE

GPR

❧

The *Irish Mail on Sunday* decided there was something they could do straight away to try and get to the bottom of this mystery. They organised a ground penetrating radar survey.

I had to look up what a ground penetrating survey was, and how it worked. Basically, it seemed that equipment that used radar pulses would create images of what was below the surface of the ground. It was a non-intrusive method of surveying underground areas. It was typically used in construction, but in this kind of scenario, it might just show up anomalies under the surface.

I was delighted that the newspaper was taking such an initiative. It was more than anyone else had done to date. And sure enough, their survey revealed 'likely human activity' in the ground. They ran with the story, reporting that their survey recommended 'further investigation', that the experts were of the view that 'if we are to find out anything more a dig would be necessary'.

The paper also revealed that the Bon Secours sisters 'had the remains of 12 members of the order exhumed and reburied in a cemetery in Knock before they abandoned their base in Galway in 2001 – after selling property to the Western Health Board for a reported €4m'.

Well, this was news to me. It was such a relief to have other people investigating the issue. Suddenly I didn't feel so alone with it all. So this meant that the sisters had made the effort to rebury their own before they left Tuam, but had not thought to do the same for all the children buried there. One rule for them, another for those they were meant to care for.

CHAPTER FORTY-FOUR

The High Nelly

━━━⌒⌒━━━

I t was around this time, in the summer of 2014, when Fr Fintan Monahan arrived at the Tuam home site, pedalling in on his high nelly bicycle. He was known for cycling around the town.

There was mounting pressure on Archbishop Michael Neary to give some sort of statement on the whole matter and Fr Monahan, being his secretary, was asked to speak on his behalf, as the RTÉ reporters were on site and wanted a statement for that evening's six o'clock news.

I met Fr Monahan at the site. The RTÉ news reporters were there too – waiting to see what the local clergy's statement would be. I wondered if this might be a sign that the church was ready to apologise and perhaps make a reparation of some kind to the mothers and babies who had suffered so horrifically at their hands.

I walked the priest through the playground, to the little patch of grass beyond it. 'This is where the babies are,' I said. I watched for a reaction. He gave none. I showed him the various places where we believed the remains to be and talked him through my research and what I had found. I explained that we believed the babies' remains had been discarded in the area, many of whom may be in the sewage tank. '796, we believe,' I said. I could see him flinch just a little as I said it.

RTÉ reporters asked Fr Monahan for a statement on what he had seen. I listened in.

'I suppose we can't really view the past from our point of view, from our lens. All we can do is mark it appropriately, and make sure there is a suitable place here where people can come and remember the babies that died.'

I couldn't believe what he was saying. In that moment I had a flashback, to the day my family had painted the house to prepare for the stations. I thought of all our friends and neighbours gathered in our little sitting room, people who had come from miles around, all of us saying our prayers, uttering our Hail Marys again and again, looking for forgiveness, doing all the 'right things' so that the church would absolve us of our sins. How we atoned, how we tried to appease those in the church, us and every family like us. And yet, here was the church, guilty of the greatest sin of all, and *that* was all he could say? That's all he felt the mothers and babies deserved? It was deplorable.

I decided at that very moment that I was done with religion. I was finished with it all. I was raised a Catholic, but this was not something I wanted any part of now. I felt sick to my very being. I could hear the babies in the sewage tank screaming out for help. And if it was the last thing I did, I was going to help them. I was going to show this church just how sorry they should be. They were not going to get away with this.

They had been given a golden opportunity to repent and make reparation for their involvement in this tragic scenario, on the spot where we stood, where underneath our feet lay the tiny remains of babies and children in a sewage tank.

Although Archbishop Neary stated that the church had nothing to do with the running of the home, that was not true. I knew from my research that the diocese of Tuam had commissioned a chaplain to the home at a yearly salary of £120 to oversee all events. His job was to ensure that those incarcerated attended mass, confession, and other religious duties in the little chapel that was contained within the home building; that births, baptisms and deaths were recorded; and that burials were carried out in a Christian manner, with the attendance of a priest.

And sure enough, all the babies were baptised by the local priest in that chapel. Details of their baptisms were written in red ink in the church's baptism book, to differentiate them from those who were 'legitimate'. There was no trace though of a single record of a burial or service for the babies who died. The chaplain would have known this, but of course those babies didn't matter. In the eyes of the church they were illegitimate, born into sin. It has also transpired that any adoptions that took place from the Tuam home had to be sanctioned by the archbishop. There is written evidence of this. So to say there wasn't church involvement is ludicrous.

As I drove home, past the cemetery, I tried to digest what had just happened. When I had started my research back in 2010, I had known very little about the home. I had set out to write an essay about an orphanage run by the kind sisters of the Bon Secours, a French nursing order. That is what we had been taught to believe, and who could dispute it, as the home was guarded on all sides of its seven-acre site by a ten-foot-high wall and high boarded gates, where no one entered except for the odd delivery of milk and necessities. How could we have known what was going on inside?

But now that we knew, why was the narrative not changing? I thought about that idea that we can't view the past through the prism of the present. So the question I had was: what's the cut-off point? When does something so sinister become 'the past'? Is it five months? Five years? Fifty? Who decides when it becomes the past? When is it something we no longer have to deal with because it belongs in the past?

If this story had happened five years ago – human remains found in the grounds of a state-run school, for example – would we leave the children's bones buried there? Would we say it didn't matter, it belonged to history? Of course we wouldn't. We would find out who each and every one of those children were. We would do everything we could to tell their surviving family members. We would bury them with dignity.

And yet, because this happened 50 years ago, somehow we don't?

So was this really about how much time had elapsed or was it still because they were born out of wedlock?

I had expected the story of the babies to be met with shock and empathy, but the reaction was more complicated than that, as I was about to discover.

CHAPTER FORTY-FIVE

What Mary Saw

‘ Who do you think you are, coming in here? What do you
know? We have looked after this site for the last 20
years; we want those babies left in peace.’

I was showing a journalist where the babies were buried, when
a man came up to us, yelling and pointing his finger at me. It
was someone I recognised. He had some of his family members
with him, standing behind him.

I let him have his say, and calmly replied that I understood how
he felt, and that I continually reported to the journalists how he
and others had maintained the site so beautifully over the years,
and that indeed only for their loving care of those babies, I may
not have discovered their whereabouts. I tried to tell him how my
research had revealed that this was not a proper resting place for
the home babies, that they had been callously discarded into what
I now knew was a defunct sewage tank, and that it was not right
to leave them in such a distasteful way.

I also made the point that it was because of the journalists
and documentary makers that the government was beginning to

take action, and that it was not just Tuam's tragic story but that of all the other mother and baby homes throughout Ireland.

I managed to calm the situation, though the group still seemed rather disgruntled as they left the site. I thought about it afterwards, as I sat in my car – the anger of that man. I had a feeling he was not the only one who was thinking those things.

I had wondered if I was imagining it, if it was my anxiety playing out somehow, getting the better of me. I had tried to put it down to that. Since the story had broken in the media, I had started to feel as though the whole town was angry. Everywhere I went I felt eyes on me. I could hear the hushed whispers between people as I passed. Then it became clear that I wasn't imagining it when I received a call from a stranger telling me what she had overheard people saying.

'Is that Catherine Corless?' the woman asked as I answered the phone.

'It is . . .' I said.

'You don't know me,' she said. 'I hope you don't mind me getting in touch.'

The woman introduced herself as Mary Moriarty. I listened with interest. She told me she had been in the hair salon and had overheard some women talking about me. 'They were saying things about you: "Who's that one, Corless? Who does she think she is? Nothing happened here. What would she know, that one from out the country? She's just doing this for a bit of notice . . ."'

She told me she had held her tongue, until she couldn't stand it any longer. She got out of her chair, she told me, and said, 'I know what I saw. That woman is right. You leave her alone!' It made her angry, she said, to hear me being talked about that way, especially after what she had seen.

And this is what she had phoned to tell me. In 1975 Mary was living in one of the houses in the Dublin road housing estate, built on the site of the old mother and baby home. She'd never forget the day, she said, when a neighbour told her that there was a boy running around with something very peculiar. She went to have a look, and sure enough she saw a young boy whom she recognised, who lived in the housing estate, with something in his hand which he was proudly showing to his friends.

Mary called over the wall to the child. 'Come here for a minute,' she said, "til I have a look at what you have there.'

The boy walked over to her, sheepishly. As he got closer, Mary felt her blood run cold. The boy was holding a stick, and on top of the stick was a human skull. The skull didn't look plastic, it looked like a real human skull. She examined it closely. It had a full set of teeth. But she could never have been prepared for what happened next . . . something that would stay with her for the rest of her life.

She recounted her story to me. I couldn't believe what I was hearing. I asked if she would be willing to tell RTÉ what she had told me. She said she would, of course, if I thought it would help. It would, I said.

I made contact with Philip Boucher-Hayes from RTÉ Radio 1. He agreed to come to Tuam to speak with Mary, and with me too. He arrived at our house the following day. We spoke for a long time. He was easy to talk to. He had a lovely, warm personality and I could tell he cared about the story, that he wanted to get to the truth of the matter, as much as I did. I showed him all my research and laid it out on the kitchen table so that he could examine it and take notes.

Then he interviewed Mary and went to the Tuam site to have a look around and edit his report. He told me the time the piece would be going out on air. I tuned in. I listened intently as the ads came to a close and the familiar *Drivetime* signature tune played. Philip announced that he had an exclusive: new information pertaining to the mother and baby home in Tuam. I felt a shiver down my spine. I listened as Mary recounted the story she had told me over the phone: how she had followed the child to where he had found the skull.

Mary Moriarty: We went out into my back garden and I called over the wall to the child – I knew him and I asked him if I could have a look at it. And he said, 'It's plastic; it's from Halloween.' But when I looked at it I knew it wasn't because it had teeth.

    I said, 'No, put it back wherever you got it, because that's a proper skull. It must be from the home.' I went out with the lady, with my neighbour, and there were two other women in it and we went down to have a look and it took ages to get through the rubble and the bushes and everything and eventually we got in there – two, three of us. We were looking down at the ground, and the next thing, the grass was wet and my feet went from under me and I slid down, part of the way down, into it and the women caught hold of me to pull me up and I said, 'Hold on.' I was just trying to get my bearings, my sight, you know, in a dark place, and looking, and I could see. There would seem to be rises of steps or something on the far wall opposite me and the babies were placed on that – you could see they were swaddled up. Rolled up in cloth and placed one after another in each raise and there was quite a lot of them there.

Philip Boucher-Hayes (PBH): Describe your impression of the space to me – was it purpose-built? Were there walls? Could you see concrete?

Mary Moriarty: I don't know, you see, because I understood it was a crypt.

PBH: You've obviously heard the reports about there being a septic tank in the area as well and that that might be a possible burial site. Did the space that you fell into, did that strike you as being like that or did it seem like something more purpose-built?

Mary Moriarty: I don't know. I cannot answer that and I won't tell a lie.

PBH: What age were the babies, though? Were they newborn, do you think, or were they a bit older?

Mary Moriarty: What I seen seemed to be newborn babies, like I couldn't tell for that they were babies or not, but from the way they were wrapped they seemed to me they were.

PBH: On the basis of what you saw, though, you made the presumption, did you, at the time that these might have been or must have been stillborn babies?

Mary Moriarty: Yes, that's what I thought and that's what the people who was along with me at the time thought as well.

PBH: How many did you see? Was it anything like the 796 deaths that we know occurred there?

Mary Moriarty: I don't know, you see, because I didn't see the whole of the place. I only seen what was facing me that day.

PBH: But what did you see? How many did you see?

Mary Moriarty: There was quite a lot in it – there was three or four, I thought, levels, or five maybe. From the ground, up to the roof that was filled with those parcels. They were like little parcels set on shelves.

PBH: *If I said 20 to you would that sound like an under-estimation?*

Mary Moriarty: *Probably an under-estimate, yeah.*

PBH: *If I said 50 . . .*

Mary Moriarty: *Maybe still under-estimated.*

PBH: *If I said over a hundred . . .*

Mary Moriarty: *Maybe, in that area, that's what I assumed was in it. I never realised it was anything more.*

PBH: *Mary and her neighbours were so horrified by what they had found that they started asking questions locally, but by 1975 the Bon Secours nuns still in Tuam, in the nearby hospital, were too young to recall anything about the running of the home. They did direct Mary though to a lady called Julia Devaney who had been a resident [in the home] and later worked there. Mary then showed Julia Devaney the burial site that she had slipped into . . .*

Mary Moriarty: *'Ah yes,' she said, 'that's it. That is the little place where the babies are. And I brought most of them out there. There's a tunnel,' and she pointed back to her left with her left hand. 'There's a tunnel coming out there from the hospital part. And that's where we would have carried the baby out, or babies, if they were dead, and placed them in there.'*

PBH: *This would have been, going by her age . . . what . . . something that happened in the '40s, '50s and '60s?*

Mary Moriarty: It would have been. The home closed in 1961. At the time in '75 I suppose she [Julia Devaney] was a woman in her late sixties at the time. 'Ah I did,' she said, 'I carried a lot of them out of there.' And we took that as what was the truth.

PBH: You had no reason to disbelieve her?

Mary Moriarty: I had no reason to disbelieve the woman.

PBH: She seemed credible to you?

Mary Moriarty: Very credible woman she was.

PBH: Did she say why they went through the tunnel?

Mary Moriarty: Well, we understood that was the direct access to it from the hospital, rather than coming out and lifting a lid and going into it.

PBH: The existence of a tunnel is confirmed in minutes of the county home committee meetings of 1940. Local historian Catherine Corless has established that the committee intended during World War II to use the tunnel as an air-raid shelter if the need arose.

Then he played a clip from my interview, where I read from a report of a committee meeting.

Catherine: The County Galway Homes and Homes Assistance Committee at their monthly meeting held in the Children's Home Tuam on Wednesday decided to prepare a tunnel for use as an air-raid shelter by the occupants of the home. Mr Corbett suggests that a tunnel in the institution be used as a shelter and the secretary mentioned, yes, it could be used and the assistant county surveyor for this area could have it prepared to be used as such.

PBH: *I've asked around in Tuam and there are some people who remember either a tunnel or tunnels at the back of the home. Among them Frannie Hopkins, who explored one as a young boy before the home was knocked down.*

Frannie Hopkins: *And it would have been a tunnel that would have been accessible enough for us to run and play in and we would emerge halfway through the garden or the back field or whatever you want to call it and when you came to the end of the tunnel you could either exit left or right. And you would emerge out in the centre of the garden.*

PBH: *But not near the actual burial site.*

Frannie Hopkins: *No, it wouldn't have been near the burial site as such. It wouldn't have been leading to the burial site. That's the way I would have put it.*

PBH: *Suffice to say there was a tunnel there. It was accessible from one end from inside the building and from the other end in the garden.*

Frannie Hopkins: *There was plenty of headroom and plenty wide enough. You could run through it, through the best of it, like. It was a proper tunnel. It wasn't just a makeshift-type thing.*

At this point the *Drivetime* presenter, Mary Wilson, interjected with a question for the reporter.

Mary Wilson: *To sum up – what might be the significance of this additional information that you've brought us this evening?*

PBH: I think it significantly advances our understanding of what is contained in this plot and what was going on there. It does provide anecdotal evidence that the nuns were burying children in these sites.

It also raises more questions, though – if that skull did indeed have teeth, it certainly was not a newborn baby but a significantly older child. You also wonder why weren't the nuns using the cemetery on the side of the road. Even if these were unbaptised babies, there was an angels' plot in that graveyard so it's quite perplexing as to why they wouldn't have been using it.

But ultimately it is yet more evidence that these remains were from the mid-twentieth century and not from the famine era, as had been contended by some. It still doesn't explain why, I suppose, why so many died in Tuam and where exactly they are all buried.

But I think that possibly the most significant aspect of this, whatever cruelties that you could lay at the nuns' feet, however harsh or however medically incompetent the regimes were that they ran in the mother and babies home, particularly in Tuam, it was always hard to believe that they would have knowingly put babies into a septic tank, not least because of their own religious sensitivities, but because there may have been a tunnel running up to and into this one particular burial plot. In this case it would seem highly unlikely that it is a septic tank. We can't say that of the other burial plot which is a couple of yards from it, because the plans do, as I've said to you before, indicate the presence of some kind of sewage tank in the vicinity.

Mary Wilson: Philip, just ahead of getting the terms of reference, which we expect to get at the end of the month, *into this commission of inquiry now into the mother and baby homes, is there any sign on the ground in Tuam that the government is gathering evidence on the ground?*

PBH: *Not on the ground, but I know that any attempts that I've been making relatively recently to get access to public records have all been politely declined because all of those records are now being gathered together by civil servants into one place to facilitate this scoping exercise before the inquiry. I suppose one thing of perhaps small significance today to indicate the government's intent on this now is that the minister for children, Charlie Flanagan, called Catherine Corless this afternoon. They talked for some time. He thanked her for her work and complimented her, indeed, as well on her work. But beyond that he didn't tell or relate to her anything of any significance about possible terms of reference or how this inquiry was going to be conducted.*

It was a good piece, I felt. It was comprehensive, and it was significant that Mary's testimony was now on the record. It was evidence that supported Frannie and Barry's discovery all those years ago.

I closed my eyes and thought of the part of the story Mary had not mentioned on the radio – something she told me that will stay with me for the rest of my life.

About two years after falling into the hole, Mary had given birth to a baby boy in the private hospital in Tuam which was run by the Bon Secours nuns. Mary said she would never forget the moment when the nun presented her baby to her. He was swaddled tightly in several white cloths, like table linen. An image flashed across her mind: the memory of all those dead babies she had seen wrapped in rags in the very same way, all stacked one on top of the other in that dark hole in the ground. In a moment of panic she grabbed her baby from the nun, pulled the swaddling cloths off him and held him close.

CHAPTER FORTY-SIX

The Locked Room

~

Even though the story had broken internationally, there was still one part of the puzzle which remained a mystery to me: the owners of the site, Galway County Council.

I had been trying for some time to secure a meeting with them. Now with international media attention gaining momentum, I hoped they might be more obliging. I requested a meeting again, this time with the help of a senator named Trevor Ó Clochartaigh who was proving himself to be a great advocate for the Tuam babies. He wrote to Kevin Kelly, acting CEO of Galway County Council at the time, to see if they would meet with me. This time the request was granted.

The meeting was arranged for the following week, on 27 August. I spent the next few days going over my presentation, studying the material, meticulously going through it all, in case I had missed something, anything that could weaken the case. I wanted to be sure I could make the best possible argument to them. I had one chance and I needed to figure out how I could convey to them the importance of what I had found out and how critical they were in it all – that only they had the power to do something about this.

The day of the meeting came around. I left the house with my file under my arm. Aidan drove. I was glad about that. I would have been too tetchy for the drive. We arrived at the county council offices and they ushered us towards the boardroom, where we were introduced to the acting manager and his team.

I laid the maps and records out across the boardroom table and began my presentation. As I looked around the room, I got the feeling they weren't overly interested in what I had to say. At the end of the presentation I asked them if they had more detailed records from the Tuam home.

They told me I was not an academic and therefore wouldn't be granted access to the files.

I felt a hot rush of blood to my cheeks. I knew they must have looked red. Aidan looked defensive. I cut in before he had a chance to say something inappropriate. I still needed the council onside. I tried to leave the meeting on a positive note. But in reality I felt very deflated as we got back into the car. Aidan and I looked at one another.

'Well, that was a waste of time,' I said.

'You did very well,' he replied.

'Not well enough. We got nothing out of it.'

I decided I was going to need some help to persuade the council. I rang Trevor Ó Clochartaigh again, and asked if there was anything we could do, then got in touch with solicitor Kevin Higgins, who was helping some of the Magdalene women with their cases.

It was some months later before I finally made any progress. A call came through from the council saying that I would be granted 'limited' access to 'some' of their records. It was better than nothing, I thought. At least it would be a start.

My mother Kathleen O'Hare (under the dot), aged 12,
at Manooney School in County Armagh, 1924.

My mother in the middle in the hayfield, with neighbours and my brothers
Michael and Martin and my sister Mary on her knee. In the background
is our old house, which was once an RIC Barracks, c.1953.

Aidan with his parents Paddy and Josie.

Me aged 13 with three of the
Ryan children. The family lived
close by and I have many happy
memories of them.

Me during my year at art college, 1974.

Aidan and I on our wedding day, March 1978.

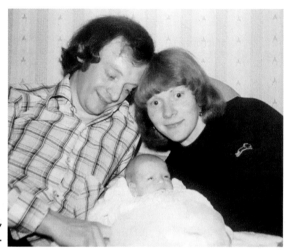

Adrienne's christening day, June 1979.

Our four beauties (left-right): Aaron, Adrienne, Alan and Alicia, getting ready for a school concert in Tuam, c.1990.

Our first place together – a mobile.

Aidan with my parents Paddy and Kathleen on Lough Key in County Roscommon, 1976.

A joyous occasion! The birth of our first grandchild, Aoife Moriarty, January 2008.

Bringing the grandchildren for a walk. I'm holding Sophia and in the buggies are Cormac, Beinean and Sophia's twin Ethan.

Aidan walks Alicia down the aisle on her wedding day to Tom Dilleen.

Liam Neeson, when he called to our house in July 2018, replaying the line 'I will find you ...'

Ray Ryan, Tuam Herald ©

During my investigations into the Tuam Home, I made this model of how it would have looked.

Michael Duffy, far right, who was born in the Tuam Home, on his First Holy Communion day with four other Tuam children. Michael's mother paid for his keep while he was there and took this photo.

Opposite page: Images from the burial site and surrounding area at the old Tuam Mother and Baby Home.

Ray Ryan, Tuam Herald ©

Pointing out other potential burials outside the walled off area at the babies site, to Minister Zappone, on her visit to Tuam, April 2017.

Ray Ryan, Tuam Herald ©

With home survivors, P.J. Haverty, to my immediate right, and Walter Francis on the day of the minister's visit.

On the day I received my Bar of Ireland Human Rights Award with my Tuam Home survivor friends, 2017.

Front, l-r: Peter Mulryan, Aidan, myself, Carmel Larkin and Walter Francis; back, l-r: John Egan, Tom Warde, Michael O'Flaherty and P.J. Haverty.

Men, women and children – including home survivors Michael Flaherty, left, and Peter Mulryan, right – hold funeral boxes, each representing a dead child, at a procession from the Garden of Remembrance to the GPO, Dublin, 2018.

This was on the day of our ceremony to coincide with the Pope's visit to Knock. The sculpture in the middle was surrounded by little ceramic booties, August 2018.

Our very first vigil for the Tuam babies. Aoife, our granddaughter,
at the heart-shaped lighted candles, November 2016.

Me speaking at a gathering in 2019, to highlight the exact
area where the archaeologists discovered the chambers which held
the skeletal remains of the Tuam Home babies. We marked that area
with white paper lilies, which we also wore. The microphone was
handed to each person there who wanted to say a few words.

I arrived back at the council offices at the agreed time. A woman was there to meet me. This time, instead of the boardroom, I was brought into a tiny room with a small table and two chairs in the centre. 'Please, have a seat,' she said, pointing towards the table and chairs.

'Thank you,' I replied, wondering why I was in this empty room.

'I'll be right back,' she said.

I sat looking at the walls around me. She returned a few minutes later with several large, weathered-looking files. She placed them on the table. 'I was told these are the files you are looking for,' she said. She locked the door behind her and sat opposite me.

I looked at her for a moment, bemused. I couldn't believe this is how the interaction had to take place. In a tiny locked room, with a supervisor. Regardless, I got to work, quickly. 'Thank you,' I said.

I started peeling through the files, reading the pages one by one. Half an hour went by. I could see my supervisor was getting restless. I started to wonder if this was a pointless exercise. Just then, as I turned the page, something caught my eye. I read over it again and again, imprinting it in my mind, in case I was not allowed to take a copy.

'Would it be possible to get a photocopy?' I asked, tentatively.

'Sure,' the woman said, looking bored. 'But I will have to make a note of what you have photocopied.'

'Of course,' I said quickly. I wondered if she would have to ask permission to photocopy the pages, and if, when they saw the contents, they would refuse me a copy.

The woman left the room with the pages in question. I waited. She returned five minutes later, with the photocopies in hand. I tried to remain cool. I didn't want her to pick up on my astonishment.

'Thanks,' I said, placing the pages on the desk beside me as I continued to flick through the file. 'I think that's enough for one day,' I said, after I had looked through the remaining files.

The supervisor seemed relieved. I tucked the photocopies into my bag, so as not to draw attention to them on the way out. I made small talk with her as she checked me out at reception, thanking her and asking what time she would get off work. We joked about the traffic on the way out, and I left on a cordial note.

I got into the car and as soon as I was on the main road towards home, I felt a sense of elation come over me. As I picked up speed and was sure I was out of sight of the council, I banged the steering wheel. 'Yes!' I cried.

I couldn't wait to show Aidan what I had found. When I got home I placed the photocopies carefully across the dining room table. I had studied them several times to be sure they said what I thought they said. I wanted Aidan to see it and confirm it. Though I was sure I had found what I was looking for.

'I have to show you something,' I said, when he got home that evening. 'Have a look.'

'Papers from the council?' he asked.

'Yes – I think it's proof,' I said, pointing to the pages, and explaining. 'This one is the architect's drawing of the plan for the Dublin road housing estate. Construction was to begin around 1972.'

'Oh my God,' said Aidan. 'Does that say what I think it says?'
'Yep.'

We looked at one another in disbelief. Stamped across the map were the words 'Children's burial ground' exactly at the spot Frannie and Barry had fallen into, and 'Adjoining burial ground' was written across the surrounding area.

Aidan looked stunned. It was the first time either of us had seen it written in black and white: 'Children's burial ground'. It meant they knew that the children were buried there when they went to build the housing estate. All this time the authorities had denied any knowledge of the children being buried there. And yet, here it was – the truth, buried deep in a file at the county council offices.

'That's not all,' I said. 'Look at these.'

I showed Aidan the memos that I had found in the file, written in advance of building the estate. One read: 'Take great care putting in a playground, because of the children's burial ground.'

This is the same county council that had stated to the commission of inquiry that it had no knowledge of the babies being buried in the tank.

There were more details of the building of the estate houses in printed and handwritten notes, one of which stated: 'Galway County Council develop the unused ground at the Dublin Road Housing Estate as a playground for the area with due respect for the sensitive nature of the area.'

There was also a cost sheet for the project, which read: 'Provide playing equipment on children's burial ground: £2,000.'

And there was a paragraph on the expenditure sheet explaining the delay in the building of houses. The Tuam branch of the blocklayers' union insisted on local men being employed, and, as a consequence, the contractor could not use his own blocklayers on the job. Although he eventually managed to get three local craftsmen, they stayed for only four weeks, and despite repeated advertising for blocklayers, the contractor managed to get only one.

'What's that about?' asked Aidan, after he read the paragraph about the blocklayers.

'I think locals knew about the babies, so no one wanted the job,' I said. 'But I suppose we can't know for sure. Just strange he couldn't get anyone locally.'

I told Aidan about my day at the council and about the tiny locked room. It didn't seem right. This was a story which had been covered by major newspapers across the world, with people demanding answers. And yet still, here at the very heart of the story, despite the international media attention and the public outcry, everything was still going on behind locked doors.

Now I just needed to figure out what to do with the information I had found. Did this mean that the council had known about the babies all along and that the playground was built with full knowledge of the bodies lying in the ground surrounding it? This was a sick and sobering thought.

My mind was racing when I went to bed. Though I was glad I had found the information, somehow it made it worse. Had someone known about the babies and just ignored it? I found that hard to fathom.

I couldn't sleep. Eventually I got up as I didn't want to keep Aidan awake. I went downstairs and made a cup of tea. I hoped it would settle me. The more I thought about what I had seen, the more anxious it made me. I didn't know what to do next. Whom should I tell about the files I had found? I felt like there was nowhere to turn. Who do you go to when it's the people in charge who are the ones in the wrong? Where can you turn when the gatekeepers are the ones you can't trust?

CHAPTER FORTY-SEVEN

Exaggerated Religiosity

❧

Journalists were flooding the house for the next few months. Every day, it seemed, there were calls from documentary teams from all over the world. We set up a system: Aidan took on the role of organiser and Alan manned both the house phone and my mobile, which rang continuously. Each room of our small home was turned into a separate studio for film crews to interview survivors and talk to me about my research. The interviews were difficult, often under very hot lights for long periods of time, but I was glad the story was getting out there finally and that there was such interest from around the globe. And, yet, one very important part of the story was still missing: someone from the Bon Secours nuns to speak out and tell their side of the story. No one yet knew what their stance was or how they accounted for what had happened.

It wasn't until a lady named Saskia Weber, who was making a documentary for the television channel France 2, sent an email requesting that someone from the order come on the programme to speak about the Tuam mother and baby home, that people finally saw the attitude the nuns, or the spokespeople for the nuns, were displaying. This was the email reply Saskia Weber received from PR agency The Communications Clinic, working on behalf of the Bon Secours sisters.

Terry Prone
Bon Secours

Your letter was sent on to me by the Provincial of the Irish Bon Secours congregation with instructions that I should help you. I'm not sure how I can. Let me explain. When the 'O My God – mass grave in West of Ireland' broke in an English-owned paper (the *Mail*) it surprised the hell out of everybody, not least the Sisters of Bon Secours in Ireland, none of whom had ever worked in Tuam and most of whom had never heard of it. If you come here, you'll find no mass grave, no evidence that children were ever so buried, and a local police force casting their eyes to heaven and saying 'Yeah, a few bones were found – but this was an area where Famine victims were buried. So?' Several international TV stations have aborted their plans to make documentaries, because essentially all that can be said is 'Ireland in the first half of the twentieth century was a moralistic, inward-looking, anti-feminist country of exagerrated [sic] religiousity.' Which most of us knew already. The overwhelming majority of the surviving Sisters of Bon Secours in Ireland are over eighty. The handful (literally) still in active ministry are in their seventies. None of them is an historian or sociologist or theologian and so wouldn't have the competence to be good on your programme.

    If you'd like me to point you at a few reputable historians who might be good, I'll certainly do that.

Terry Prone (Ms)
Chairman
The Communications Clinic

Perhaps the PR company hoped that this would be enough to deter Saskia, and others like her, from further investigation. If that was the objective, it achieved the opposite result, because Saskia went public with the email, and showed us all how the order was responding.

It made me wonder if we would ever get to the truth. We needed the nuns and the government to be committed to the cause. If not, I feared we would never get justice for the babies. Then, one cold January morning things seemed to be taking a turn for the better. I received a call from then Minister for Children James Reilly's office. He had taken over from Charlie Flanagan in the Cabinet reshuffle the previous July. They were calling to invite me and Aidan to see the minister – there was something he wanted to discuss with us. Of course, we'd be delighted, I said. I hoped that finally things were going to move forward. It had been over six months since the government had announced the inquiry and still we had no terms of reference for how it was going to operate.

A few days later we got up early and made the trip to Dublin. I had never been inside Government Buildings and was curious to see what they would be like. We arrived outside Leinster House and saw some of the other interest groups there – survivors' groups and the heads of various organisations who had been campaigning for rights for adopted people. Together, we made our way through the security area and out onto the plinth you often see on the news – where the politicians assemble for photocalls and to give their statements to the media. It was interesting to be there in person. I wondered what made people choose this way of life – politics. What was it that made them want to walk through these doors every day? I had to assume their intentions began in earnest. No doubt each in their own way once upon a time wanted to change the world, or at least their little pocket of it.

We were welcomed by some of the staff working in Minister Reilly's office. They ushered us through to a meeting room with about 40 chairs laid out for us, and a table and some chairs at the top of the room for the minister and his colleagues. At the back wall there was tea and coffee and some scones and buns.

Minister Reilly entered the room, said hello, and we all engaged in small talk about our journeys to Dublin. And then it was down to business. What had he brought us here to say?

He wanted to let us know, he said, that the government was going to announce the terms of reference for the Commission of Inquiry. I could feel the tension rising. The thing everyone wanted to know was: what would they be looking into?

He went on to explain that the inquiry would be a nationwide investigation into mother and baby homes across the country, not just in Tuam. There was a sigh of relief from everyone in the room. This is what many of the groups had been looking for, for decades.

At last, the government would investigate what had gone on in those institutions which had for a long time hidden their sins behind their high stone walls. The Commission would look at why women and children ended up in the homes, how they were treated when they were there and how adoptions were handled. It would also investigate the high mortality rates, whether vaccine trials were carried out and – crucially, from my perspective – the burial practices.

Television reporters and journalists were waiting outside the gates, hoping to interview us, to get our reaction to what the minister had said.

I spoke to the reporters, welcoming the establishment of the Commission, but made the point that the nuns, in my opinion, had not been forthcoming enough in providing information. I left Leinster House feeling relieved. I felt reassured that the government was taking this seriously.

That is until a few months later, in June, when a new piece of information came to light – something I really wasn't expecting. Someone told me to look at the *Irish Examiner*. There was a shocking exposé about the home, they said. I logged on to the paper's website immediately. It was a piece by Connall Ó Fátharta, under the headline 'Special Investigation: Government Already Knew of Baby Deaths'.

The article said that the newspaper had obtained evidence that showed that the Health Service Executive (HSE) had looked into both the Tuam and Bessborough homes as part of the Magdalene laundries inquiry in 2012. It would be almost another two years before the inquiry was announced, on the back of my research, the article pointed out.

It went on to say that senior HSE figures had recommended a full investigation, that a state inquiry be launched and that the minister should be informed immediately.

I couldn't believe what I was reading. They knew? All that time, the government actually knew about all this? And they did nothing? Could this be true?

All this time I had thought that I had stumbled upon something that the state at the highest level wasn't aware of – because surely, if they'd known, they would have done something about it. If this new information was correct – and I had no reason to believe it wasn't – then for two years the government had sat on this. Perhaps they hoped it would go away, that it would be brushed under the carpet and consigned to history, like so many other atrocities.

I could only hope that the current government was committed to finding out the truth and to investigating fully, but that remained to be seen.

CHAPTER FORTY-EIGHT

Scratching the Surface

~

In October 2015 the government announced that the commission had organised its own ground-penetrating survey. I was glad to see some kind of action being taken. It made sense that the commission couldn't go by the newspaper's survey and needed to do their own independent investigation. The survey would take place with the cooperation of Galway County Council, it said, and would take approximately one day to complete.

One day. I found it difficult to accept that that's all the effort it would take to know whether the children may be buried there, and yet it had been such a fight to get to this point. And sure enough, the stratigraphic survey identified a number of 'sub-surface anomalies' that the commission deemed worthy of further investigation.

But then everything ground to a halt again. A general election was called for February 2016. When the new government was formed, the new minister for children was announced, a woman named Katherine Zappone. I wondered what this change in government would mean for the Tuam babies. Everything

depended on how committed the government – and, more specifically, the children's minister – was to the cause.

Aidan suggested I write to her, to make a connection – it would
be a good idea, he said, ever the business head on his shoulders.
So I did. I wrote to the new minister and asked her what she
intended to do about Tuam.

In reply I received an invitation from Katherine Zappone, asking
if Aidan and I would like to come and speak with her. So we
made the trip to Dublin and spoke with her about what had
happened to date, and why we felt so strongly that something
had to be done.

She listened. She really did. By the time we were leaving, I felt
we had been heard. But what would be done about it remained
to be seen.

Just before we left, I asked the minister if she would come to
Tuam, to meet with the survivors. She would, she said. And what
happened next showed what could be done, if someone in power
actually wanted something to happen – how things *could* be
actioned.

Not long afterwards, Katherine Zappone came to visit Tuam.
She brought the minister for housing, planning and local government, Simon Coveney, with her. They didn't come with a huge
fanfare or a convoy, the way I imagined they might. They had
two men with them – their assistants, perhaps.

We arranged to meet at the site, and I sent them directions on
how to get there. When I arrived I saw their cars parked up beside
the playground. It all looked very official. We greeted one another
and then walked across the playground to the site, where we met
with some of the survivors. The ministers spoke with them,
listened to them as they told their stories and showed them the
grotto, with babies' shoes hanging from the branches surrounding
it, as well as little baby soothers and teddy bears, all stark

reminders of what it was all about: the babies and children who had lost their lives.

As I watched her listening to the stories of the survivors, I was thankful that the minister was a woman, and someone who originally came from outside Ireland. Katherine Zappone was born in the US, though she was now an Irish citizen. She was gay too, so no doubt she knew of the struggles that can sometimes come with being a minority in a religious society. I felt she might have an outside perspective. Politics in Ireland can be very local – very attached to the parish – with the church and state historically hand in glove. Maybe this would finally be the change that was needed.

CHAPTER FORTY-NINE

A Knock at the Door

M y phone rang. It was a woman asking me to give a talk.
'A talk?' I said, surprised. I'd never given a talk in my
life.

'To some students at the university,' she said.

I paused. I couldn't imagine myself at the top of a lecture hall
talking to a room full of educated students. The thought of it
terrified me. 'Oh . . . I don't know,' I said.

'I think they'd really get a lot out of it,' she said. I could hear
she was disappointed I hadn't said yes.

I told her I would think about it. That night I told Aidan. He
thought it was a great idea.

'I can't do it,' I said.

'Why?' said Aidan.

'You *know* why,' I said.

Sometimes it was frustrating when he pretended my anxiety
didn't exist. I knew he did it to give me more confidence, but it
wasn't logical to me, because it did exist, it was there, lurking in
my brain every day.

'How could I do something like that? Stand up in front of all those people. I can't do it,' I said. I was disappointed with myself. I wanted to be the kind of person who could do that, who could be confident and self-assured, who didn't have to overthink things. But I knew I wasn't that person.

'I'll help you,' Aidan said.

'How will that work?' I asked.

'I'll come with you, and I'll give an introduction . . . warm up the crowd. And if you get stuck at any point, I'll jump in. We'll be a double act.' He smiled at me as he said it.

Somehow that made it easier. I didn't want to disappoint him. I knew he'd be great with the crowd. He had a way with people. He could put them at ease. People liked him, instinctively. I could see why. I told him I'd sleep on it. That night I turned it over and over in my mind. When I woke the next morning I felt delirious from all the deliberation.

'I'll do it,' I said, in a moment of frustration.

'Great!' he replied. 'That's settled, then.'

Things felt easier once I had made the decision. Now I had to step into the role. I spent the next few weeks thinking about what I would say – how I would showcase my research and how best to describe what I had discovered. I had learned so much from my lecturer on the history course, I felt a type of responsibility to be a good teacher, or as good as I could be. Good teachers were important. It was a privilege to be asked to speak in front of people and I wanted to take that seriously.

It seemed like no time at all before I found myself at the college. A glass of water beside me, I sat on the cushioned metal chair looking out at the crowd, all the fresh young faces watching from their tiered seats. They laughed as Aidan told a few jokes to warm them up – making fun of himself, as he always did, but in a way that put everyone at ease.

I laughed too. Somehow it didn't seem as frightening when Aidan was there with me. He spoke a little bit about what the past few years had been like – how I had become dedicated to this quest for answers. He said things I couldn't really say about myself, and then he welcomed me to the stage to take over. He broke the ice with another little joke and I took to my feet, smiling.

I had my note cards with me. I began by reading my introduction. I could hear my voice shaking. I powered through. And then, as I began to get into a flow, it became easier. I had a natural passion for what I was talking about. I didn't have to feign it. After a while I starting going off-script. I liked knowing my note cards were there if I needed them, but I knew the material so well, it made sense to speak from the heart.

Time seemed to go very quickly. I looked up at the clock at the back of the room. It was nearly time to finish up. I asked if anyone would like to ask any questions. Several hands flew up. The students were very respectful and engaged in the topic. They seemed to really care about the subject matter. Their questions were very considered – about how to go about accessing information in the way that I had done. Where did I learn to do my research, they wondered, and how did I know how to trust the sources I found. They were all very interesting discussion points. Other students chimed in with their ideas. It was electric. I felt like I was back on my history course again. Ideas flying around the room, people energised by thinking about things. I looked over at Aidan, who gave me a subtle thumbs-up under the table. This was going well, I thought. I was actually enjoying it and I felt the students were too.

When the lecture was over, the students began talking with one another. That's when I noticed an elderly couple walking towards me. I had seen them in the crowd while I was speaking. They introduced themselves. 'I'm Peter,' said the man, 'and this is my wife Kathleen.'

We shook hands. They had a gentle way about them. 'I was one of those children,' Peter said.

'Sorry?' I asked, not quite understanding what he meant.

'I was in the Tuam home,' he explained.

'We heard you were going to be talking here, and we had to come and see you,' said Kathleen.

I thanked them for coming and asked Peter about his time in the home and his experience. This is what he told me. Like most of the Tuam babies, his story began with his mother's story.

'Late at night there was a knock on my grandfather's door. It was the parish priest. He said: "You know your family has been causing scandal in the parish. Your daughter is pregnant outside of marriage." He insisted that the young woman needed to be taken out of the parish, immediately.

'"I know where she can go," the priest said. There was a county home in Loughrea. He could take her there that very night, he said. And so, my mother at seven and a half months' pregnant was forced to leave her family, and the house she grew up in, not knowing whether she would ever see her parents again.'

As Peter tells me the story, I try to imagine what that night must have been like for his grandparents, having someone come to their house and tell them their daughter had to be taken away, feeling powerless to stop it.

'My mother was told to sit on the crossbar of her father's bicycle.' Peter winces as he says it.

'And off they went, into the darkness of the night.' Her father, he tells me, cycled 20 miles to reach the home in Loughrea.

I try to remember what it was like to be seven and a half months' pregnant. I think back to when I was pregnant with

Aaron, our youngest. Pregnancy is a time of great strength and great vulnerability – somehow at the same time.

I could not imagine the discomfort that that woman must have felt, and the fear, not knowing where she was being taken. It was a kind of kidnapping. What happened when she arrived at her destination, I wondered. What 'welcome' did she receive from these strangers in habits? Was it cold there? Where did she sleep that night, suddenly finding herself away from the comfort of her own bed, her own room, the safety of home? She must have been afraid.

Once under the auspices of the church, Peter's mother was transferred to the Tuam mother and baby home. Some weeks later, Peter was born. Instead of being born into the homestead that was his family farm, he was born into an institution. He spent the next four and a half years in the home before being fostered out to a family to work for them. His mother meanwhile was sent to the Magdalene laundry in Galway, where she lived and worked for the rest of her life.

What must it have been like for her, the day they took her son away, the day another family came to collect him, at just four and a half years old? She must have hoped they would be kind to him. That they might love him, like a son, the way she did.

But that was wishful thinking. It was a far cry from the reality, and she must have known that, in her heart. Peter had a hard life, from the very beginning, and it didn't get any easier when he was sent to his foster family. Subjected to beatings and regular punishments, he was forced to do hard labour for the family, in return for his bed and board. The mother of the family was kind. He remembers her berating her husband for being hard on him. But the man was relentless.

'I dreaded summer as a child,' he said, his eyes filling with tears.

'Why?' I asked.

'Because it was nettle season,' he said. I could see the memory of the pain in his eyes. 'I was beaten, with nettles. They were stuffed down my clothes . . .' His voice choked up at the thought of it.

Kathleen put her hand on Peter's back. She looked at me as if to say, 'How could they?' It must have pained her to think of people treating him this way – the man she loved so dearly. And when he was just an innocent little boy.

I could see the boy standing in front of me now. 'I'm sorry,' I said, 'that's really terrible.' It's all I could think of to say. We sat down on the lecture hall seats and talked a little while longer. Then when we felt it was time to clear the room, we said our goodbyes and promised to keep in touch.

For days afterwards I felt a sadness, a heavy weight in my chest, thinking of all that Peter had been through. It was starting to become apparent what had happened in the home, what damage had been done to so many people, mothers and children, who were put through this gruelling system.

It was around this time that I met P.J. Haverty. His story was similar to Peter's in some ways, though the outcomes were very different.

P.J. was born in 1951. His mother did not have a teenage pregnancy. She was 27, but, being unmarried, she was sent to the Tuam mother and baby home where she gave birth to a baby boy, P.J. And it is in the home that P.J. would live for the next seven years under the auspices of the Bon Secours nuns, before finally being fostered out to a couple named Teresa and Mikey Hansbury from Menlough, near Tuam.

P.J. remembers the day he stepped out of the home, into the world, for the first time. He was leaving the only place he'd ever known, to be taken to the Hansburys', who were strangers to him. They were to become his foster parents. He didn't know what to expect – who they were or what life would be like with them. For a little child it must have been very frightening. When he reached their house, he stepped out of the car and saw a dog in the driveway. He had never seen a dog before, so he quickly jumped back into the car in fear. So sheltered had his life been in the home, so far removed from the outside world. Suddenly everything was new – as though he was a baby all over again, when in fact he was seven years old. Things that seemed normal to most people had to be explained to him. He couldn't understand why their house was so small. He was used to the big old institution of the mother and baby home, where he slept in dormitories with all the other children.

Luckily for P.J., his foster parents were kind. They treated him like one of their own – like a son – though they were strict too and believed in hard work. They wouldn't stand for anyone being soft either. But they were good to him. He was one of the lucky few. He remembers a happy childhood – being cared for and respected.

When he was in his twenties, P.J. became curious about his birth mother, and his foster mother was very happy to help him find her. They discovered that his mother was from a place called Eyrecourt, near Portumna, which was not very far away. P.J. decided he would go there and see what he could find out.

He asked people locally if they knew of the Haverty family (his mother's maiden name). Nobody seemed to know of them. It felt like a dead end. But then he came across a man on a bicycle who said he remembered a Haverty family in the area. He said that the elder generation had passed away but that they had had two daughters – one had become pregnant and disappeared, and the other was married and living in Eyrecourt.

P.J. was very excited to hear this news. The old man gave him directions to the house where the woman lived and P.J. decided to pay a visit. If this was the right family, the chances were this woman was his aunt. He found the house and knocked on the door. A woman appeared. She seemed to get a fright when she saw him. She only opened the door a little and then called for her husband.

P.J. thought the whole encounter very strange and didn't feel welcome, so he apologised and said he must have the wrong house. It must have been very difficult for him to leave, without getting a chance to ask about his mother, having come so close to finding her.

And then one day, when he least expected it, P.J. received a letter from his birth mother. His aunt had recognised P.J. and had written to his mother to tell her that a young man who looked like P.J. had shown up at her door.

They began a correspondence and P.J. arranged to meet his mother, who now lived in Brixton in England. He headed off early one morning and made his way to the ferry, and drove all the way to Brixton, anxious to meet his mother for the first time. He had so many questions he wanted to ask her.

But when he arrived, it wasn't quite the Hollywood reunion he had envisaged. They had an awkward hug and shook hands, as he introduced himself to his mother and her husband. It was difficult to think of this stranger he had only just met as his mother. The mother he had grown up with all his life was back home in Ireland, his foster mother, Teresa.

His birth mother had the tea all laid out in the sitting room and she had made up a bed for him, expecting that he might stay the night. But as he had arrived with several relatives (who had helped him along his journey), P.J. and his mother didn't really get a chance to speak privately, and so they parted ways again after the tea and a brief chat, with just as many questions left unanswered.

It wasn't until years later that they would be reunited again. P.J. received another letter from his mother asking if she could be a part of his family. She had resisted contacting him all this time as she didn't want to interfere in his life. Her husband had passed away since they had met and a lot had happened in her life. But she hoped that they could meet again.

So P.J. planned another meeting, this time with his wife and their three children, so that his mother could finally meet her grandsons. He still had a question he needed answered, one that had haunted him all his life: why had she left him at the home? Why had she not taken him with her?

This time they met in a café in Brixton. P.J. was just about to ask the question, when something very unexpected happened. His mother smiled and gave a look that he suddenly recognised. A memory came flooding back to him.

It was of an ordinary afternoon when P.J. was about 14 years old. He was helping to bring the cows in. He had just moved them out of the field and on to the road when a car pulled up.

The car came to a stop close to where he was. The back window wound down slowly and in the back seat P.J. saw a woman looking out at him. She asked him where the Hansburys lived, and P.J. told her, pointing over towards his house. He apologised for having the cows out on the road. The woman smiled and thanked him, before rolling up the window.

Now, looking at his mother, he recognised that same smile. The woman in the back of the car, all those years before, was her. She had come to find him. P.J. asked his mother about it.

'Yes, that was me,' she said.

She was always looking for him, despite warnings from the nuns that there would be big trouble if she tried to find him. It was then that P.J. finally heard the story, the full story, of his birth and why he had been given away, or taken away, contrary to what he had always believed.

His mother told him of her pregnancy out of wedlock at the age of 27. A priest came to the house and told her to stay inside. She was not to leave the house, in case she was seen by other girls, with her stomach protruding. He instructed that she would be taken to the Tuam mother and baby home, where the nuns would look after her.

It was there that she gave birth to P.J. and stayed for a year after he was born – working for the nuns and minding her child. Then when her twelve months were up, she was told to leave, like all the mothers at the home. They were given no choice but to go.

'If she had a hundred pounds, which you couldn't have had back in those days, my mother could have bought me, but she didn't have it,' P.J. explained.

And so his mother looked for work nearby in Tuam because she didn't want to leave P.J. there. She wanted to be close by. Eventually she got a job as a cleaner in the hospital in Tuam, in the hope that she would earn enough money to buy her son back.

Every week for five and a half years she walked up to the home and banged on the door and pleaded with the nuns to let her take her son home. They told her to go away, that he was going to be fostered out and that was that. And that is what happened. That was the day P.J. remembered so clearly – walking out of the mother and baby home to live with two strangers, who would become his parents.

His mother found out that P.J. had been fostered out to a couple in Menlough and made it her business to find out where he had been taken. Though she knew she could get in a lot of trouble for doing it, one day she managed to convince someone to drive her out to the farm, so that she could see for herself if P.J. was okay.

She sat in the back of the car and when they spotted P.J. out on the road, his mother said, 'Stop, that's him!' And so the car stopped and she rolled down the window and took a long look at her son, who had grown into a little boy. She longed to go and hug him and steal him away with her. But she couldn't. She knew the law would not be on her side, even though he was her son. She took one last look at P.J. and rolled the window up and the car drove away and she took the boat to England to get away from everything that Ireland stood for, to escape from the oppression and run as far away from the mother and baby home as she could.

And that was the last she heard of him, until she received that letter from her sister many years later, saying that P.J. had shown up at her door. As she told him the story of what had happened, P.J. could see the pain in her eyes, and the love for the child she had lost all those years ago.

But soon after P.J. and his mother met up, she developed Alzheimer's. The next time he went to see her, she didn't recognise him.

'I'm your son,' he said.

'I have no son,' she told him. And he knew he had lost her all over again.

She died a short time later. He felt so lucky to have known her before she died, even though it was brief. I can only imagine what it meant for her to have the chance to finally tell him the full story, after all the years she'd mourned for the son who was stolen from her. She must have worried that he felt abandoned, that he thought she didn't love him. At least he would finally know the truth, and know how hard she had fought to keep him.

I thought of the bravery of that woman, knocking on the door of the home, week after week, for years on end, begging for her son back. It wasn't that she didn't love him. Quite the contrary. It was church and state that were the loveless ones.

'We were known as bastards,' said P.J. 'That was the name that was put on us, because we were born out of marriage.'

That word always made me wince. It was so full of venom, and hearing it made me wonder all over again if that was the real reason nothing was being done for the Tuam babies. Were they still seen, in some way, as 'bastards' not worth saving?

CHAPTER FIFTY

A Truth Deep Buried

⌒

Meanwhile, emails and letters were flooding in from people all over Ireland who had been born in mother and baby homes. They were hoping I could help them to find their birth mothers or at least to try and find out who they were, where they came from and what had happened to them in the Tuam home.

One such email caught my attention, for a different reason. It was from a man living in America who discovered that he was adopted when he found some papers in the attic after his parents died. Among the papers was a letter which the mother superior had written to his parents to tell them she had a lovely little boy available for adoption, and another letter thanking the adoptive parents for their 'very generous donation'.

Then, another woman contacted me looking for help to trace her mother's origins in Ireland. Her mother had also been adopted to America. She had the solicitor's letter and adoption papers which were dated 1951.

I noticed that the children were sometimes baptised with the adoptive parents' name. This was making tracing very difficult

271

because it was harder to know who the birth mother was. I wondered if this had been done on purpose – to cover the trail.

As I was researching the various cases for people, trying to link them back to their families, I took out my papers and looked through the list of children who had died. That's when I spotted something I hadn't seen before. On the long list I noticed the name Marian Bridget Mulryan.

I tried to remember . . . that man at the lecture, had he said his name was Peter *Mulryan*? I checked my notebook where I had written down his contact details. Yes – Peter Mulryan. I wondered if there was any chance that Marian Bridget Mulryan could be a relation of his.

I didn't want to upset him until I had more information. I emailed the births, deaths and marriages office in Galway (HSE West) and asked them to source a birth cert for a Marian Bridget Mulryan who was born in the Tuam home. I was able to give an approximate date of birth because I knew the age she was when she died. They found a birth certificate for her, which I purchased.

It was as I suspected. Bridget Mulryan was born in the Tuam home, and the certificate had her mother's name and address. The section under 'father's name' was blank. I went to my notebook, found Peter's contact details, and called him. 'Hi Peter, this is Catherine Corless here – we met at the university recently . . .'

'Ah yes, Catherine, good to hear from you,'

'Can you talk, Peter? There's something I was hoping to discuss with you.'

'Of course,' he said.

'It's just . . . I've found something . . . and I'm not sure yet whether it's relevant to you, but I thought I had better call you.'

'Oh?'

'I just wanted to check one or two things with you first . . . Where did you say your mother was from?'

'Corrandulla, County Galway.'

'And her name?'

'Delia.'

It was a match. I was silent for a moment while I tried to take it all in – what it meant.

'Hello? Catherine, are you there?'

'Sorry, Peter . . . yes . . . I . . . I'm not sure how to tell you this . . . but, did your mother ever mention a sister to you?'

'A sister? No . . . no, she never said anything about a sister.'

'Well, it's just – I have a list of names of the children who . . .'

Suddenly it was difficult to complete the sentence. I hadn't fully appreciated how hard this conversation might be, how much new information this would be for Peter to hear all at once, out of the blue.

'Who?' said Peter, prompting me to continue.

'Well, a list of names of children who died in the home.'

Peter was silent. I could almost hear his mind casting back to the memories of the home – to the faces of the other children he had known.

'And there's a name – Bridget Marian Mulryan. She is listed as one of the children who died. I took the liberty of getting a birth cert for her. And, Peter, it matches what you've just told me about your mother.'

I could tell this was a lot for Peter to absorb. 'I'm sorry,' I said, 'I can only imagine this is very difficult and confusing news to receive.'

'She never said anything about a sister . . .' he said.

He seemed to be in disbelief. Peter had been reunited with his mother in her old age. But by the time they met, she was very affected by having been institutionalised all her life. She had worked at the Tuam home and then at the Magdalene laundry in Galway, where she had lived out her days.

Peter and I arranged to speak again in the next day or two, once he'd had a chance to digest the news. This seemed like the best thing to do. It was a lot to take in.

When I hung up, I wondered if I had done the right thing. Was it useful for Peter to know that information? Or was it all the more hurtful? I tried to imagine how he might be feeling. He must have been searching his mind for clues from the conversations he and his mother had had in later years.

I tried to imagine their relationship, what it must have been like to be reunited as mother and son so late in life, together again after so many years, both shaped by the experience they had, each traumatised in their own way, a chasm between them – all the unspoken hurt that life had cast upon them both, through no fault or choosing of their own. Simply because there was no marriage involved. A pregnant woman. Her son. Their story. Society moves on, but it is the people it has hurt who have to pick up the pieces for the rest of their lives.

It is often said of people who lived through wartime that they can be reluctant to talk about their experiences because the hurt is too deep, the damage irreparable. I wondered whether that might also be true of people who had gone through the trauma of this kind of separation and institutionalisation. Somehow, as a society we have come to accept that this is what happened during that time in Ireland – that this was just normal then, without fully acknowledging the degree of trauma that was inflicted upon a generation of women and their children. After atrocities often come healing and reconciliation. But in Ireland there seems to be a lack of acceptance that this is what is needed.

Like the stoic generations whose stereotype is not to discuss feelings or sentimentality, to get on with things and brush over difficulties, so it seems we were taking this approach when it came to dealing with the difficult past of mothers and their children – leaving them to suffer in silence with no supports, emotional or practical.

It just didn't seem right. For so long I had been focused on what had happened to the children who had died. Only now I was starting to see the impact on those who had lived. The ones who had been spared the sewage tank, but who were left to live through their own kind of hell – the truth of what they'd been through buried deep inside them.

CHAPTER FIFTY-ONE

Digging

It was October 2016 when hoardings went up around the site and a 24-hour garda surveillance team was stationed outside it. The archaeologists moved in. As part of the commission of investigation the site was being excavated. They called in the state pathologist too and the coroner.

I kept driving past, every few days. I watched as teams of archaeologists came and went. I wanted so badly to know what was going on behind the tall temporary walls that had been erected.

It pained me to think that there were so many people employed to undertake the excavation who now knew the answer that had plagued me for nearly six years. Were the remains of the children buried there, in that sewage tank? And if so, how many of them, and how old were they? I needed to see with my own eyes, to know exactly, without doubt, what was there.

I tried to be patient. But it was getting too much for me – knowing that the ground had now been opened, at last, and that the answer was just metres away, if only I could get into the site.

I decided I was going to try. I arrived at the Dublin road housing estate and parked my car a little distance from the site. I walked through the puddle-pocked lane, holding on tight to the file under my arm. I headed towards the playground, sheepishly, subtly looking around to see if I had been spotted by anyone. I was nearly there. All I needed to do was get through the door in the hoarding and I would know, finally, what lay beneath the surface of the soil.

I was trying to peek through the hoarding door, when a garda appeared beside me. 'Can I help you?'

'Oh.' I could feel my face go red. 'I just need to bring this file in to the archaeologists,' I said. 'It's full of maps that might help them with their work.'

He told me to wait there, outside the site, and that he would call on one of the team to come and collect it. He disappeared behind the high wooden wall. One of the archaeologists appeared from behind the hoarding and apologised that he could not let me see the dig, but thanked me for the maps that I had given him.

I hurried away. When I was back in the safety of my car, I closed my eyes and tried to imagine how things could have been – if those children had been allowed to stay with their mothers, if they'd been cared for in the safety of their grandparents' homes. There was something so sick about the fact that it was us, the adults, who were responsible for what happened to them and now here we were, digging up their bones, which had been discarded in the most undignified of ways.

I worried that they wouldn't find what I truly believed to be there. Or that the official story would be different from the reality. Part of me just wanted to break in and pick up those little bundles wrapped up in cloth and hug them and tell them that they are loved. That there are people who care. That they are not forgotten.

At least in death, if not in life. They were born into a cruel society, but was that society any better now? Only if it did the right thing, at last, for these children. Only then would we have redeemed ourselves, to say this could never happen again.

Still, I had no choice but to drive away. And to hope that the teams enlisted to do this most important work would be able to uncover the truth. It would be many months before I'd finally learn what they'd discovered behind that tall wooden hoarding – what they'd found when they'd finally removed the earth and looked just a few metres beneath the soil.

CHAPTER FIFTY-TWO

The Truth

⁓

The third of March 2017 was a day I will never forget.

The radio was on in the kitchen. As I was opening the back door for our dog Shadow, I heard Aidan shout, 'Did you hear that?'

'Hear what?' I called back.

'They said that Katherine Zappone would be making a big announcement later today on the Tuam mother and baby home.'

'I wonder what that's about,' I said.

A few minutes later, the phone rang. It was the local radio station. They were looking for a comment – wondering what the announcement was going to be from Katherine Zappone.

'I haven't a clue,' I said, 'but I hope it's something good.'

'Call the commission and ask them,' said Aidan, ever the pragmatist. 'The least they could do is tell you what's going to be announced.'

I wasn't so sure. I didn't want to overstep the mark. But then I decided there was no harm in trying. So I rang the team involved with the commission of inquiry to ask if there was going to be an announcement.

'They are going to announce that the carbon dating has proven that the bones are definitely those of the babies associated with the home, and not famine bones,' said the woman on the other end of the line.

'Sorry, could you repeat that,' I said. I called Aidan over and put the phone on loudspeaker.

Aidan put his arms around me.

The woman repeated, 'The carbon dating has shown that the bones are definitively those of the children in the home.'

'Thank you,' I said. I could feel the tears welling up in my eyes.

Aidan hugged me tight. I hung up and we held each other. It wasn't good news, but it was news that good had finally triumphed over evil.

The truth. Finally, the truth. After so many years of fighting, the truth was finally emerging.

In that moment, I thought the battle had been won, at last. But it would seem the truth can often mean different things to different people, as I was about to discover.

CHAPTER FIFTY-THREE

Like a Lion

I was listening to the radio a few days later when *Liveline* came on. Joe Duffy introduced his guest, a Fr Paul Churchill, who had come on air to speak about the Tuam mother and baby home. I turned up the volume and sat down by the range, expecting to hear another difficult survivor's story. I was intrigued that this particular survivor was a priest.

But that wasn't the story at all. Fr Churchill wasn't a survivor. He wanted to tell Joe Duffy how wonderful the Bon Secours sisters were and about the great love and care that they had shown to his father, Patrick, who was in their care from 1926 until he left the home in 1937. He said he had heard of the happy memories that his father had of the Tuam home.

'*What*? Okay, that's it!' I said. And before I knew it, I was dialling the number for RTÉ.

'Can you put me through to *Liveline*, please?' I asked. I couldn't believe what I was doing. But I was so incensed, I couldn't let this go unopposed.

For the next half hour or so Fr Churchill and I 'exchanged

views' on the matter, with presenter Joe Duffy officiating. I recounted the painful stories of the survivors I had met, while Fr Churchill repeatedly stated 'the impression' he got from his father about his time in the home. I tried to remind him that my research showed a lot of evidence to the contrary.

The show wrapped up. I thought about it for a long time afterwards. But it wasn't until some time later, when I came across a ledger from the 1930s, that it all started to make sense. Someone had saved the ledger from a skip during a house renovation, and gave it to me in the hope it would help with my research.

In it was a small file with references to the Tuam home. Going through the file, to my astonishment, was the name 'Paddy Churchill, Tuam Home'. It immediately jumped out at me. There were several pages relating to him where it appeared that he was being singled out by the local clergy for a brighter future. They intended to send him at the age of eleven to a good educational facility in a Dublin orphanage. There was a stipulation that only orphans could be admitted, and as Paddy Churchill did not fit this criteria, Fr Fergus, secretary to the archbishop of Tuam, visited the Dublin orphanage in person to ensure that Paddy Churchill would be admitted.

I placed the ledger with the file on my kitchen table, asking myself why this one child, out of all the others in the Tuam home, was singled out for such special treatment. His experience was far removed from that of the other survivors in the files on my kitchen table, which were overflowing with evidence of the cruelty and neglect of children in the home. Fr Paul had also mentioned on live radio that two of his father's friends from the home who were still living had also been horrified when the story of the Tuam home babies went public, and that they denied my findings of neglect and cruelty.

I believe I have figured out who those people might be, though

I cannot know for sure. Because they came from more privileged backgrounds, I believe they may have enjoyed special privileges, such as going to secondary school in Tuam to further their education and being allowed to visit their school friends' houses in the town, and even sharing a bedroom with the nuns' special aid, Bina Rabbitte.

So, evidently, there were exceptions to the norm – children who had a better experience of the home – but that seemed to depend on who you were and where you came from: if you were one of the privileged few. It somehow made it worse, to know that they were capable of caring but chose not to treat the majority of the children with dignity.

In his book *@Tuambabies: A Critical Look at the Tuam Children's Home Scandal*, the author Brian Nugent challenged my theories, claiming that the babies were reinterred in a type of crypt. Included in the book was a piece by Fr Churchill:

My father was one of the children reared in the Bon Secours home in Tuam in the 1920s and 1930s, the one in the news recently. Through him I came to know several of the other children who were taken care of by the nuns in that institution and I still have contact with several of them to this day.

Across my whole life the constant impression I had from my father and these children was that the children were treated well and cared for with much love. Some of them although old still affirm that they were cared for well. Our family has photographs from that time showing them well fed. I know of one case, she is still alive, of a baby on the point of death when she was given to the nuns, and they pulled her back from death. My father never had a bad word about them, indeed he gave me every impression of having felt loved by them and cried over the death of one who had been like a mother to him.

I do recall talk when I was much younger of the angels' plot. I never heard anything negative about it nor anything irregular about burials and had the impression that there was a sense of warmth and love towards the little ones buried there and that they were buried with dignity.

The recent media hype has had one tragic consequence. Many of the surviving children from the home have been very hurt by the suggestions that the sisters were harsh or uncaring or unloving. When they were abandoned by the society of the time they were welcomed and cared for and loved by the sisters. To hear that the only group who cared for and loved them are now being portrayed as evil women has been a horrible experience for them. They don't believe that the same women who were so good to them could have mistreated babies as it is suggested. What a tragedy that those who were rejected in their origins by society should find their truth rejected by modern society. They don't deserve that. When something so contrary to truth is portrayed in the media I can think of only one source of this lie. I'll call it as Pope Francis would: The devil.

When I heard that Brian Nugent was coming to Tuam to give a talk to promote his book, I decided that rather than sit at home wondering what was being said, I would go and hear for myself. When he stood up to speak and looked into the crowd, we caught eyes for a moment. I think the sight of me unnerved him. He probably wasn't expecting to see me there.

I stayed quiet until the end of the talk, when I raised my hand to speak. During his speech he had stated that the chambers attached to the sewage tank were built as catacombs (respectful burial vaults). I asked him if he knew what the definition of a catacomb was, reminding him that the chambers in the sewage tank only had an opening at the top, not big enough for an adult to enter, and that the babies had to be lowered down and piled one on top of the other without a coffin. Catacombs would have a stairwell entrance with chambers that one could walk through. I felt I had made my point, and I was glad of that.

As I drove home that night, I was reminded of one of my favourite quotes. Ironically, it was by St Augustine, and was one that I was starting to live by: 'The truth is like a lion, you do not have to defend it. Let it loose, it can defend itself.' And that's precisely what I intended to do. Let it loose.

CHAPTER FIFTY-FOUR

Chamber of Horrors

❧

We heard that the taoiseach was going to make a statement on Tuam, so we tuned in to the news that evening. I watched as he made his impassioned speech to the Dáil. Finally, I thought, a head of government seemed to care about what had happened. It was 8 March, just five days since the news of the carbon dating had been announced.

Enda Kenny took to his feet. He looked genuinely emotional.

Tuam is not just a burial ground, it is a social and
cultural sepulchre. That is what it is. As a society in the
so-called 'good old days', we did not just hide away the
dead bodies of tiny human beings, we dug deep and
deeper still to bury our compassion, our mercy and our
humanity itself. No nuns broke into our homes to kidnap
our children. We gave them up to what we convinced
ourselves was the nuns' care. We gave them up maybe to
spare them the savagery of gossip, the wink-and-elbow
language of delight in which the 'holier than thous' were

particularly fluent. We gave them up because of our perverse, in fact morbid, relationship with what is called respectability. Indeed, for a while it seemed as if in Ireland our women had the amazing capacity to self-impregnate. For their trouble, we took their babies and gifted them, sold them, trafficked them, starved them, neglected them or denied them to the point of their disappearance from our hearts, our sight, our country and, in the case of Tuam and possibly other places, from life itself.

We are all shocked now. If the fruit of her religious and social transgression could be discarded, what treatment was meted out to the transgressor herself? We had better deal with this now because if we do not, some other taoiseach will be standing here in 20 years saying, 'If only we knew then, if only we had done then.' What will be his or her then is our now. Now, we do know. Now, we have to do. All of us in this House must do so together.

This commission of investigation has completed some of its work and has carried out the physical excavations on this chamber of horrors in Tuam. What is now needed is some reflection on the processes required. There is an independence for the coroner. There is an independence for the Garda. There is a duty in terms of the local authority. Obviously, those whose siblings and families were affected are distraught. There is a role for the coroner in north Galway to consider what steps may be necessary and appropriate in accordance with his statutory functions. The commission has not made formal findings yet. What it has done is complete the physical excavation, so we now know that there are substantial remains of very young children in this spot.

This wasn't the first time the issue had been raised with concern in the Dáil. I could see from my research that as far back as 1934 the government had been aware of what was happening in Tuam. The mortality rate at the home was significantly higher than it was for children generally at the time in Ireland. A Dáil debate in February of that year noted that one in three children born outside of marriage died within one year of their birth – a rate that was about five times higher than the mortality rate for other children.

'From the abnormally high death rate amongst this class of children,' Fianna Fáil TD Dr Conn Ward told the Dáil at the time, 'one must come to the conclusion that they are not looked after with the same care and attention as that given to ordinary children.'

And yet nothing was done about it. The Tuam home continued to exist for nearly three more decades, despite the high death rate. Where is the accountability for that, I wondered. It was important too to remember that all this had happened very recently. It wasn't something long consigned to history. Many of the children who lived through this terrible situation were still alive.

As I listened to the taoiseach's words – 'No nuns broke into our homes to kidnap our children. We gave them up to what we convinced ourselves was the nuns' care' – I thought of Peter's story, of the priest arriving to his grandparents' house in the middle of the night. I thought of the terrible pressure people were under to obey the church.

The taoiseach seemed to be saying that we were all responsible. That society was responsible. But what is a society if not the set of values and principles by which it is governed and policed. And who was policing it? The state and the Catholic Church.

CHAPTER FIFTY-FIVE

Where That Angel
Sleeps Tonight

T here were a lot of calls from journalists after the taoiseach's address in the Dáil. The story was dominating the news agenda.

Then a call came from *The Late Late Show* – would I be willing to come on live television on Friday night to talk about the Tuam babies? Live television sounded very daunting, and I didn't know if I'd be able for it, or if my nerves would get too much for me. I told the researcher that I wasn't sure about it. They were very kind and understanding. I said I'd call them back.

I spoke to Aidan. He tried to convince me that it was the best platform to share the story. I knew he was right, but it was difficult to explain to anyone how anxiety affects your mind and body. It wasn't about being a little bit nervous, as I'm sure a lot of people are on television. You can get past that, I've no doubt. Anxiety is different. I was scared my body would clam up, that I would open my mouth and nothing would come out or that I might collapse again as I had done before, with everyone watching.

These were the thoughts going through my head. I went for a walk around the farm, heading out into the fields so that Shadow could run around. I thought my head would be clearer when I returned, but I felt just as conflicted as when I'd set out.

I rang the researcher and explained how I was feeling – that I was very sorry but I didn't think I would be able to do it, that I wouldn't have it in me to go on live television. I thanked them profusely for their interest in the Tuam babies, and wondered if there might be another way to cover the topic on the show.

She said she would talk to the producers and come back to me.

A few hours later the phone rang again. I thought it might be the researcher.

'Hello.'

'Hi, Catherine, this is Ryan Tubridy.'

'Oh my goodness,' I said. 'I wasn't expecting that!'

Ryan was very kind – he was calling to reassure me. He wanted me to feel safe coming on the programme and said that his team would help me in any way they could and that I shouldn't feel any pressure . . . that it would just be a chat about my research.

I felt a bit embarrassed. It was so nice of him to call. I didn't want to appear silly. I told him about my anxiety and I felt he really understood. It wasn't about just being nervous, I explained.

'Okay, I'll give it a go,' I said, cautiously. 'But do you think I could bring a survivor of the home with me?' I asked. 'I feel it is their story to tell.'

That would be great, he said. He thanked me and reassured me again that they would all help me through it and that it would be a warm and welcoming environment.

I rang Peter Mulryan and asked if he would come with us to Dublin to appear on *The Late Late* – if he would be willing to tell his story. He was a bit taken aback; I could tell he was still trying to process everything he had heard about his sister. But he agreed that he would come on the programme. It was an important story to tell, he said, and he wanted to share it.

Friday came around quickly. RTÉ had booked us a hotel for the night, so we packed our things and headed off. We wanted to get there early so we left in plenty of time. Aidan was dressed in his best suit. The drive to Dublin was very quiet. I wasn't in the mood for chit-chat. I was nervous. Every so often Aidan leaned over and gave me a reassuring pat and told me it was going to be just fine. By the time we reached Dublin, I felt a little more relaxed. Once I'm in the flow of things, I tend to get less anxious. It's the anticipation that gets to me most.

We arrived at the RTÉ studios. A friendly team greeted us and made us feel very welcome. Before we knew it we were in the green room backstage along with the other guests of the show that night. We were an eclectic lot: the magician Keith Barry; a panel of women farmers to talk about farming in Ireland – I could relate to them; a lovely young man named Adam Harris with a panel of contributors to promote their new documentary about living with autism; Ted Walsh the horse trainer; and some musicians and singers too.

Peter was sitting in the audience. He would do his interview from there, the team told us.

We heard the iconic theme tune playing and the backstage team told us that it was time to go live. There was great excitement in the air. All the other guests around me seemed very relaxed. They had all done this before, I presumed. They must be used to live television. We were watching on a screen in the green room. It was hard to believe that the stage was just metres from where we were, as it felt like we were at home watching the television.

When I was talking to Ryan on the phone, I had asked if it

would be possible to go on early in the show, so that I could get my bit over with; otherwise I felt I would become too anxious backstage. He agreed this would be no problem. I also asked if it would be okay not to do the iconic walk onto the stage with the music playing. If it was possible to begin the interview with me sitting on stage with Ryan, without the walk-on, it would help me a great deal. He was very understanding and reassured me that that would be fine.

Then, suddenly, it was time to go on. Someone came over to check my mic and get me ready. I looked at Aidan. He gave me a wink and a smile. 'You'll be fine,' he said, 'it's for the babies.' That helped me to relax. I focused on the purpose of the interview, and I felt grounded then. I could feel the babies helping me through it. I had them on my side.

I stepped out on to the stage and made my way to the couch. The lights were so strong, and beyond them I could just about make out the rows and rows of people sitting in the audience. I was glad I couldn't see their faces properly. I sat down and waited silently for the ads to finish.

Ryan began by introducing the piece and introducing me. Suddenly there was no going back. We were live. I tried to stay focused, looking only at Ryan, pretending there wasn't a live studio audience or an audience watching at home.

He asked me about the babies.

I told him that I had found 798 death records of children who had died in the home.

'What age-group?' he asked.

'They were from a few hours old, a few days old, right up to three years old. The oldest was eight years old.'

'Typically, what do they tell us about how those children died?'

'There were various causes – there was a lot of measles, whooping cough. There was diphtheria, there was gastroenteritis and a lot of different bits and pieces. There was one with an abscess on the hip and another one with laryngitis – I don't know, I don't understand. It's just a bit peculiar.'

Ryan clarified for the audience: 'Just shy of 800 children registered as dying.'

'Yes,' I confirmed.

'But none as being buried.'

'No, no burial records whatsoever.'

Then, near the end of the piece, Ryan walked into the studio audience, introducing Peter Mulryan.

Peter bravely told his story of the four and half years he spent in the Tuam mother and baby home. And then, what it was like to find out that he may have a sister.

'Out of the blue, Catherine rang me one day and she says, I'm looking through the registers that we got from Galway County Council, she says, and something here rings a bell to me, she says, the area where your mother's from and also the name, of course, seems to coincide . . . And I never heard anything of [my mother] having a baby. She was always afraid to talk. She was institutionalised by the time I met her.'

'What happened to your sister, if you don't mind me asking?' said Ryan.

'I don't know what happened to her. I have a birth cert and a death cert and a register of her being baptised, but they can't tell me where she is.'

'Nothing?'

'Nothing. And it's odd, it says on the register that she died of convulsions at 19 months old.'

'So you know she died, but you have no record of where her remains are?'

'But there's no medical record from anyone, from a nurse or a doctor, saying who attended to her. It's only a woman who's also a single parent in there working, who signed all those documents — she's all over the place.'

'What do you want to happen — you were there, you were in the home . . .'

'I was there until four and a half years of age. What I want to know is, where is she? Is she there? Where is she tonight? She could be like a number of other people — documents falsified. She could have been sent to America and sold off. I don't know, but I need to know, and I will not rest until I find out.'

Then Ryan came back to me to finish the interview. He asked me to sum up what I thought was going on. Why were there no burial records for these children.

'Well, that's the question I asked myself. I knew then I wanted to make this public,' I said. I told him about all the theories that had been put forward: 'I had been told that perhaps the grandparents brought them home to their own plots when they died but I knew that wasn't very likely because, I mean, these poor women had to leave their own homes and go into this home. Now, there were a lot of arguments this week about whether the parents put them in, but my argument is, we have to go back to Catholicism . . . women were condemned if they got pregnant outside marriage.'

At that moment, the audience began to clap. I looked up and through the bright studio lights I saw someone stand up. And then another person beside them stood up, then another and another, and in a matter of seconds, the whole audience had risen to their feet in a standing ovation.

'Now that's something,' said Ryan, looking out at the audience. 'Now that's something I haven't seen for a long time. I don't think I've ever seen something like that happen in a spontaneous way on this programme . . . and all it says to me is there's a hunger in this country. If that audience represents the people watching tonight, there is a hunger in this country for the truth.'

'There is, Ryan, and thankfully it's coming out now, and thank you for highlighting it.'

I was shaking as I stepped off the stage, back into the darkness of the long corridor to the *Late Late* green room. Aidan was there waiting for me. He gave me a hug. 'Well done!' he said. 'You did it!'

We watched the rest of the show from the green room. Afterwards, we went back to our hotel as we were exhausted from the adrenaline of it all. The next morning, we arranged to meet Peter and Kathleen early in the breakfast room, where we chatted excitedly about the night before, all in disbelief at what had happened, at the way the audience had reacted.

It proved, at long last, that people may just be on our side with this. People wanted the right thing to happen as much as we did, and this would deliver a strong message to the government. Finally, I felt, we were a little less alone with it all. People cared about the babies. And that's what mattered most.

CHAPTER FIFTY-SIX

Missing Pieces

~——

It must have been Peter's story that inspired people to get in touch. After *The Late Late*, my inbox was flooded with emails. There were hundreds – from people all over the country, and all over the world.

One was from a woman who said she had six brothers and sisters, and when the news broke about the Tuam home, her father turned to her and said, 'I was in that home.' They had lived their whole lives without knowing this part of their father's past. The woman asked if I would be able to help her father, Martin, to find his birth mother. She told me it would mean the world to him to find her.

I set to work. She had given me some details – his birth name and date, his mother's name. Once I traced Martin's birth cert, I was able to follow up on the townland in Mayo where his mother was born. Many townlands in Ireland have family namesakes, not only in surname but first name as well, so you may find for example two or three Molly O'Sheas, Pat Dunleavys or Mick Donnellans and they might all be around the same age, which makes searching quite difficult. Using websites, such as Irishgenealogy.ie and the 1901 and 1911 censuses, proved very helpful. One can work back from the mother's name on the birth cert to find her identity. I also used fee-paying sites such as Ancestry.com, Findmypast.ie and Irishnewsarchive.com.

Then I looked through the newspaper archives. These were always very useful. Some papers go back to the mid-1800s, and continue right up to the present. It's amazing what the Irish newspapers covered, especially in the 1940s, '50s and '60s – everything from petty court cases, brawls in pubs, people charged with not having a bicycle light . . . This might seem irrelevant, but for a person named within the report it will include his or her townland, sometimes their parents' names, and with that information you have confirmation that this person was in that area at a certain time.

I found it could also be very useful to find details of an accidental death because it would give details of the person's family, or a death notice that would sometimes give the names of the whole family in offering them condolences and may include the marriage name of sisters of the deceased, along with their county or country of residence, for example '. . . his sisters Mary (McCarthy, Wales), Susan (O'Connor, NY) Jane (Kavanagh, Dublin)', etc. Those details are invaluable for tracing forward, and ensuring you have the correct family.

Ancestry.com also has shipping details for those who emigrated to America, particularly detailed for the period circa 1900 up to 1930, where you may find the home address of the person, who their next of kin is, who they are going to stay with in America, their age, details of their hair colour, eye colour and height. This site will also give indexes of births and marriages up to 1958, which is useful as the Irish genealogy site will only give births up to 1919 and marriages up to 1945.

I used a combination of all these methods in the search for Martin's mother, and I narrowed it down to a woman who lived in County Mayo. I gave Martin's daughter the information I had gathered, and suggested that Martin go for a pint in the local pub in the village in Mayo I had pinpointed and ask some of the locals if they knew of his mother. Even with all the research methods, it was often the easiest way to find out local information.

She thanked me and told me she would pass the message on to her father.

A few days later, there was a knock at the door. I opened it to find a stranger standing there, a man who introduced himself as Martin. He held out a bunch of flowers. 'These are for you,' he said, 'to thank you for finding my mother.'

I was taken aback. I invited him in for a cup of tea. That's when he told me the story of what happened when he went to find his mother. In the pub he'd got talking to a few local people and, sure enough, they were able to tell him the house he should go to.

He went to the house on the outskirts of the village and knocked on the door and waited. No answer. He tried again. Nothing. He waited a while, in case someone had gone out. He tried one last time, knocking a little louder this time. Still nothing. He turned to leave. Just as he was about to walk away, the door of the house next door opened and an old man appeared. 'Well, where were you?' he said.

Martin was taken aback. 'Do you know who I am?' he asked.

'I do. You're Mary's son. You're the image of her. We looked for you when your mother died, and we couldn't find you. We searched and searched.'

Martin's eyes welled up with tears. 'When did she . . .?' he said.

'A few years ago,' said the neighbour. 'Would you like to see her house?'

The old man brought Martin in to see his mother's house. He had been entrusted with a key. The house had been empty since she died. As Martin walked through the kitchen he looked around at the remaining pots and pans, and speckled delph – remnants of the life she lived. They went into her bedroom and Martin opened the wardrobe. It was empty, except for one thing. At the bottom of the wardrobe he found a hat, with a feather in it.

'That was your mother's hat,' the old man said.

Martin picked it up. He tried to smell it, to see if there was any trace of her – a perfume, perhaps. He held it close. At last, he had a piece of his mother, something to remember her by, something to prove that she existed, that he was loved, that he was mothered, once upon a time.

The neighbour pointed him towards his mother's grave. Martin went to pay his respects. I try to imagine him there, standing in front of her headstone. Not the reunion he had hoped for. A one-way conversation, a silence that will never now be broken. A secret that has gone to the grave. Why had they been separated, this mother and her son?

As we sat and talked, Martin produced the hat, with the feather in it, and placed it on the table. He smiled, and then the tears fell from his eyes. 'My mother's hat,' he told me proudly. 'How can I thank you?'

I could see how much it meant to him, to know some part of her. Perhaps now he could imagine her, he could paint a picture in his mind, to fill the gaps that he had lived with all his life.

He would never sit with her, or ask her questions or talk with her. He would never truly know what happened, or how he ended up in a home in Tuam, but at least now he had seen some glimpse of where he was from, the life he could have lived, if things were different, if Ireland was different.

I'll never forget that feathered hat placed so delicately on my kitchen table, and everything it meant to Martin. A symbol of a life lived with dignity, the ghost of a mother who never had a chance to know her child.

CHAPTER FIFTY-SEVEN

The Power of Information

⌒

I magine getting a call out of nowhere from a stranger to say that your beloved wife, now passed away, had a child she never told you about. It was a scenario I could never have imagined, until the day a man named Philip wrote to me to see if I could help him. He gave me his mother's name and birth date and some information he had been given by social services. They had told him that his mother had moved to a small town in England, and had given him some scant details. Philip was able to piece it all together, and found a woman with the same name as his mother in the place they identified. I listened and took down all the information.

I set about researching but soon realised that something didn't add up. I contacted Philip again and mentioned my suspicion. 'That can't have been your mother,' I suggested. The woman in question would have been 11 years old when she had Philip. The dates didn't work. That was too young. Maybe if she had been 13, it might have been plausible, but not 11.

Philip wrote to social services to question the information he had been given, but they insisted it was correct. They then wrote to the husband of the woman in England, now widowed, who was named Robert, looking for confirmation. That man died some time later. The news had been very difficult for him, to hear out of the blue that his wife had a son in Ireland she had never told him about. So many unanswered questions about a woman he thought he knew.

Robert and his late wife had two sons. They contacted Philip and asked if he would be willing to do a specialised DNA test, which would determine whether they were in fact half-brothers. Philip agreed, and when they received the results some weeks later it proved that they were not related in any way. Robert had died before he had a chance to know the truth.

Meanwhile, I had tracked down a woman in Sligo with the same name, who I thought was more likely to be Philip's biological mother. I was determined to get to the bottom of this, for everyone's sake.

I suggested to Philip that perhaps he would do another type of DNA test, with one of the UK companies that, for a fee, would send out a DNA kit, where he could provide a saliva sample and it would show up through a database if anyone else in the world had matching DNA. He took my advice and some weeks later he gave me his password to go through the many second, third and fourth cousins who showed up on the database.

And, bingo! Some of the second cousins that the site identified were connected to the woman I had pinpointed in Sligo as Philip's mother. She had passed away, but she had a son who was still living in Sligo. Philip decided to go and visit the area to try to find out a bit more. Eventually, he met with the woman's son, who agreed to do a specialised DNA test to see if they were half-brothers, and it turned out, to Philip's delight, that yes, they shared the same mother. She had died just a few years previously, his brother told him.

It made me furious to think that if the social workers had taken the time to check his file properly some years before, Philip might have had the chance to meet his mother, and it was also heartbreaking to think that Robert had died before finding out the truth.

I gave all the details to Tusla, the state's child and family agency, in case they wanted to rectify their records. I wrote to them twice but all they said was that they couldn't communicate with me about someone else's personal data.

All these individual cases were proof as to why information is so important, why facts are so important, because the wrong information can ruin lives and the right information can bring families and loved ones together.

It was true of the next person who reached out to me too – a man from Dublin. He was adopted, he explained, and it was his adoptive parents' names that were on his baptismal record, rather than his biological parents, and that was making it very difficult to trace his biological mother. He had tiny bits of information that he managed to piece together over the years. He thought that his biological mother's family might be involved in a farm business as he had been given a glimpse of a name on a record once.

I tried to do some research for him. It really struck me what people who are adopted have to go through to try to find out information about themselves.

He was unlucky in that his adoptive mother wouldn't tell him much at all. All she said was that she paid a lot for him. They were having an argument one day and she had thrown that comment at him. I'm sure it must have hurt him to hear that – as though you were a commodity, something to be bartered, and bought.

He told me he had an adopted sister whom he didn't get on

with. She and her husband had subsequently moved back to the family home to live with his adoptive mother. His brother-in-law was kind to him and was trying to inconspicuously help him to get information.

He knew that his adoptive mother had kept a diary all her life, so his brother-in-law was going to try and sneak a look at the diary when his wife and mother-in-law were out of the house – to see if it said anything about his birth mother.

To think that he was depending on someone snooping through a diary to try and find out who his birth mother was. It was a sad, sad reality for so many people.

It struck me how terrible it is that in Ireland the balance of power still rests entirely with the mother. She gets to choose whether the child she gave up for adoption may have access to information about her or not.

I was learning that there seemed to be a big difference between being fostered and being adopted, with regard to getting access to records. A fostered child often knows their birth date, and therefore, as all Irish birth, marriage and death records are public, there is no reason why they cannot order their own birth certificate. The birth cert will show where they were born, and will include their mother's name, and, most importantly, her home address. This is a great lead to have, for with a bit of research they could then trace her back to her townland, to find out who her parents were and her siblings. Even if the mother had long emigrated to the UK, a good way to find her marriage name there (if she married in the UK) is to check back with her local parish priest (or his secretary), who could check the baptism book, where in a separate column on her baptism record will be written her prospective husband's name. This is because most Irish women who married in the UK would have written back to their parish priest, as is requested, for a 'letter of freedom' to state that she was not married in Ireland. Armed with this information, one can work forward to locate the birth mother.

As regards the adopted child, they will have been registered by the mother in her surname and whatever Christian name she gave to the child. Then, on adoption, the adoptive parents will have re-registered the child in their own names, though the date of birth always remained the same. This is what makes it so difficult for adopted people to discover their true identity.

Currently, the law states that if adopted people approach Tusla for their birth information, Tusla is not allowed to reveal it. What Tusla will do is inform the mother (if they know who she is) that their child is looking for information about them and ask the mother if she wants to be contacted. The right to refuse is entirely in her hands. The adopted person has no such rights.

To this day, adopted people in Ireland are lobbying the government to change this ruling, and to give equal rights to the mother and the adopted child. The government claims that either a referendum would be required, or it would have to pass some law to allow this to happen. So far there has been no progress on this issue.

However, I had discovered that there was a way around this for adopted people, and it was coming into play more and more because the technology existed to make it possible. By doing a simple DNA test with Ancestry.com or any of the other DNA test companies (there is a fee of up to 90 euro for the service), results will come back usually with a few dozen first to fourth cousins to sift through, and sometimes people are lucky and actually find the information they are looking for.

Another way is to check the 'adoption books' in the GRO (General Register Office, either in Dublin or in the head office in Roscommon). You can go through those books by your date of birth, and if you know where you were born, there will be a

305

list of names relevant to that date and place. You may have to buy several birth certs (at a cost of five euro a cert) and then go through a laborious process of studying those certs until you find out if any of the information fits. Barnardos will also help to find out what adoption agency handled a particular adoption.

I was learning a lot about the process, and the best ways of dealing with it, but I felt so sorry that it was all so difficult for some people. The system was working against them, not for them. I really hoped that the government would pass the law that was so badly needed to give adopted people rights to their own information.

It's awful the lengths people have to go to, the hoops they have to jump through, to try and find out who they are. Often it comes down to chance whether they manage to trace their birth mother or not. And it doesn't always work out the way they think it will. As I was about to find out.

CHAPTER FIFTY-EIGHT

A Stranger Parked Outside

❧

'Hello, is this Catherine Corless?'
I was getting used to hearing these words when I picked up the phone. This time, it was a woman's voice. She sounded like she was from Cork.

'I'm so sorry to call like this, out of the blue . . . but I got your number from a friend, and I was wondering if you might be able to help me. You see . . . I'm trying to find my mother.'

I listened to her story. Her name was Nora. She was adopted and had never met her biological parents.

'All my life I've wondered who my mother is,' she said. 'Sometimes when an elderly woman walks past me in the street, I wonder – just for a moment – what if, what *if*, that was her.'

In a way it's comforting, she told me, because when everyone could possibly be your mother, you hold out hope. You look to connect with strangers, because who knows – they might just be the person you've been looking for all your life. But it could be lonely too, the not knowing.

I listened intently, then asked her for the details I needed to get started. 'I'll call you and let you know if I find anything,' I promised.

And with that I started my search. I began by looking through the online records and slowly I pieced it together and whittled it down to one possible woman. 'I think I may have found your mother . . .' I said.

There was a silence for a moment, as though Nora had stopped breathing. 'Are you sure it's her?' she said, softly.

'I suppose I can't know for sure without speaking to her,' I said, 'but it looks likely.' I was worried about getting her hopes up. 'And you're not going to believe this . . .'

'What?'

'She lives very close to you in Cork.'

'Here . . . in Cork?' she said, in disbelief.

I gave her the details and wished her luck. The next part was up to her. She said she would sleep on it and thanked me for all I had done.

When I put down the phone, I felt uneasy. I could only imagine how much it meant to her to find her mother. I had checked and re-checked the information. I felt I was probably right about this one, but I was always afraid of getting it wrong. There was a lot of emotion attached to finding one's biological parents. Everything we feel about our parents carries with it so much meaning. It's complicated, inevitably, because life is complicated and our parents and our relationship with them brings us back to the very core of our being. They are our source of life. Our reason for it.

Nora rang me several weeks later to give me an update. I knew immediately from the sound of her voice that it hadn't gone well.

She had decided to go to Tusla with the information I had given her and had asked them to contact her mother, she told me, to arrange a meeting. She felt the more official channel was best. To give the meeting the best chance of success, she explained.

Then she waited anxiously for news of the meeting. When no news came, she called Tusla, to check in on her request. The official took her details. 'Okay, just connecting you now . . .'

Little did they know the meaning of those words. Connection was exactly what Nora was looking for.

As the dial tone sounded, Nora waited to be connected. It rang and rang. Eventually, a woman answered and took Nora's details. 'Okay, just a moment,' she said.

Nora waited.

'Hello?' the woman said, coming back to the phone.

'Hello . . .' said Nora.

'Yes, we have your file here,' the woman said. 'I'm afraid we have bad news. Your mother does not wish to meet you.'

Nora was silent. The news came as a shock. As the weeks passed, she had imagined over and over again what it would be like to meet her mother: where they might meet; would she take her to her favourite places and find out her mother loved them too; how it might go; would they look alike or have similar mannerisms; would they talk into the night and realise they had been missing one another all this time? She imagined the conversations they might have – played them out in her mind. In a way she felt she'd almost got to know her mother – at least, this imagined version of her mother.

Then, suddenly, it was like she had lost her all over again, only this time it was worse. Her mother had said no. She did not want any of these experiences with her daughter – now or ever.

'Pardon?' she said, though she had heard it the first time.

'She has decided she does not want to meet,' said the official. 'I'm sorry. It often happens.'

'Are you sure?' Nora said.

'Yes. I'm sorry.' The woman sounded rushed.

Nora could hear the noise of a busy office in the background. 'I . . . I won't keep you,' she said. 'Thank you for your help.'

And with that Nora put down the phone.

Her mind was full of new questions, which only her mother held the answers to. Why didn't she want to meet her? Did she think Nora would be angry with her for abandoning her or would hold it against her? Was the guilt too much for her? What was she so afraid of? What memories would Nora bring back for her that she didn't want to face?

Maybe all the years Nora had spent trying to imagine her mother, perhaps her mother had spent the years trying to forget her baby. Each suffering in their own way. One trying to imagine a future, the other trying to forget the past.

After a few sleepless nights, Nora made a bold decision. She would go and meet her mother. Confront her. Force her to see what she was missing. Nora felt sure if she could just speak to her mother she would change her mind. And if her mother never wanted to see her again, at least she would know what she was saying no to, *who* she was saying no to. Nora wasn't a concept. She wasn't a baby who had been frozen in time in the Tuam mother and baby home. She was a person. She was that baby whose cries went unanswered. She was that little girl who always felt like she didn't belong. She was that woman searching for answers. She was all those people. All without a mother to call her own.

I imagined her knocking on her mother's door. Knock. Knock. Knock. Like the kick, kick, kick of the baby in the womb.

Nora managed to find her mother's address. A few days later she got into her car and drove along a quiet country road until she saw a house surrounded by a beautiful garden with colourful flowers – carefully manicured beds of hydrangeas, with sweet pea poking over the stone wall. She checked the address. This was the house. She slowed as she approached and took a deep breath. Just as she was about to turn into the driveway she saw the door of the house open. And out stepped a woman – an elderly woman. Her mother. Nora froze as she watched the old woman closing the door behind her and placing her key in her handbag before turning around.

Nora stared, trying to take in every bit of her. Her hair was grey and her face was old and weathered. She looked like she had kind eyes.

The woman looked over towards the car, and with that Nora lost her nerve, put the foot to the accelerator and drove away. She drove and drove until she was out of sight. When she felt she was far enough away she pulled the car over and collapsed onto the steering wheel. She closed her eyes and tried to process what she had just seen. It was all too much. It was all too real.

The old woman must have wondered who had stopped outside her house, as not many cars passed her cottage. Someone lost and looking for directions, perhaps. Little did she know that it was the baby she had lost some 50 years earlier.

Nora couldn't bring herself to do it in the end, she told me. She thought she'd have the courage to approach her. She had hoped that when her mother met her, she would soften. She would feel moved. She would want to welcome her daughter back into her life. But when Nora finally saw the woman she believed to be her mother, a strong urge came over her to leave. She wondered again why her mother had said no to meeting her and if she would be angry with her for coming anyway. She obviously wanted nothing to do with her daughter. Maybe that decision had come easily to her. She might have hated the idea of being 'found'.

Nora thought of the image of a baby being left on a doorstep in a Moses basket. It's an image we've all seen in folklore. Perhaps there is a reason you never see the grown-up baby – now an adult – arrive back on the doorstep. Perhaps that Moses basket is where the story ends. The giving away. All these thoughts rushed through Nora's mind as she stared out the windscreen of her car. Then something broke her train of thought – a noise, getting ever louder. She looked up. It was a car, coming up behind her. It trundled towards her and slowed down as it passed her on the road. It was the car from the house. The woman looked back through the rear-view mirror. For a split second Nora made eye contact with her. The woman smiled. Nora quickly looked away. When she looked back the car was gone. Around the next bend.

Nora and I kept in touch over the months that followed.

She confided in me that she often drove to that house and sat outside in the car, hoping to catch sight of her mother again, but not knowing what she would do if she did.

'I get the paper every day,' she said, 'for the death notices. If I can't meet her in life, then maybe I can at least be at her funeral.'

She paused. I didn't know what to say.

'Maybe then I will find out if I have brothers and sisters.'

'Because they would be at the funeral?' I asked.

'Yes,' she said solemnly.

There was something tragic about Nora's story, but equally tragic about her mother's. In another time and place they would have shared a relationship. They would have been family. But here they were, strangers passing one another by. A lost past and a lost future. I felt guilty, in a way, for finding out the information for her. Maybe if she'd never known her mother was alive, she might have lived in that realm of their imaginary relationship. Without meaning to, I felt somehow that I had killed both – the ability for her to imagine, and the hope that she would no longer have to.

Time passed. I often thought of Nora. And of her mother.

Each with their crosses to bear. Different, but equally difficult. I tried to imagine a scenario in which all the years I had known my own daughters were suddenly erased from memory. I tried to imagine meeting my daughters for the first time, as they were now, as adults, with all the gaps of those years – all those shared experiences. I cannot imagine what that would be like.

Then one day, quite unexpectedly, I received an email from Nora. 'I have something I need to tell you . . .' it read, 'something I'm not proud of.'

I would never have guessed what she was about to tell me.

'I had a son . . . when I was very young. Is there any way you can help me to find him?'

I rang Nora that afternoon.

She thought of him often, she told me, but even more so now, after the experience of looking for her own mother. She imagined him, perhaps going through what she was going through, searching for his mother. Now she was the one looking through the rear-view mirror. She worried that they too might be strangers passing one another by, and that some day he might be at her funeral. She wanted to make things right for him, for both of them, before that day came, so that they might meet in life, and maybe, just maybe, he would forgive her, the way she would forgive her mother, if only she had a chance to talk to her.

She had gone in search of her son. She had spoken to the social worker.

'I can't give you the information you're looking for,' the social worker had said. 'It's against the law.'

Before Nora could protest, the social worker lowered her voice to a whisper. 'But I will tell you that his name is David. And his adoptive mother's name is Mary. That's all I can say.'

David. Nora repeated the name all the way home. David.

'So that's all I have for you to work with,' she said to me. 'I was very young when I had him,' she added. 'His father was Moroccan. When David was a baby, he was the most beautiful baby. His colouring was beautiful. They took him off me. I couldn't do a thing.'

She gave me his date of birth.

He would be 35 now, I thought. Same as my son.

Somehow it made me want to find him all the more. I imagined what it would be like if my son was out there in the world and I didn't know him. I would do anything to find him. I thought about all the years I had had with my son. All the laughs and giggles when he was a baby, the sleepless nights, the feeling that I would do anything in the world for him. His first steps. His first day at school. She had missed all these things in her son's life. There were missing parts of her heart, scattered somewhere.

I told her I would do anything I could to help her find him. I put down the phone and got to work, though it was hard to know where to start. All I had to go on was his first name, David. She had said he was in the west of Ireland. I knew his age. I knew that he might look Moroccan.

I thought about it and decided that in this case an archival search wouldn't yield much, so I needed to move with the times. With the kids' help, I tried a Facebook search, to see if that might give me some clues. There were many Davids on Facebook. I trawled through some possibilities, but my eyes were drawn to one David in particular. I clicked on his profile. Up came some photos of a tall, dark, handsome young man. I opened his page. One of his posts was a press cutting of two middle-aged women after their charity swim; one of the names underneath the photo was 'Mary'. I asked myself why a young man would include this photo on his page, unless he had a close connection to one of the women featured. It looked as though he was proud of their achievement. I went along with that theory, so now I had a Mary and a David, and Facebook had given me a clue as to where they might live.

Luckily, I had an acquaintance who lived in the same area. She was a real community person. She knew everyone. I rang her and asked, confidentially, if she knew anyone by that description.

'Leave it with me,' she said.

She rang me two days later as I was doing the grocery shopping. 'Guess what?' she said.

I was standing by my trolley in the middle of the aisle.

'I think you have found the right David. He was adopted.'

I rang Nora as soon as I came home and gave her the good news.

Now it was up to her what she chose to do. She had a name and an address to write to if she wished to take the chance that this David might be her son.

Nora decided she would write to David's adoptive mother and ask her if she thought David would like to meet with her. She didn't want to sidestep Mary by writing directly to David. Though she felt a sense of envy towards her, she was also grateful to her – whoever she was – for raising her son.

Nora sent the letter, then waited anxiously. She tried to prepare herself in case the same thing might happen, that David might say no to meeting her. Some weeks later she received a reply from Mary. She braced herself for bad news.

But it was a lovely letter from Mary saying that David would like to meet his mother, and she gave contact details for how to get in touch by phone to make the arrangements.

A wave of emotion passed over Nora. They arranged to meet.

Nora wondered if David had felt abandoned all his life, if he might hold it against her. She wanted so badly to tell him that he was wanted. That she had wanted him every single day since he was born. Perhaps she could give David the reunion that she had always hoped for with her own mother.

And that was the last I heard from Nora, until a few weeks later when I received a letter in the post. When I opened the envelope, a photograph fell to the floor. I picked it up and turned it around. Instantly I knew who it was. A photo of Nora and David. Reunited at last. The words 'Thank you x' were written on the back of the photograph.

She had her son. He had his mother.

But that was not the end of the story.

Some months later, through a bit of research, Nora discovered that she had a brother. She plucked up the courage to call him one day. She explained who she was and that she had tried to contact her mother – their mother – in the hope of meeting her, but that her mother had decided it would be best not to meet. Her brother listened to her story. He was so delighted to hear from her, he said, though the news had come as quite a shock. He sounded like a nice man. He said he would talk to his mother, and find out how she felt about it all, and he promised he would be back in touch with Nora. He was sorry she had gone through all this, he said. He would do his best to help; after all, he was her brother.

A few days later, he called back with some very unexpected news. He said that his mother had known nothing about Nora trying to contact her. She had not been contacted by social services, she said, and had not declined the meeting. She would, in fact, love to meet Nora, as would his brothers and sisters.

Nora couldn't believe what she was hearing. All this time she had assumed her mother wanted nothing to do with her. They made the arrangements to meet at her mother's house.

'Will I give you the address?' her brother asked.

'I know it well,' Nora said.

And so the day came when Nora drove down that quiet country lane once more, but this time, instead of parking on the road, she turned into the neat little driveway, past the hydrangeas and the sweetpea poking out over the wall, and parked outside her mother's house. She knocked on the door. Knock. Knock. Knock. Like the kick, kick, kick of the baby in the womb.

Her mother answered. And they were reunited at last.

And so, in a matter of months, Nora had gone from having no family, to having a son, a mother and brothers and sisters. Her life was full, in a way it had never been before. She was back where she belonged.

CHAPTER FIFTY-NINE

A Mother's Love

The sense of attachment to one's mother runs deep. It's something that never leaves us. Whether our mother is alive or dead. Where do you get your genes, your talents, your sense of self? It's in you, it's in your blood.

When the officials refuse to hand over the records, the case is made that it is to protect the privacy of the mother, but I don't buy that. It's all about power, and its misuse.

And it was time for someone to apologise. As I read through more and more stories of what people went through in the mother and baby homes, I really wanted the Bon Secours sisters to come out and say sorry because I knew that would mean so much to so many people. They had been through enough heartache. Many carried a sense of guilt for having been born, and a feeling of betrayal in having been deserted.

Surely, they deserved an apology. For someone to say: it's not your fault, it's ours. This was more than important, it was vital.

There was one man I'll never forget. I helped him to trace his mother. He found her. She was in England. But she had died. He went to visit her grave. He came back to me and said, 'I'm bringing my mother home.'

I didn't know what he meant at first. I thought there had been a mix-up. His mother was dead, I was sure of it.

He explained that he was going to get his mother's body exhumed, to bring her back to Glenamaddy, to the place she should have been all along, to her home, at last – at least in death, if not in life.

He wanted to make it up to his mother, he told me, to do something for her. Because he knew that she had been forced to lead a very difficult life because he was born. She had fled to England because she was pregnant. Now, finally, he was able to bring her back home.

And as I spoke to more and more people, trying desperately to find some part of their mothers, some part of where they came from, it made me yearn for that part of myself too.

My mother had been in front of me for most of my life. I had grown up with her, and yet I hadn't known her. Now, for the first time, I felt I was beginning to understand her, beginning to understand why she was the way she was. I knew what she had been through.

You wonder where different things come from in you, why you're this way or that – why you like this work or that work. It's not where you come from, it's who you come from. That's what matters.

The discovery that my mother was born outside marriage was a major turning point. As far as I could tell, her own mother tried to hold on to her for a while. But to little baby Kathleen I'm sure that didn't matter, as she found herself suddenly in and out of foster care. She had a tough life, like many of the people with whom I was now in contact.

I'm sure my mother must have missed her mother for the rest

of her life. It was a missing piece for her. And so, when it came time for her to be a mother to us, she didn't know how, or didn't want to get attached, she was so hurt by her own abandonment. So she stayed aloof, remained a relative stranger her whole life.

I would never compare my experience to that of someone who has been through a mother and baby home, but hearing how people felt, it made me think of all the conversations I never got to have with my mother. I imagined that she must have had all the same feelings that the people emailing me had – the sense of loss, of abandonment.

I know what it feels like to miss your mother. To want to know her – who she was, and why you are the way you are. I can understand when people come to me looking for their mothers. In some small way, I know their pain, though my life was very different to theirs. But I can empathise, because I've felt that missing piece. I've longed to fill it. And maybe, just maybe, for those whose mothers are still alive, they might still have a chance, a chance to put things right, and for those whose mothers have passed on, at least understanding part of their story might help to bring them peace, to help them look in the mirror, and know who they are.

To this day, my search goes on, and despite finding family for many of those who contacted me over the years looking for help, my own search for answers remains a mystery. If there is no paper trail, and no relatives to fill in the gaps, with not a single O'Hare relative among the cousins on my DNA test results, then there isn't much more I can do.

I can almost picture my mother with a wry smile telling me to leave things be, in her own way, saying, 'That's enough now, that's enough.'

CHAPTER SIXTY

Happy Birthday

⌒

A social worker from Tusla got in touch to ask if she could meet with me, and if I would bring a photo of the model of the Tuam mother and baby home that I had built.

I agreed to meet, but I was a little cautious about it. I knew that Tusla would not approve of the work I was doing. I was carrying out a task I had been told was the exclusive remit of Tusla, but I was only helping because survivors had come to me telling me that there was up to a year's waiting list with the state agency, and that it was unbearable for them to wait that long, as they worried they might be running out of time. If there was any chance their mother was still alive, she would be elderly, and time was critical.

I wondered if they were bringing me in to reprimand me for my actions. Nevertheless, I knew I had to go. There were two social workers at the meeting, and sure enough, they quizzed me on my research methods. But I assured them that I always advised survivors to contact Tusla as their first port of call. What I didn't say is that most came to me after they had tried to engage with Tusla.

Towards the end of the meeting, one of the social workers did something I really didn't expect. She handed me a piece of paper. 'Here,' she said, 'this might be of interest to you,' she explained that it was an account written by a woman named Bridget, who had been a mother in the Tuam home, and that Bridget had given them permission to use the testimony in whatever way they saw fit. So they wanted me to have it.

I thanked her, and when I was back in my car I read the piece. A real testimony, from a mother, from someone who had been inside the home. I was captivated.

This is Bridget's story, in her own words.

My Time at St Mary's

I went into the home in mid April 1955. My first sight of the home was very scary. It was a big gloomy building surrounded by big iron gates. The gates were opened by a woman dressed in long black clothes. It turned out that this woman had a terrible life and received a few beatings in her time from the nuns. I was brought into an office and was asked by the Revered Mother my name and the name of the child's father. My suitcase and coat were taken off me and locked away. The Revered Mother then took me to the maternity ward where I was put into bed. It was 3 p.m. I was told to wait for the doctor who would visit me the next morning; he never turned up until the following morning. I saw nobody until the doctor arrived. The doctor examined me and told me the baby would be due on XXX 1955. XXX was born on the XXX 1955. I never saw the doctor again in the whole 12 months I was in the home. After the doctor examined me I was brought to a big room that was known as St Patrick's. This room held about 20 children aged between two and two-and-a-half years old. There was a long table running down the room where the children sat to eat their meals. There were no toys in the room, in fact the children never had any toys to play with. The children who could walk trotted around and those that couldn't or were handicapped just sat and rocked back and forth. There was nothing to stimulate them with. There was a bucket in the corner with some kind of disinfectant to mop up the 'accidents' the children continuously had. They were always soiling themselves even though there was a potty in the room which they were put on every half an hour. They couldn't help it, their diet consisted of porridge for breakfast, mashed potato for lunch and bread and milk mashed together for dinner. They never had any solid food. There were several of these rooms, all named after Saints, for different age groups, then there was a dormitory for the school children at the back of the home. They would be taken to a school outside of the home by one of the girls who were born there. We rarely saw the school children. I would be working in St. Patrick's and was known as a waiting girl. My duties included cleaning up after the children, feeding them and covering the other girl I worked with. There were 2 girls assigned to each room. At feeding time we would go around with a big pot of porridge or mashed potato and spoon feed the children, they never had their own plate, cup or cutlery. Some girls worked as waiting girls while others worked in the launderette, sewing room or kitchen. One girl helped the nuns cook, she would tell us about all the lovely food they would get to eat while we were fed slops. We had a tin mug of porridge for breakfast, lunch was like a watery stew and dinner was bread and butter served on a big plate that was put in the middle of the table. You had to be quick or you wouldn't get any. We also had a mug of tea. Once a week our cook would make a fruit cake. This was done without the nun's knowledge, how she did it I will never know but we looked forward to it all week. The daily routine was at 6 a.m., you were woken up by the night shift. The night shift was made up of girls who had 6 weeks left until they would be leaving. You would attend to your baby straight away, you didn't have a wash, only once a week were you allowed to the wash-room. We were all covered in a huge itchy rash, including the children. We were given a lotion to put on it once a week after your bath but there was a bottle of the stuff in the nursery that you could put on the babies every day, this was only allowed so that they wouldn't be crying from the itch and disturbing the nuns. After you fed your baby you put them into their pram in the nursery, you would then go and get the toddlers and dress and feed them. At 8.30 a.m. you went to Mass. 9 a.m. you fed your baby again and then had breakfast at 9.30 a.m. 10 a.m. you went back to work until 12 p.m. where you attended your child again. From 1 p.m. – 1.30 p.m. you had your lunch, then back to work. 3 p.m. you went back down to the nursery and fed and changed your child. 3.30 p.m. you were back at work until 5.30 p.m. where you would go and fetch your child from the nursery and see to them before they were put to bed. 7 p.m. you had your dinner and into bed at 7.30 p.m. You would be so tired that you would be glad to get into bed. Your baby slept in the bed with you and all night long the night shift would be shouting at us not to have our backs to our babies. We didn't get much sleep.

When my time came to have my baby I was brought down to the maternity ward. This would be when you went into labour, you worked right up until the end. I was put into bed at 3 a.m. and a nurse came and examined me, left after 10 minutes and I didn't see her until 2 p.m. the following afternoon. I was left to get on with it. I had no pain relief, not even a drink. I gave birth to XXX at 3.10 p.m. on XXX 1955. I was told I had a baby girl and that it would have been better for the child if it had been a boy as it would have a better life.

I was put into a little ward next door and XXX was put into a separate room. The inmate who worked on the maternity ward brought XXX into me; her hands were filthy as she had been out planting potatoes. She put XXX to my breast but she was very sleepy and wouldn't feed so the inmate slapped XXX hard across the face to wake her up. You were kept on the ward for 10 days and then you were sent back to work as normal. My time there was very hard as we were treated so badly. We were never allowed any kind of recreation, no talking was allowed during meal times or when you were in the nursery attending your baby. We were allowed to write 1 letter a month which was censored, as was the one coming in. This was done by XXXX the nun's secretary and [she] was born in the home. She never attended to any of the children nor did she attend any births, she only stood for the children when they were baptised. You were allowed visitors but they seldom came, no one wanted to know you while you were in there. I think about 3 girls had a visitor while I was there. I had none. Christmas was no different to any other day. We never had a Christmas dinner or a tree nor were any decorations put up. The children were never given any presents. They may have had presents sent in by their mothers but they certainly never received them. Some mothers sent parcels in after they had left the home. They would have new clothes and some toys in them but the children never got them. The nuns would keep them though in case the mother came to visit and seen the state he was in. A few of the children stuck in my mind. There was one child that was a result of a sister/brother relationship and she was so pale like a porcelain doll. They said she probably wouldn't live past 5. Another child had a terrible condition where every time she went to the toilet her bowel would protrude through her bottom. She was never seen by a doctor. They would just push her bowels back inside her. One of the friends I made during my time there had a little boy called XXX. I always thought there was something wrong with him as he couldn't sit up properly and his nappies always smelled horrendous and he should have been seen to by a doctor; one day poor Pat got taken off and was never seen again. My friend told me he had died and she had been told she would be leaving the home very soon. The children were never seen by a doctor or had any kind of medical checks. It was very hard knowing you would have to leave your child behind in that place.

XXX was 11 months old when I was taken into Galway by the Reverend Mother and another nun to see a solicitor to sign some documents. At the time I didn't know what they were nor did I dare ask as the journey to and from Galway in the car was done in total silence. After seeing the solicitor the three of us went into a restaurant and we had fish and chips, the one decent meal I had the whole time I was there. I'm sure we were only there as the nuns were hungry, it wasn't done for my benefit. Anytime you had any dealings with the Reverend Mother and asked what would happen to XXX she would tell you she was going to be sent to America. I was hoping XXX would be adopted as soon as possible so she didn't have to stay in the home to suffer. You carried on as normal with your work until you were called up and told you were being put on night shift. Then you had 6 weeks until you would leave.

On XXX 1956 it was XXX's first birthday and I had dressed her in the little dress my uncle's wife had sent to me a few days before. We were sitting in the nursery when I was told Reverend Mother wanted to see me. I went into her office and the door was shut behind me. On her desk was my suitcase and coat. She told me I had to leave immediately and would be going to the Convent down the road. I asked if I could say goodbye to XXX, but she said no, that wouldn't be allowed. I was brought to the Convent, where I stayed for 3 weeks until my uncle's wife wrote a letter to say that she was willing to take me in. If she hadn't have written that note I would have had to stay and work in the Convent. When I left the Convent I had managed to get a job in Galway looking after an elderly lady, with whom I stayed until 1957 when I left for England. I visited the home a week after I left the Convent. They brought XXX to see me, but she was crying and I was told to leave as I had upset her and was not to come back upsetting her anymore. I never did.

CHAPTER SIXTY-ONE

Hands Up

⌒

'You'll never guess who's on *The Late Late* tonight,' Aidan said, rushing into the kitchen one morning.

'Who?' I asked, as I placed my cup of tea on the table.

'That PR woman – the one who wrote the email . . .'

'Terry Prone?'

'That's the one.'

Aidan seemed very excited about the prospect. I knew he must be up to something. 'Why don't you call in?' he said.

'What? Like, for a prize?'

'No . . . to see if Ryan will ask her about the email. It'd be a great opportunity to know why she wrote it.'

'Ah . . . I couldn't do that.'

'Why not?' said Aidan.

I was always amazed at how his brain worked. So different from my own. I mulled it over for a moment. I was suddenly very nervous.

'What would I say?' I asked after a few minutes had passed.

'See if Ryan will ask her if she regrets sending the email . . .'

It was a question that I had been wondering about ever since it had happened.

'Okay,' I said.

Aidan's face broke into a smile. 'Really?'

'Yes, really. I'd always wonder about it otherwise, and I may never get a chance to meet her myself.'

I rang the researcher for the show. No answer. I sent a text message. He phoned me back minutes later.

I asked if it would be possible to put a question to one of the guests on that evening's show.

He said I had caught him at just the right time, as he was on his way into the production meeting. He noted my request and said he would have to run it by the producer. He was very nice about it.

I walked back into the room.

'Did you do it?' Aidan asked.

'Yes,' I said, 'but I'm not sure if they will be able to ask her . . . you know, it might not fit in with what they're doing.'

That evening, we made ourselves comfortable in the sitting room. When the familiar theme tune played, I felt a flutter in my stomach. We watched the programme in anticipation, waiting for Terry Prone to appear on set. Then Ryan Tubridy announced that she would be joining the programme after the commercial break.

They were the longest set of ads I have ever sat through. When they were over, Terry Prone appeared alongside some other guests for a panel discussion about the sexual harassment of women, a discussion brought about because of the infamous Harvey Weinstein case.

Ms Prone gave examples of times in her own career when she had been aware of inappropriate behaviour by men. The discussion was interesting to watch – to me it seemed that the same objectification and abuse of women that had gone on in the time of Tuam was still happening around the world, just in a different kind of way.

As the panel discussion drew to a conclusion, I thought to myself, Well, that's it, they aren't going to ask her. And then Ryan Tubridy picked up the pen that was on his desk and began a new line of inquiry.

'Can I mention Catherine Corless briefly, Terry? You know, Catherine Corless and the Tuam babies. She was on to us and she brought up the email that you wrote when you represented the Bon Secours sisters and she just wanted to make the point that: Do you think that you feel the same way now as you did then with regard to saying that there was no evidence and that it might have been a famine area, and so forth?'

It felt like the world stood still for a moment while I waited for her answer.

Sitting on the couch in her pink dress, Ms Prone answered quickly and with the expertise of a PR professional.

'Oh, I mean, it's a great question. I will never forget the day, it was the third of March, that the commission came out with their first report, and reading it and realising, this is not famine remains. This is babies, toddlers, little children, and that they were from that time in that mother and baby home. And it was just the most shocking thing. And I actually should have contacted Catherine and said I'm really sorry because I believed, based on the evidence that I had, that it was famine burials, but you were absolutely right, and you were right to fight it through.'

'Well, that's an honest hands-up on your part,' said Ryan.

And with that Terry Prone threw her hands into the air. 'Oh yeah,' she said, nodding. And the audience broke into applause.

I looked at Aidan. 'There you go,' he said.

I couldn't believe what had just happened. It felt like a small victory, at last. A tiny win. It wasn't about Terry Prone. It was about all the people who denied that this could be a possibility, who blocked the search for answers, rather than assisted it. It wasn't personal. If only it was. It was systemic. That was the problem.

CHAPTER SIXTY-TWO

A Humanitarian Issue

~

I was driving back from the shop with the groceries, when the phone rang. I pulled over and took the call.

It was a woman from the Bar Council of Ireland. She wanted to know if I would be willing to accept a humanitarian award from the council, in recognition of my work with the Tuam babies.

The Bar of Ireland's Human Rights Award is presented to a person or organisation who has shown exceptional humanitarian service, she explained. The year before it had been awarded to the Irish Naval Service for its work on the migrant crisis in the Mediterranean.

I couldn't believe what I was hearing. It wasn't so much the award aspect, though I was incredibly honoured by the gesture. It was the fact that it was a humanitarian award. For years I had been trying to tell the government that this was a humanitarian issue. It seemed that others were in agreement. This was about human rights.

On 26 October 2017 I stepped up to the podium to receive the award. I was nervous, but I knew what I wanted to say. I spoke of the terrible injustice that had been done to 'both the people who went through the home and survived it and also . . . the children who died there'.

I explained what had kept me searching all these years, why I had to know the truth:

I couldn't get my mind around how the sisters could leave that home in 1961, close the gates when it closed down, with 796 children buried . . . a lot of them in the sewage tank area, as we now know. What kind of mentality would leave that place without acknowledging that so many burials were there, so many precious lives were lost?

I went on to talk about what I hoped would happen next. What needed to happen next.

The ideal would be to exhume those little bodies and just show them some dignity and reverence and to perhaps re-inter them in the main Tuam graveyard which is only across the road. Hopefully the commission of inquiry will give them [the survivors] justice. All they want is an apology and an acknowledgment of what happened to them and their mothers.

My work campaigning on behalf of the survivors of mother and baby homes continues and I hope that this special award will give even more survivors the strength to come forward to tell their story. With each and every testimony, the truth is uncovered further and our campaign for justice to prevail is strengthened.

I share this award with the all survivors – this is for them.

As I looked out into the crowd, I thought of Bridget, being separated from her daughter on her first birthday; I thought of P.J.'s mother knocking on the door of the home, week after week, begging for her child; of Peter searching for the sister he never knew he had. I thought of Martin bringing home his mother's hat. I thought of all the survivors I had met, and those I hadn't, and all those who had not survived. The forgotten ones.

CHAPTER SIXTY-THREE

Leaked Information

After that day, I thought that things were turning a corner, that people finally recognised the babies and all they had been through.

But less than two months later, we were dealt another blow.

A report was leaked in *The Irish Times* that the children buried in the Tuam site may never be identified. DNA testing was what many of the survivors really wanted. They wanted to know for sure who the children buried there were.

Minister Zappone came out to apologise after what she described as 'highly confidential information' being leaked to the media. She said she was 'disappointed beyond words' that this information had got out in this way. 'This goes against my promise to the survivors and families that I would inform them of developments in advance of information entering the public domain,' she said, and she really did seem sorry.

Experts from the UK later confirmed that DNA testing was quite possible, even from whatever tiny remains were there, which indicated to me that the government was using outdated information when they said that garnering DNA evidence may not be possible.

And though the minister was sorry, something about the whole episode shook our confidence in the government. The leaking of such sensitive information – how was this allowed to happen? And was the government really doing all it could for the babies or was this a half-hearted approach to dampen down demands from campaigners and survivors?

We were on the defensive again, unsure of whom to trust.

The quest for DNA evidence from the site had become a much more critical task in recent years. In the early stages of my research, my main aim was to have the babies exhumed from the sewage tank and surrounding areas and to have them interred in the main Tuam cemetery in an angels' plot. As time progressed, I could see that the survivors who had family buried there were lobbying for DNA testing to be carried out on the babies' remains in the hope of re-interring them with their own families.

But that possibility was receding, as I realised that the government was 'pulling a fast one'.

CHAPTER SIXTY-FOUR

In the Heart of the Church

~

I t is not often you get an insight into the Vatican. It wasn't until
some time later that I came to learn what had gone on there,
the day the news of the Tuam babies broke.

That day, by pure coincidence, Diarmuid Martin, the archbishop of Dublin, was in the Vatican for a meeting with the pope.

I try to picture where he might have been – what it looked
like. In my mind the Vatican is a palace made of gold, where
people in white gowns and hats walk about being very quiet. It
might be nothing like that, but it is what I imagine. And here
he was, Ireland's envoy, face to face with the highest authority
in the Catholic Church, and news of a mass children's grave in
a Catholic-run institution in Ireland had broken that very
morning.

I found this out on Easter Sunday. I was driving to the shops
and turned on RTÉ Radio 1. Miriam O'Callaghan was interviewing a guest. After a few moments, I figured out it was
Archbishop Diarmuid Martin. I listened as he spoke about a
number of things, from his faith, to clerical abuse scandals, and

the state of the church in Ireland. Well, there's one scandal they never talk about, I thought to myself.

But then, near the end of the piece, he spoke about Pope Francis and their recent conversations, and something the pope had said to him one day: '"I often think of you; you got a difficult task. I'm sure there's many a morning you wake up and say, 'Why did I ever leave Geneva?'" Because that's where I was before,' Diarmuid Martin explained. He had been stationed in Geneva before coming to Ireland. Presumably the pope was implying that Ireland was a difficult posting. No one could argue with that, I suppose.

Then Archbishop Martin paused. His voice cracked. He was starting to get upset. 'I remember the day . . .' he said, pausing again to gather himself as he recounted his conversation with the pope, '. . . the story of the Tuam babies came out.'

I turned up the volume.

'He said to me, "How are things in Ireland?" I said, "There's a terrible . . . a terrible story." Sorry . . . ' Archbishop Martin was getting emotional.

Miriam O'Callaghan intervened. 'No, I can see you're upset, and it's important for my listeners to know how upset you are about it. Take your time . . .'

The archbishop explained, 'Someone said to me today, "Why do you get emotional?" I get emotional when I'm tired. But, anyway, that's another story.

'I said to him, "There's a terrible story emerging about children . . . bodies being found."'

He went on to explain how the news had affected the pope: 'Afterwards a number of people came to me and said, "What did you say to the pope? Because he was visibly upset. And he kept looking after you when you went away." You know, he has that sensitivity to things. And I hope that the people around him allow him, when he comes to Ireland – and that would include our own people – will allow him to say what he wants to. And what he should say.'

Was he suggesting that the pope was going to say something about the mother and baby homes? Or that he wouldn't be able to say what he wanted to say? The pope was due to visit Ireland the following August. Now that he knew about the babies, what was he going to do about it? Surely he of all people had the power to make something happen. It remained to be seen.

CHAPTER SIXTY-FIVE

Tea, for Three

❧

Life was full of surprises around that time. I'll never forget the day, not long after that, that a Hollywood star came for tea.

It all started when a journalist from *The New York Times* phoned me, saying he hoped to travel to Tuam to write an article about the Tuam babies. He wanted to spend some time with me, getting to know me and the work I had done.

I told him I'd be happy to talk with him.

Dan Barry arrived several weeks later. He spent a lot of time with me. He wanted to travel the route I walked to school, to get to know where my homeplace was and what life was like when I was a child. I got the feeling he really cared about the story. He asked so many questions. He was meticulous about detail. I hadn't anticipated we would spend so much time together.

But when he returned to America and the piece was published, I was in awe. It was an eight-page special report inserted in *The New York Times*, with digital moving photographs on the paper's website. The piece was so moving, and was a fitting tribute to the children who spent time in the Tuam mother and baby home and those who died there.

I phoned Dan and thanked him for all his work. He had put so much time and effort into making the piece the powerful and moving account it was. I appreciated that so much. So few people had managed to capture the essence of the Tuam babies and what went on in the mother and baby home.

A few weeks later Dan rang me and said that there had been a lot of interest in the film rights to the story. He said there were two people in particular who were very interested in the project and asked if I would be okay with him passing on my contact details to Liam Neeson.

'Liam Neeson?' I asked, in disbelief. '*The* Liam Neeson?'

'The very one.' He laughed as he said it. He told me to expect a call from him in the next few days.

I hung up in disbelief.

'Go 'way,' said Aidan. 'That didn't happen.'

'I swear,' I said.

And sure enough, a few days later, the phone rang.

'Hello,' I said.

'Hello,' said the voice, 'is this Catherine Corless?'

'It is,' I said. The voice was somewhat familiar.

'This is Liam Neeson,' he said.

I tripped over my words. 'He-hello. . .' I said.

He was very pleasant. He asked me how I was and told me how interested he was in the Tuam babies and what a powerful story he thought it was. He was very kind about it all. I was very taken aback by the whole experience. I don't think I said very much at all! I just listened, and then he said something I really wasn't expecting. He asked if he could come and visit me and Aidan.

'What, here at the house?'

If that was okay, he said.

I was half-expecting him to say his famous line from *Taken*: 'I don't know who you are, I don't know what you want ... [but] I will look for you, I will find you. . .'.'

Of course he didn't say that.

'Absolutely,' I said, 'we'd love that.'

He would be visiting his home in Antrim in the coming weeks, he told me, so it would make sense for him to come then, if that suited us. As the weeks went by, we received further communication from him, and we arranged a day for him to call. Both Aidan and I were thrilled. It all seemed very surreal.

He was to travel by helicopter, and wanted to know if it would be possible to land near the house. Aidan was straight out the door, on to the quad, out to measure the top field, to see if it was suitable for a helicopter landing. I laughed as I watched him rushing out the door. He was like a little boy all of a sudden, excited and nervous at the same time.

As it turned out, because the Galway races were on, there was a shortage of twin-engine helicopters, which was what was required for the journey. So instead Liam would travel by car.

The day arrived, and we were up early, getting the house ready for our famous guest. I still didn't believe it was happening, until I saw the car pull up outside. I was watching from the kitchen window. The car door opened, and Liam Neeson stepped out. He looked just like he did in the movies.

We welcomed him in. He looked so out of place – this movie star in our modest house, sitting by the range in the kitchen. I put the kettle on to make a cup of tea. Liam was as lovely as I'd imagined he'd be. He explained, bashfully, that he was on a diet for a new movie, so he had brought his own, special tea bag – mint tea.

We sat over our tea and we told him the journey we had been

on. It felt strange to have a Hollywood actor asking you questions about yourself; surely it should be the other way around. We were a little embarrassed, but he insisted that he was interested and wanted to know all about it.

We had a long chat, and at the end of it he explained that he would love to make a movie about the Tuam babies and everything we had been through on their behalf. Something that would pay tribute to the lives the babies had led. I liked the sound of that. He had integrity and was doing it for the right reasons, I could see that. And I loved the idea of the children's story being brought to life at last.

He asked us if we would promise him the film rights, and we wholeheartedly agreed. And just like that, a deal was struck.

He thanked us for our hospitality and went on his way. We waved him off at the door, but not before taking a picture or two, 'for the grandchildren, of course'. When his car had pulled out of the driveway and made its way back up our quiet little lane, Aidan and I turned to one another in disbelief.

'Did that just happen?' Aidan asked. We both laughed. It was as though we had just imagined it. No trace of our famous Hollywood guest left behind. Except, of course, his mint tea bag, which I decided to keep, to remind myself that I hadn't been dreaming.

What followed were calls from movie agents and solicitors, and a contract was drawn up. It all happened very quickly. They asked if the screenwriter could come to stay with us for a few days – to get to know us and see at first-hand how we lived. Okay, we said, of course, that's no problem, if that's what was needed. It was fascinating to see how the film world worked.

A few weeks later a woman came to stay. She was writing the screenplay. We welcomed her in and showed her around the house and made her feel at home in the spare bedroom. She had a lovely way about her. Somehow she was able to be a stranger in the house but not make it feel that way. She subtly joined in with our everyday life. Aidan brought her up to the farm, I showed her the model of the home I had made, and talked her through the story of the Tuam babies and everything that had happened over the years. She stayed for four days. We said our goodbyes and wished her luck. It was a strange experience. I felt a bit shy about the whole thing, wondering what they would think of our set-up here in the west of Ireland. There was nothing glamorous about it. Tuam was a long way from Hollywood; there was nothing surer than that.

As part of the contract, I was given a small advance. Very small in terms of the film world, I would imagine, but more than we would have ourselves. I knew exactly what I wanted to do with the money.

Some time previously, the head of the committee had shown me the grave where Julia Devaney was buried. It was a single plot as her husband was buried with his first wife. It had a cement base with a simple iron cross with her name and age and date of death, which had rusted over time. It had been inscribed by an artist who had lived next door to Julia on the Gilmartin road. There was no headstone, which made me very sad. From listening to her voice on the tapes, I had come to know her and I admired her greatly. I wanted to give her the dignity she deserved.

I wouldn't have had the money for a headstone. Now, with the advance for the film, we did have it. I mentioned the idea to one of Julia's neighbours, a woman also named Catherine, who had been a great friend of hers. I asked if she thought it would be appropriate for me to install a headstone for Julia. As Julia had no family to be found, I reckoned no one else was likely to do it. I felt I owed it to her and everything she had been through, I explained. She thought it was a lovely idea and insisted that she wanted to be part of the project and to contribute. It would mean the world to her to be involved, she told me. So we agreed – that's what we would do: we would buy a headstone for Julia.

Another old neighbour of Julia's, Dom, also wanted to be involved. He adored Julia. He had known her as a child as he grew up in a busy house full of brothers and sisters, and Julia was the old lady who lived next door. Every evening, to help his mother out, Julia would visit their house to read Dom a bedtime story. He remembered it so fondly – the nightly story time he had with her.

Together we chose a headstone and an inscription. A few months later, it was installed. I went out to see it and stood there as the rain fell gently on Julia's grave. It was lovely to see her name written there, committed to history – a tribute to her at last, some evidence that she had lived and died.

I went to visit the grave regularly, to tend to it, and keep it looking the way she would have wanted it. I liked being there with her. I felt close to her, knowing she was being looked after now, having worked so hard for others her whole life.

Dom had wanted a dove on the headstone, but somehow it hadn't been possible. One day, I managed to find a little silver dove in a shop in Galway. I brought it out to the grave and superglued it on.

It was important to him, as the dove was a symbol of peace and he wanted more than anything to know that she would rest in peace – this beautiful soul who had given so much and expected so little.

CHAPTER SIXTY-SIX

Straw Poll

⁓

When I learned about the questionnaire Galway County Council was passing around, I was furious. The council had been charged with conducting a consultation process to see what the preferred options were for memorialising the babies. They were to consult with the various stakeholders: the survivors of the Tuam home, the residents of the Dublin road housing estate, the wider network of local residents of Tuam and the general public.

After it was confirmed in 2017 that there were human remains at the site in Tuam, the government was unsure what the next course of action should be. Katherine Zappone decided to enlist the help of an independent agency – a group of international experts associated with the UN who had arranged for reburials in war-torn countries. They were to examine the issues relating to Tuam and report back with their analysis and recommendations for action. I thought this seemed very positive. Being from outside Ireland, I felt they would be more independent. They had seen atrocities elsewhere, and I was confident they would appreciate the human rights violation that had happened in Tuam.

• In December 2017, the expert technical group published its report, which recommended that an exhumation take place. But as per their remit, the group also outlined other possibilities for further action, if exhumation was not preferable. The group outlined five different options in relation to Tuam:

• memorialisation

• exhumation of known human remains

• forensic excavation and recovery of known human remains

• forensic excavation and recovery of known human remains with further excavation of other areas of interest

• a full forensic excavation of the site.

They also advised that Galway County Council, as the owners of the site, would be best placed to undergo the consultation process to find out what the preferred option was among the various stakeholders, with the support of the Department of Children and Youth Affairs.

It was now over a year since the group had been established. It took seven months for Galway County Council to act, and the idea that they came up with, in my opinion, was nothing short of insulting – it was literally a voting page, a 'tick the box' exercise.

They organised a series of talks to be held in Tuam – one for survivors, one for the general public and one for the residents of the Dublin road housing estate.

Only a couple of people turned up to the event held for the housing estate residents. And so, the council took it upon themselves to go door to door around the estate, delivering the docket through letterboxes and knocking on doors to encourage people to vote and put an X beside their preferred choice, out of the five options.

I was very upset when I heard about this. I knew it was important for people to have a say in the process, but I was concerned that it was all being done in a very simplistic way. I was worried that such an important decision might end up being derailed. Surely there was a better way to do this.

I objected every chance I got. I contacted our local radio station, and Keith Finnegan of Galway Bay FM decided to discuss the issue, and invited me and the manager of Galway County Council, Kevin Kelly, on air. I've never been one for confrontation but I felt so strongly that this was not the right way to go about making this decision.

You might as well be voting for the Eurovision with this "tick the box" exercise, I said during the radio discussion. And I didn't stop there. I told him I thought it was horrific what they were doing, that it was disrespectful to the survivors and to the babies. Those babies should have been taken out long ago, I said.

I couldn't believe that the organisation that was responsible for running the home, all those years ago, was now being charged with running the consultation process to see what should be done to redress the terrible injustices that occurred under its watch. Of course none of the people involved in today's council had anything to do with it, but the body itself had once been responsible for the home's operation, and during that time Galway County Council even held their meetings there.

I couldn't believe that we had enlisted the help of an independent UN agency and now we were back to the very organisation that was involved in perpetrating these injustices, tasked with conducting a process to determine what would happen next.

It made me feel sick. I thought of the day I had stood in front of Galway County Council asking them for information – thinking they would want to help – and they had told me they wouldn't help, and had instead questioned who I was and what I was doing, because I wasn't an academic.

Survivors were getting very upset about the process. We were all upset about it.

So Minister Katherine Zappone called a meeting – it was to be held in the Ard Rí House Hotel in Tuam on 23 July at 7 p.m. She was calling on those who felt they had yet to be heard to attend. She was preparing to give her recommendation to government but she wanted to hear from people on the ground, first-hand, before she made her decision.

On the day of the meeting Denise Gormley, a volunteer who had always been very helpful with all the events, went around to the houses of the neighbourhood asking for old teddy bears and dolls. She tied them to the railings outside the hotel along with a handmade sign which read: Bury Our Babies with Dignity.

We arrived at the hotel that evening. It was a beautiful summer's day. The colourful wall of children's toys made a powerful impact as you entered. The room was packed. The media was excluded from the event as the minister had made the point that it wasn't a media opportunity; it was a chance for the survivors and residents of Tuam to be heard.

The straw poll, as far as I could see, had not returned any meaningful result.

Katherine Zappone thanked everyone for coming. The topic under consideration was the possible exhumation of the babies. This is what I personally wanted to happen; to me, it was of the utmost importance. Those babies had no voice now, no one to fight their corner, if we didn't.

The minister explained that legislation was needed to exhume the babies and that she was doing her best to make this happen.

My daughter Adrienne was in the audience. She also felt very strongly about what had happened to the Tuam babies and had started a blog about it which had amassed a huge following. Her blog was called 'Kettle on the Range' as a tribute to me, doing my research beside the old range in our kitchen.

When the invitation came for people to speak from the floor, Adrienne stood up and challenged the minister. 'I'm an archaeologist,' she said, 'we have often come across skeletons on our digs where there are motorways being proposed. We always have to dig to examine the site before a motorway is put in. When skeletons are found, we exhume them and they are reburied. Sometimes motorways go through old famine plots,' she explained. 'What's this about the Tuam babies? Why are they different? It's a delaying tactic. We have exhumed many skeletons like that and they were just reburied. Why is there a law needed?'

For a moment the minister seemed stumped by the question. Then she went on to explain that legislation was needed in this case because it would be a mass exhumation, that if there were 796 babies there, that would be an exhumation on a scale never before carried out in the history of the state.

It was left at that and the conversation turned to other things – including adoption, and access to files and people's personal information.

I was impressed with the minister. She stayed for two hours and listened to what everyone had to say. She had the courtesy to come to Tuam in person and listen to survivors. To her, it wasn't a 'tick the box' exercise – I could see that. She seemed to really care. It was her third time coming to Tuam. But would it produce any results? We waited to see what would happen next.

CHAPTER SIXTY-SEVEN

El Papa

～

It was August 2018, and the pope's visit to Ireland was fast approaching. We decided we would host an alternative ceremony to coincide with the Papal mass in the Phoenix Park. There had been some media interest in it, but not much.

I had a telephone interview with a reporter from the *Tuam Herald* for a short piece about the upcoming vigil. I talked him through our plans for the day and why it was so important to us that the Tuam babies be recognised in this way, because all eyes would be on the pope. Meanwhile, we wanted to draw attention to the people who had suffered at the hands of the Catholic Church. Where was their ceremony?

'Uh-huh.' I could hear the reporter taking notes on his computer. 'Okay, that's great. Thanks, Catherine.'

When the interview was over I stared out the kitchen window. I wondered whether the story would even make it into the paper. No doubt the pope's visit would be the only news in town. I felt that familiar sense of frustration. They were about to win again. How could anyone ever attempt to compete with the fanfare and showmanship of one of the most powerful organisations on earth? Once again, the Catholic Church would shout loudest, and the Tuam babies would have no voice at all.

At that moment the phone rang. I thought it might be the journalist calling back. I'd become used to calls from unknown numbers. But nothing could have prepared me for what I was about to hear.

The caller introduced himself and explained that he was calling from the taoiseach's office. I waited tentatively, wondering if he had news from the commission of investigation.

'As you are probably aware, the pope is coming to Ireland this week . . .'

I was all too aware.

'I'm calling to issue an invitation to you,' he said.

'Oh . . .' I said, curious as to what was coming next.

He went on to say that a civic reception was being organised for the pope in Dublin Castle, for a small, select group of people to meet him in person. Twenty-five people had been chosen to attend. I was one of them.

I couldn't believe what I was hearing. I said nothing for a moment.

'Hello? Are you there?' said the voice.

'Oh . . . yes,' I said. 'Sorry, would you mind if I called you back in a few minutes?'

'Of course,' he said. And he told me that he would email me the invitation in the meantime, so that I would have the details to hand.

I hung up and tried to digest what I had just heard. Meet the pope? I couldn't possibly meet the pope – not after all that the church had done to the women and children of Ireland. For a moment I wondered if I had heard correctly. I started doubting myself. I went to the computer and opened my inbox, and sure enough, there at the top of the list of emails was an invitation from the taoiseach's office to attend a reception for Pope Francis.

I rang Aidan. I needed to tell him, so that he could help me get my head around it. He was at work, so I had to be quick. 'You're not going to believe what's just happened,' I said. 'I've been invited to meet the pope . . .'

'What did you say?' Aidan was sure he must have misheard me.

'The taoiseach's office just rang . . . they've asked me if I would like to attend an audience with the pope, when he's in Ireland this weekend.'

'What did you tell them?' I could hear the worry in Aidan's voice. We were talking about the head of the Catholic Church – this was getting serious.

'I said I'd ring them back. I wanted to talk to you about it, but I'm going to say no. How *could* I meet him?'

I told him about my plan to use the opportunity to make a bigger story in the *Tuam Herald*; the fact that I had turned down the invitation might be of interest to the newspaper. I needed to tell the church that I was serious about this – I wasn't going to be *plámásed* into a photo opportunity with the pope.

'What do you think?' I asked.

Aidan paused. I could tell he was thinking about it. 'What if there was another way to use the opportunity,' he said.

He was always able to turn the situation on its head and look for the best in it. I loved that about him.

'Before you turn it down,' he continued, 'why don't you ask if you could speak to the pope. You could tell him about Tuam.'

I hadn't considered that idea. I thought about it for a moment, then decided that's exactly what I would do. Then I would know for sure that the pope was aware of the full story of Tuam and what had happened there. If I could tell him myself, there could be no doubt in my mind that the message had reached the highest office in the Catholic Church.

I rang the taoiseach's office. 'I'm just ringing back about the invitation I received . . .'

I could hear the scramble for a pen on the other end of the line.

'I was wondering if it would be possible to have a word with the pope, on behalf of the Tuam survivors and other mother and baby home survivors?' I asked.

No, I was told. No one would be speaking with the pope at Dublin Castle.

'Well then, there's no point,' I said. 'Thank you for the invitation, but I'm afraid I cannot attend. I am going to stand with the babies who were buried in a sewage tank in Tuam. I am needed at the vigil we're holding on the same day, in their honour.'

I hung up and suddenly felt giddy at the thought of it all. How life can take a turn, so quickly. There was a bit of devilment in me, and I knew I couldn't let this opportunity pass.

I rang the reporter from the *Tuam Herald*. 'I was just thinking, if it's of any interest . . . if you want to add this to your story . . .'

'Yes?' said the reporter.

'. . . I've just declined an audience with the pope.'

The reporter listened with interest.

I recounted the whole event to him and told him I was taking a stand with the babies.

The next day I was in the local shop when I caught sight of the *Tuam Herald* on the newspaper rack. The front-page headline read, 'Corless Rejects Invite to Reception for Pope'.

We had done it. I had a chuckle to myself and I could feel the home babies egging me on, like a little secret we shared. It was a small victory, but a victory nonetheless.

The national media soon caught on and I spoke about my stand with the babies on various radio stations. At least I could make the point now about the injustices that continued to exist, and all the hurt that had been caused in Ireland at the hands of the Catholic Church, and yet here we were, about to host its leader, pulling out all the stops for him. But what about the babies? Those women and children whose lives were destroyed. What did we do for them?

On Saturday, instead of going to Dublin Castle as I had been invited to do, I sat at home with Aidan watching events unfold on RTÉ.

It was the pope's first official engagement – a meeting with President Michael D. Higgins in Áras an Uachtaráin. It was a beautiful morning. The Áras was dazzling white in the sunshine, the type of weather that the thousands of people flocking to the Phoenix Park the following day would be hoping for.

Several Mercedes cars pulled up and out came men in expensive-looking Italian suits carrying briefcases. Then a people carrier arrived, out of which stepped Archbishop of Dublin Diarmuid Martin, Archbishop of Armagh Eamon Martin, some monsignors, I'm sure, and other members of the clergy I didn't recognise, all in their official garb: gowns and skull caps. Members of the Irish defence forces stood to attention, their medals on show on their pristine uniforms. High-ranking gardaí were there in number, along with a guard of honour from the naval service.

The army band played as the pomp and ceremony kicked off. Then, when the time was right, the pope was introduced to President Higgins and his wife Sabina. Other introductions were made, and then came the introduction to Katherine Zappone, Minister for Children. I watched closely as she went to greet him under the portico of the Áras. They clasped hands for what seemed an inordinate amount of time. I could see she was speaking to him. He looked surprised. He was listening intently.

'What is she doing?' Aidan remarked. 'What's happening?'

We both watched as the minister broke with protocol, and then moved away.

'What was she saying?' Aidan asked.

'I don't know,' I said, 'but I'd be very curious to find out.'

Later that day at Dublin Castle, at the event which I had been invited to attend, the pope made reference to the words spoken to him by Katherine Zappone.

In his speech he addressed many topics, giving a little time to the church's wrongdoings in Ireland:

I am very conscious of the circumstances of our most vulnerable brothers and sisters – I think especially of those women and children who in the past endured particularly difficult situations, and to the orphans of that time. With regard to the reality of the most vulnerable, I cannot fail to acknowledge the grave scandal caused in Ireland by the abuse of young people by members of the church charged with responsibility for their protection and education. The words spoken to me by the minister for children and youth affairs still resonate in my heart; I thank her for those words. The failure of ecclesiastical authorities – bishops, religious superiors, priests and others – to adequately address these repugnant crimes has rightly given rise to outrage, and remains a source of pain and shame for the Catholic community. I myself share those sentiments.

What had she said? I wondered.

The pope continued:

My predecessor, Pope Benedict, spared no words in recognising both the gravity of the situation and in demanding that 'truly evangelical, just and effective' measures be taken in response to this betrayal of trust [cf. Pastoral Letter to the Catholics of Ireland, 10]. His frank and decisive intervention continues to serve as an incentive for the efforts of the church's leadership both to remedy past mistakes and to adopt stringent norms meant to ensure that they do not happen again. More recently, in a Letter to the People of God, I reaffirmed the commitment, actually a greater commitment, to eliminating this scourge in the church, at any cost, moral and of suffering.

Each child is, in fact, a precious gift of God, to be cherished, encouraged to develop his or her gifts, and guided to spiritual maturity and human flourishing. The church in Ireland, past and present, has played a role in promoting the welfare of children that cannot be obscured. It is my hope that the gravity of the abuse scandals, which have cast light on the failings of many, will serve to emphasise the importance of the protection of minors and vulnerable adults on the part of society as a whole. In this regard, all of us are aware of how urgent it is to provide our young people with wise guidance and sound values on their journey to maturity.

I didn't know what to think of that. Somehow the church always seemed to be able to say two things at the same time. In a sense, he seemed to be acknowledging the wrongs of the church but at the same time praising it for promoting the welfare of children.

Later that night, in a room in Drumcondra, a most unusual meeting took place. A secret meeting that no one would ever have imagined possible.

CHAPTER SIXTY-EIGHT

The Circle of Truth

$\backsim$

For some time Archbishop Diarmuid Martin had been requesting that the pope meet with survivors of church abuse while in Ireland. And for a long time no positive response was forthcoming from the Vatican.

Until a week before the pope's arrival, when eight survivors of church abuse received an invitation to meet with him. The time and location was not arranged until the day before.

According to the *Irish Times*, the eight selected were: Mother and Baby Home survivors Clodagh Malone and Paul Redmond; Damian O'Farrell, a Dublin city councillor who was sexually abused as a child by a Christian Brother; Bernadette Fahy, who had spent a great deal of time in Goldenbridge orphanage; victim of clerical abuse Marie Collins; and an anonymous victim of notorious paedophile priest Fr Tony Walsh. Two outspoken priests who had also been victims of clerical abuse were there too – Fr Joe McDonald from Ballyfermot with fellow priest Fr Paddy McCafferty of the Corpus Christi parish in Belfast.

At the last minute, all eight made their way to the archbishop of Dublin's residence in Drumcondra. They were then taken by garda escort, transported in people carriers, to the papal nuncio's residence on the Navan Road. It must have been a very surreal experience for them.

When they arrived they were guided into a room and asked to take a seat. The survivors had very little information about what the meeting would entail. They had thought there might be hundreds of other survivors invited, but instead there were just eight of them, the pope, and his translators. They thought the meeting would be quick – a half hour or so. Instead it went on for an hour and a half.

I read about the meeting in the paper afterwards. I tried to imagine how the scene unfolded.

They all sat in a circle, including the pope. It was informal, but it seemed there was a structure to the meeting all the same, and a deference to the fact that the pope was an elderly gentleman.

One by one each of the survivors was invited to tell the pope their story. Their words were translated into Italian by a translator, so that the pope could understand. His responses were then translated back into English. After telling their stories, they each asked him questions that they had prepared on note cards.

I cannot imagine how that must have felt for them, to sit opposite the pope, the head of the Catholic Church, and tell their story, after a lifetime of hurt and trauma. This was their chance to look him straight in the eye and ask him why. Why did this have to happen to them? Why did it have to be part of their story, their one life on earth?

CHAPTER SIXTY-NINE

The Big Day

⌒

The following morning, the pope travelled to Knock by plane for a visit to the Apparition Chapel and a recitation of the Angelus.

I followed the news all morning, waiting for him to say something about Tuam. Knock was in the same diocese as Tuam. It made sense that he should address the issue while in the vicinity. But nothing. No mention of Tuam or the babies or anything of the sort. I was disappointed. But, sadly, I wasn't surprised.

We had made all the preparations and we were ready to hold a special ceremony in honour of the babies. Meanwhile, there was only one story dominating the headlines: reporters followed the pope's every move throughout the morning, with minute-by-minute coverage on every radio station.

We had planned the ceremony for the babies to coincide with the pope's appearance in the Phoenix Park in Dublin. So at around two o'clock Aidan and I got into the car and headed towards Tuam town square, where the ceremony was due to begin. We left in plenty of time, but as we approached the town, traffic was

360

unusually heavy. We were inching forward. I was worried we would miss the beginning of the ceremony.

'What could possibly be causing all this build-up?' I said.

'Must be the throngs arriving for the ceremony!' Aidan joked.

I threw my eyes to heaven. 'Of course it is . . .'

I knew that the only show in town was taking place some miles away in Knock and was on its way to the Phoenix Park in Dublin where the pope would address the crowds who had gathered there to see him.

We decided to park the car and walk the rest of the way, as we would be quicker by foot. Aidan found a spot. We hastily unpacked the car, and carried all the bits and pieces we needed for the ceremony. We hurried towards the square, but as we rounded the corner, something stopped me in my tracks. 'Look, Aidan,' I said.

I couldn't believe what I was seeing. Huge crowds of people were gathered in the square. It was as though all of Tuam was out in force. Someone waved over at me. I recognised them. It was one of the Tuam home survivors. As I looked around, through the crowd, I noticed more survivors, from all over the country, whom I had met or been in touch with over the past few years. I knew that many of them had travelled a long way to be there.

There must have been a thousand people there. It was a humbling moment: to see all those faces, all the people of Tuam, and from farther afield, who were standing in solidarity with the babies. I could feel the tears welling up in my eyes.

Suddenly I noticed a cameraman beside me. He told me they had been following the pope from Knock to Dublin, a route that brought them through Tuam. While travelling through the town they had noticed the huge crowds gathering in the square, so they had pulled over to see what was going on. At that moment, I noticed more television crews arriving.

We all got into position, and the procession began. People lined the streets in a guard of honour as we moved through the town, giving the children the funeral they never had. Teddy bears and dolls were tied to railings. All donated by the children of Tuam.

Some carried flowers, others held up homemade placards with messages like '796', or the children's names. A big sign tied to railings had a picture of a shovel with a single word: Dignity.

Children marched alongside their parents, holding their favourite teddy bears. Some people carried a pair of children's shoes – a symbol of the missing child.

We walked solemnly from the square, the heart of the town, up the Dublin road and into the estate, through the playground to the babies' site on the home grounds. I walked beside some of the survivors at the head of the procession, carrying a small white coffin-shaped box.

As we came to the end of the walk, the crowd stopped. A circle of candles and children's shoes were laid out on the playground tarmac. In the centre was a sculpture of hundreds of children linked together. It was made and gifted to the community by an artist in Belgium who had been moved by the tragedy when she heard of it.

'Today, we're going to read the babies' names,' said Sadie Cramer, who was leading the ceremony.

'We have no speeches, we have no prayers. The babies' names speak for themselves. I'm going to start with Margaret Mary O'Connor, who died aged six months.'

The crowd called out name after name, and the age the child was when they died: 'Patrick Joseph Coleman, one month; Mary Anne Walsh, 14 months; Joseph Hannon, six weeks; Margaret Holland, two days; Patrick Burke, nine months; Eileen Quinn, two years . . .'

We stood there, in a circle, until every single child's name had been called out.

Meanwhile, in Dublin, about a hundred miles away, a very different scene was taking place: One hundred and fifty thousand people had gathered in the Phoenix Park to pay their respects to the pope and to hear him speak.

I always respect people's religious beliefs. I am not opposed to religion in the slightest, and I know that it brings a great deal of comfort and support to many people. Everyone is entitled to their own beliefs, to their own faith. That is a human right, and it's an individual's choice. I am all for that.

But I also care about justice being done when other people's human rights are violated, and in violent and repugnant ways. And if an organisation is responsible for those crimes, it should take that responsibility seriously. Instead, here we were, a nation blighted with scandal after scandal from the Catholic Church – thousands of lives ruined because of the oppressive nature of the regime and the brutal acts by some of its people – and we were putting on the greatest show on earth, to welcome the head of that institution. I couldn't understand it.

The turnout was 150,000, though they had expected many more. It was a far cry from the one million people who had turned out to see Pope John Paul II in 1979. Perhaps this was an indication of the change in religious following in Ireland.

The rain fell heavily over the park, in stark contrast to the beautiful weather the day before. But it didn't deter the many thousands of pilgrims who attended, for whom this was a very special day, a once-in-a-lifetime opportunity. And though I couldn't understand the state's response to the Catholic Church, under the circumstances, I appreciated that for many people their Catholic faith was a huge part of their lives, and therefore a chance to see the pontiff and hear him speak was something that meant a great deal to them.

Many were very elderly. Everyone stood in the pouring rain, wearing ponchos or raincoats. Others set up camping chairs to settle in and sit for the mass. Choirs performed and speeches were read.

We were watching the extended report on the RTÉ news that evening. I wanted to know exactly what had been said by all those involved.

The taoiseach welcomed the pope to Ireland, and made reference to the hundreds of thousands of people who had turned out, saying that the old Irish traditional greeting 'céad míle fáilte' seemed very appropriate under the circumstances.

He paid tribute to the manner in which the Catholic Church has stepped up to the plate in Ireland and 'filled the gap' in services.

It is easy to forget that the Irish State, founded in 1922, did not set up a Department of Health or a Department of Social Welfare until 1947.

These are now our two largest and best-funded Government Departments, accounting for more than half of Government spending between them today. Providing healthcare, education and welfare is now considered a core function of our State. When the state was founded, it was not. The Catholic Church filled that gap to the benefit of many generations of our people. We remain profoundly grateful for that contribution.

Even today, as we struggle with a housing shortage and homelessness, Catholic organizations and people inspired by their Catholic faith fill a gap in providing services, for example, through organizations like CrossCare.

Holy Father, during your papacy, we have all witnessed your compassion for those on the edge of our society, those who have not shared in our relative prosperity, those [who] have slipped through the net.

This is an argument often put forward: to appreciate the great many things the church has done right over the years, the services it has provided, particularly to those who are poor and vulnerable, and the gaps in government services that it filled. And I do understand that. I do appreciate that. It is important to acknowledge that, I agree. But, equally, when that responsibility is taken on and is not upheld in a manner that gives the poor and vulnerable the dignity and care they deserve, as in the case of Tuam and other mother and baby homes, then there has to be accountability. The same way the government or any state service should be accountable. One doesn't cancel out the other. They can be praised for the good work they have done, but also should be reprimanded when they haven't done it well, and it has harmed people.

The taoiseach then broached the issue of what happened when the church had failed in that responsibility.

> Your visit to the Capuchin Day Centre later today reminds us of work we still have to do to ensure that the promise of the New Testament is fulfilled, that we rejoice with the truth, always protect, always trust, always hope, always persevere. And never fail.
>
> At times in the past we have failed. There are 'dark aspects' of the Catholic Church's history, as one of our bishops recently said. We think of the words of the Psalm which tells us that 'children are a heritage from the Lord' and we remember the way the failures of both Church and State and wider society created a bitter and broken heritage for so many, leaving a legacy of pain and suffering.
>
> It is a history of sorrow and shame.
>
> In place of Christian charity, forgiveness and

compassion, far too often there was judgement, severity and cruelty, in particular towards women and children and those on the margins.

Magdalene Laundries, Mother and Baby Homes, industrial schools, illegal adoptions and clerical child abuse are stains on our State, our society and also [on] the Catholic Church. Wounds are still open and there is much to be done to bring about justice and truth and healing for victims and survivors.

And finally, Enda Kenny asked that there be action and zero tolerance, and that the survivors be listened to, above all else.

Holy Father, I ask that you use your office and influence to ensure this is done here in Ireland and across the World . . . There can only be zero tolerance for those who abuse innocent children or who facilitate that abuse.

We must now ensure that from words flow actions.

Above all, Holy Father, I ask you to listen to the victims.

I wondered if the words of the victims the pope had met just the night before were going through his mind at that moment. But would he use this opportunity to say something, to do something meaningful for the people who had trusted him with those terrifying testimonies?

When it was the pope's turn to speak, I listened with great interest.

To my surprise, he focused entirely on the wrongdoings of the church. It was unlike anything I would have expected from a sitting pontiff.

Yesterday I met with eight persons who are survivors of the abuse of power, the abuse of conscience and sexual abuse. In reflecting on what they told me, I wish to implore the Lord's mercy for these crimes and to ask forgiveness for them.

We ask forgiveness for the cases of abuse in Ireland, the abuse of power, the abuse of conscience and sexual abuse on the part of representatives of the Church. In a special way, we ask forgiveness for all those abuses that took place in different kinds of institutions directed by men and women religious and other members of the Church. We also ask forgiveness for cases in which many minors were exploited for their labour.

We ask forgiveness for all those times when, as a Church, we did not offer to the survivors of any type of abuse compassion and the pursuit of justice and truth by concrete actions. We ask forgiveness.

We ask forgiveness for some members of the hierarchy who took no responsibility for these painful situations and kept silent. We ask forgiveness.

We ask forgiveness those children who were taken away from their mothers and for all those times when so many single mothers who tried to find their children that had been taken away, or those children who tried to find their mothers, were told that this was a mortal sin. It is not a mortal sin; it is the fourth commandment! We ask forgiveness.

May the Lord preserve and increase this sense of shame and repentance, and grant us the strength to ensure that it never happens again and that justice is done. Amen.

He had acknowledged the pain and hurt and suffering of survivors of church scandals in front of the thousands present in the Phoenix Park and the millions more who would be watching from afar. It was a significant moment.

But the taoiseach's words echoed in my mind: 'We must now ensure that from words flow actions'. It remained to be seen if the church would in fact do anything to repent on a practical level.

CHAPTER SEVENTY

Under the Portico

~~~

For a long time I wondered what Minister Katherine Zappone had said when she spoke to the pope under the portico at Áras an Uachtaráin. Then one day, one of the newspapers revealed, under the Freedom of Information Act, what she had said, and the lengths to which the minister and her office had gone to make the most of the opportunity.

It had been decided that she was to be the government's representative to greet the pope. So, it seems, she felt this was a great chance to do something meaningful, rather than just go through the pleasantries.

The emails from Minister Zappone to members of her staff were reported in the paper. She had made it clear what it was she wanted to get across:

So, [the] message is – will he: offer [an] apology, share in costs, provide access to relevant information.

She would have only a few seconds with the pope. She couldn't waste any time. So she suggested the idea of learning her message in Italian. And, according to the article, the minister asked her advisers if she should try and get a commitment from the pope. Should she learn the Italian for 'Is that a "yes", Pope Francis?'

It was decided this would not be appropriate, particularly as the government had not yet sanctioned a recommendation on the future of the Tuam site. It would be too 'risky', they said.

She wondered if she should involve Archbishop Diarmuid Martin in some way, but, according to the report, the advisers thought it best to focus on the pope, as he was the archbishop's 'boss'. 'We are going to the top,' said one adviser.

Though she would not be pushing for a verbal commitment from the pope, her team reassured her that even raising the issue with him would be very meaningful, expecting that it would be the first time it had been raised in this way.

They agreed on the final message that the minister would deliver. It would be short, snappy and to the point. Its language should be immediate and direct. There could be no ambiguity as to whether the message was delivered.

But all this effort would be in vain if the minister's pronunciation was not correct. The report went on to say that her team sent her three separate recordings of people delivering the message in Italian so that she could study the way the words should sound and learn it off by heart.

Finally, the report revealed the historic message that Minister Katherine Zappone delivered to the pope that fateful day in the Phoenix Park. In her best Italian she said: 'Welcome, Pope Francis. I am responsible for the Tuam mother and baby home. Children's remains were found in a sewer there. I hope the church will make reparation for its part in this shameful chapter. It is important. I will write to you with details.'

And sure enough, she went on to write to him. She was thorough in her approach, according to later reports when the minister's office made the letter public.

Dear Pope Francis,

As Minister for Children and Youth Affairs and an Independent Minister of the Government of Ireland I am writing to you in the hope that the church will accept its responsibilities and make reparation for its part in a very shameful chapter of Irish history.

Mother and Baby Homes came to public attention in Ireland during the summer of 2014 following a series of disturbing reports of high mortality rates and claims of possible burials of children on the grounds of a former home in Tuam, Co. Galway. The then Government decided to have these matters investigated and a statutory Commission of Investigation was established in February 2015.

The Commission has been examining a wide range of concerns related to the institutional care of unmarried mothers and their babies during the period 1922 to 1998. The Commission is examining 14 Mother and Baby Homes and 4 County Homes. It will in time provide a full account of what happened to vulnerable women and children in these institutions; how they came to be there; and the pathways they took as they left.

An early focus of the Commission's work was to examine the Tuam site to address questions about the alleged internment [sic] of human remains. As part of this process, the Commission conducted a series of surveys and test excavations, commencing in October

2016. I visited the site myself and met former residents and relatives shortly before these works commenced.

The statutory Commission of Investigation confirmed the presence of human remains on the site of the former Bon Secours Mother and Baby Home in Tuam. The Home was run by the Bon Secours Sisters from 1925–1961 in what was previously a workhouse dating back to famine times. In the 1970s the former home was demolished to make way for a local authority housing estate. A small memorial garden is maintained by local residents and there is also a children's playground on the site.

The Commission's excavations have revealed that human remains are visible in a series of chambers that may have formed part of sewage treatment works for the Home. The Commission believes that there are a significant number of children's remains there. It recovered some juvenile remains for detailed forensic analysis. From this analysis, it has determined that the remains are between 35 foetal weeks and 2 to 3 years of age. From carbon dating it has correlated the age of these samples with the time period during which the home was in operation – between 1925 and 1961.

This news was met with widespread disgust both in Ireland and abroad. There were suspicions about burials of this kind in Tuam for some time. However, it is fair to say that the confirmation received from the Commission of Investigation caused many people to demand that dignity and respect be afforded to the memory of the children who lived their short lives in this Home. We also owe it to the families of these children to now do the right thing by their loved ones.

We have now put in place a series of actions to ensure that we have an appropriate and respectful response to the discovery.

Since then, I have instructed an expert team to do further work on the site to determine the options that are open to us to fulfil our duty to these children. The team has reported, offering options, including a complete excavation of the site and DNA analysis of the hundreds of remains contained therein.

A consultation has also been carried out with survivors and local residents about what they would like to see happen on the site in Tuam.

There was little compassion shown to children and their mothers in this home.

We cannot change what happened to them. For the little ones whose remains are in a sewage system, we owe them dignity in death. For their mothers, siblings and families we need to give them some peace.

It is my strong conviction that given the role of the Church in this shameful chapter of recent Irish history it must play a practical role in addressing the hurt and damage. I believe that the church should contribute substantially to the cost of whatever option is decided by the government. This should be done willingly, unconditionally and quickly. Nothing less will demonstrate remorse.

I look forward to receiving your response.

With every best wish, sincerely yours,

Dr Katherine Zappone TD

CHAPTER SEVENTY-ONE

Enforced Disappearances

On 30 August, which is the UN International Day of the Victims of Enforced Disappearances, the Irish Council for Civil Liberties issued a chilling response to what had happened in Tuam, and in other mother and baby homes around the country.

Enforced disappearance was a phrase I was not familiar with, but when I read about it, it made total sense. In a way it was articulating what I had been trying to wrap my head around for a long time.

The statement read:

> *On UN International Day of the Victims of Enforced Disappearances, the Irish Council for Civil Liberties (ICCL) has called on the State to ensure that family members of children who were forcibly disappeared, either through forced adoption or unidentified burials while in institutional care, are given information about the children's fate and whereabouts.*
>
> *Enforced disappearance is widely considered one of the*

gravest possible human rights violations, and is recognised in international law as a crime against humanity when widespread or systematic. Under international law, an enforced disappearance occurs when a person is detained or abducted with the involvement of the State, following which the State refuses to disclose their fate or whereabouts.

The director of the Irish Council of Civil Liberties, Liam Herrick, was quoted as saying:

The State-sponsored system of forcibly separating unmarried mothers and their children during the 20th century appears to ICCL to involve 'enforced disappearance', one of the gravest violations of European and international human rights law. Last year a European Parliament Committee recognised that a similar system in Spain – that of the 'stolen babies' – constitutes crimes against humanity. Ireland needs to wake up to the seriousness of what is at stake.

The organisation went on to call on the state to provide statutory rights to information to all those who survived the Irish system . . .

. . . including all people who were forcibly separated from their family members through the closed, secret adoption system in Ireland, as well as the family members of children who died in institutional care. This means that the bodies of children in the Tuam grave must be exhumed, identified, and all possible information about their circumstances of death given to their family members.

This is what had always made me so angry. As I read the words, I felt that, for the first time, someone was really calling it as it was. This wasn't just the repercussions from a moralistic society – like something we should regret but accept because it was 'the way of the times'. That was too simplistic. It let everyone off the hook. These were human rights violations, of the highest order.

I continued reading, with interest. Herrick went on to lambast the straw poll that had been conducted by Galway County Council.

It is simply not good enough that Galway County Council conducted a straw poll as to what should be done in the Tuam case, including the option of simply covering over the site and placing a memorial there. The State is obliged to identify the children's bodies, to conduct a full public investigation, and to provide guarantees that nothing like this can ever happen again.

We know that there are mass unmarked graves of children in places other than Tuam. We have heard adopted people and many others who were forcibly separated from their family members call repeatedly for information about what happened to them and to their relatives. Full disclosure of information is required. The secrecy must stop and the State must recognise its human rights obligations towards all of these individuals.

The piece also outlined that enforced disappearance is unique in international law 'in that it is considered an ongoing crime until family members have been informed by the State as to the fate and whereabouts of their relative'.

I had read about institutions such as the International Court of Human Rights in The Hague. Why was this issue any different?

Why were the people who suffered these violations considered victims of the time rather than victims of the church and state? All these questions were racing through my mind as I read the statement from the Irish Council of Civil Liberties.

The ICCL was right – these were state-sponsored institutions. Many, like the Tuam home, were run by the county councils, which is local government, while others were under the auspices of church authorities. There was no getting away from the fact that the conditions in the homes and the manner in which these women and babies were treated was a matter of grave concern. I found it hard to imagine a parent willingly giving up their child, in most circumstances. If they did so, it must have been because there was an oppressive state and church which made it almost impossible for them to do otherwise.

CHAPTER SEVENTY-TWO

Little by Little

⌒

I was growing weary. Every little step on this journey seemed to take years rather than months, and it was hard to tell at times if we were going forward at all, or simply standing still. No matter how hard we pushed, it always seemed a long and arduous struggle.

I no longer got excited when promises were made, simply because I'd heard it all before. What used to excite me, I now became cynical about. I hadn't given up hope. But I was tired of the constant battle, which had spanned nearly a decade at this point and involved successive governments.

Over the next two years several important things happened.

In October 2018, the Bon Secours sisters promised to contribute 2.5 million euro to the cost of the forensic excavation of the grounds at the former mother and baby home in Tuam. The total cost of the excavation was estimated at between 6 and 13 million euro. It was made clear by the minister that this was a voluntary contribution, not a settlement or an indemnity.

I wondered if Minister Zappone's word with the pope had

been a factor in the order finally agreeing to contribute. She had not received a reply from the Vatican.

It was important to take the offer in good faith, but part of me wondered if the contribution would actually come to fruition. I had no reason to believe that it wouldn't, but I had just become cynical perhaps, through it all.

Of course none of this amounted to anything if the government insisted that no exhumation could take place without a change in legislation.

Then, in April 2019, the fifth Interim Report of the Commission of Investigation was published.

This report was of most interest to me as it dealt with the sewage tank burials and the archaeologists' report into their excavation. It revealed what the archaeologists had discovered as they were digging behind the hoarding. A summary of the findings in relation to Tuam was as follows:

In the light of a great deal of inaccurate commentary about the Tuam site, the Commission considers it important to emphasise what it has established and what it has not established.

- The memorial garden site contains human remains which date from the period of the operation of the Tuam Children's Home so it is likely that a large number of the children who died in the Tuam Home are buried there.

- The human remains found by the Commission are not in a sewage tank but in a second structure with 20 chambers which was built within the decommissioned large sewage tank.

- The precise purpose of the chamber structure has not been established but it is likely to be related to the treatment/containment of sewage and/or waste water. It has not been established if it was ever used for this purpose although soil analysis illustrates that it is likely it was so used for an unspecified duration. The Commission does not consider that any of its features suggest that it was deliberately formed as a crypt or formal burial chamber. If that were the case, an entirely different type of structure would have been expected that would allow for easy human access.

- It has not been established that all the children who died in the Tuam Children's Home are buried in this chamber structure. There is some evidence that there may be burials in other parts of what were the grounds of the Home.

It seems clear that relatively extensive work and construction was conducted in and around the site of the Children's Home in Tuam, particularly during the July–December 1937 period. The Commission thinks it possible that the reworking of the old sewage tank and the construction of the second structure described above may have occurred at this time. If this is so, then the human remains found in the chambers are likely to date from after 1937. This raises the question of where the children who died before then are buried.

The more difficult question to answer is why the children were 'buried' in such an inappropriate manner.

All the residents of the Tuam Home were the responsibility of the Galway and Mayo County Councils. It seems to the Commission that responsibility for the burials of deceased children rested with the local authorities and Galway County Council had a particular responsibility as the owner of the institution.

The Sisters of Bon Secours who ran the Tuam Home were unable to provide any information about the burials there.

The Commission is surprised by the lack of knowledge about the burials on the part of Galway County Council and the Sisters of Bon Secours. Galway County Council members and staff must have known something about the manner of burial when the Home was in operation. The Board of Health and its sub-committees sometimes held their meetings in the Home. Employees of Galway County Council must have known about the burials. County Council employees would have been in the grounds of the Home quite frequently as they carried out repairs to the building and possibly also maintained the grounds. It seems very likely that Galway County Council must have been aware of the existence of burials when they were planning the Athenry Road housing scheme in 1969.

The Sisters of Bon Secours continued to live and run a private hospital in the town of Tuam until 2001. They must have been aware of the building works which were carried out on the Children's Home site in the 1970s.

The Commission considers that there must be people in Tuam and the surrounding area who know more about the burial arrangements and who did not come forward with the information.

The report was released alongside harrowing photographs taken of the excavation. The photographs showed a succession of chambers in the sewage tank. I was fascinated to finally get a glimpse inside the tank.

The photos were heavily redacted, with arrows pointing towards the human remains, which were blacked out, for the sake of dignity and the sensitivity of the site.

In one of the photos, you could see a child's blue shoe, with a little detail on the buckle. Something about it hit me hard. Over time, you could become inured to the talk of burials, but seeing that shoe, still a vibrant blue, was a stark reminder of how recently this had happened, a reminder that the child who wore the shoe lay dead in a sewage tank. The report predicted that the shoe belonged to a 'juvenile', under the age of six.

Another photograph showed that they had found an empty plastic bottle on the surface of the sediment within one of the chambers. The bottle had 'Castrol GTX' printed on it. The label read: 'Castrol GTX high performance raw oil contents 500ml Castrol (Ireland) Limited'.

The archaeologists confirmed that this particular product was released onto the UK market for the first time on 18 April 1968, so the commission concluded that it would have been available on the Irish market after that date. This was proof, according to the commission, that the chamber was accessible, either temporarily or for an extended period of time, post-1968.

All the pieces were coming together to paint a picture of what had happened. At least now the truth was undeniable. People had seen the evidence with their own eyes.

Then, in December 2019, Minister for Children Katherine Zappone put forward the bill that would be required in order to allow for the reburial of the Tuam babies.

It was called the General Scheme of a Certain Institutional Burials (Authorised Interventions) Bill 2019.

I read the statement that was published online. It outlined the main provisions of the bill. Two in particular jumped out at me as being very important:

- 'taking into account the Government Decision of 23 October 2018, that there would be a legal basis to carry out a programme of phased, forensic standard excavation, exhumation and re-interment of remains at the site of the former Mother and Baby Home in Tuam.

- there would be a legal basis for a programme of forensic analysis of any recovered remains, providing for samples to be taken from the remains as well as from family members of the deceased for the purpose of identification of the remains.'

The bill was set to go through the various stages of the Oireachtas. Surely now, something concrete was going to happen. Various groups had different wishes when it came to mother and baby homes and how to address the issue. For me, the critical point was the exhumation and reburial of the remains of the children buried in Tuam. Until that happened I could not rest. But for others, the DNA profiling was most important. It seemed this bill allowed for both to go ahead.

Finally it looked like our wishes were about to become a reality. Or so I thought. Just a few weeks later, a general election was called.

Katherine Zappone had managed to bring everything to the point where the bill was just about to go through the houses of the Oireachtas. After so many years, the barrier of legislation would finally be surmounted. And then the government she belonged to was dissolved. The campaigns and canvassing began. People wanted change. They were tired of the status quo, it seemed.

It was an election unlike any I had ever witnessed. For as long as I had lived, an election simply meant a switch between Fianna Fáil and Fine Gael. But for the first time in the history of the state, Sinn Féin was now topping the poll. It looked like the next head of government was set to be the leader of Sinn Féin, Mary Lou McDonald.

I have never held any political allegiance. In fact, I never paid any notice to the Dáil, until it became relevant to me because of my interactions with elected officials in order to try to progress the case for the babies. Aidan laughed when he saw me monitoring developments. Over the past few years I had become very interested in politics.

All that mattered to me was who would be minister for children and would the elected government be sympathetic to our cause? Typically, Fianna Fáil governments tended to be more aligned with the church. Or at least that's what I thought.

But then, an unusual turn of events. For the first time in the history of the state, the two civil war parties, Fianna Fáil and Fine Gael, decided to form a coalition, drafting in the Green Party to make up the numbers. It meant working together rather than against one another. I couldn't predict how this might affect our chances of moving things forward.

And then something happened that nobody could have anticipated. It caught the whole world off-guard, and changed all our lives, seemingly overnight.

CHAPTER SEVENTY-THREE

The New Normal

❧

Word came through that the taoiseach was going to give a state-of-the-nation address. He was in Washington on a state visit.

That night at 9 p.m, Aidan and I turned on the television and watched as Leo Varadkar took to the podium. The Irish flag had been positioned behind him.

Lá Fhéile Pádraig shona daoibh!
This is a Saint Patrick's Day like no other.
A day that none of us will ever forget.
Today's children will tell their own children and grandchildren about the national holiday in 2020 that had no parades or parties . . . but instead saw everyone staying at home to protect each other.
In years to come . . . let them say of us . . . when things were at their worst . . . we were at our best. Our country is making big demands of our healthcare staff . . . big demands of every single one of us. Tonight I want you to

385

know why these actions are being taken and what more needs to be done.

We are in the midst of a global and national emergency – a pandemic – the likes of which none of us has seen before. So far the number of cases in Ireland has been relatively small.

However, we believe that number will rise to fifteen thousand cases or more by the end of the month and rise further in the weeks thereafter. The vast majority of us who contract Covid-19 will experience a mild illness . . . but some will be hospitalised and sadly some people will die.

We cannot stop this virus but working together we can slow it in its tracks and push it back.

Aidan and I looked at one another in disbelief. It was like a science fiction movie. It was all very surreal.

The taoiseach ended his speech with a message for the world:

Tonight on our national holiday I also want to send a message around the world that we are all in this together.

To the people of China, Spain and Italy who have suffered untold heartbreak and loss – we are with you. To all of those across the world who have lost a loved one to this virus – we are with you. To all those living in the shadow of what is to come – we are with you.

Viruses pay no attention to borders . . . race . . . nationality or gender. They are the shared enemy of all humanity. So it will be the shared enterprise of all humanity that finds a treatment and a vaccine that protects us.

Tonight I send a message of friendship and of hope

from Ireland to everyone around the world this Saint Patrick's Day.

I felt like I was in a dream. Was this really happening?

The children rang, one after the other, to see if we were alright. Of course, we said. Sure, nothing's changed. We were just sitting in our living room watching the telly.

They each reiterated the need for us to stay indoors. To stay safe. I could sense they were worried.

We promised we would be careful. We'd stick to the farm. We were lucky to have it, at a time like this.

And so began the strangest time in our modern history. The whole world came to a standstill. The streets of New York City, London, Sydney – all empty. Everyone was told to stay at home, to protect one another. The scenes from Italy were frightening – makeshift medical tents were set up, there were photographs of people being taken away in body bags, the morgues were over-flowing.

It was a strange reality. For most of us, it was as if nothing had changed. And yet, there was this invisible force – this enemy which was lurking everywhere and nowhere – ready to attack. Something that you could catch at the shops or in any place where there were other people. You didn't need to go somewhere on holidays to catch it or do anything out of the ordinary. That's what was so scary about it. It was hiding in the mundane and the ordinary parts of our lives. The everyday that constituted a normal life: time spent with loved ones, going about your business with the ability to move freely. These were all things we had taken for granted. We didn't realise they could be taken away. It was being termed 'the new normal'. How long it would go on for, none of us knew for certain.

The country went into lockdown. People were instructed to

stay at home. Companies shut their offices overnight. People were told to work from home, where possible. Public transport came to a halt. We were told to keep a two-metre distance from other people, as the virus was transmissible at close proximity. The streets were eerie, with people walking aimlessly within two kilometres of their home – the permitted range for daily exercise. People were afraid to get too close to another human being. Fear was the overriding feeling for everyone. What was happening to our world? And how would we all survive it? No one seemed to know the answer.

And in the midst of all this, Alicia had a baby boy. They named him Ciarán. He was the most beautiful baby. We went to see him. We stood at a distance. I longed to hold him. I missed all our grandchildren coming to the house for sleepovers and playdates. The house felt empty without them.

On the way home from visiting Ciarán, I thought of all the parents of the women who went to the mother and baby homes, who probably never met their grandchildren. As I looked out the car window, I thought of all they missed out on. All the first steps and first words and all the ways that grandparents spoil their grandchildren. And there were parts of them, living out in the world, their offspring, whom they had never met. The concept was cruel and alien to me. I couldn't understand how that could have been allowed. Grandchildren are very special.

We were all in survival mode. We kept to ourselves and wore our masks at the shop and sanitised our hands. We stayed on the farm and tried not to venture out unless it was absolutely necessary. Our elder son, Alan, moved back home to live with us. It was lovely to have him back. He was great company, and took our minds off the pandemic.

We watched with interest as the new government was formed. Then the cabinet was announced.

'Mam, I need to show you something,' Alan said one afternoon. 'Is everything okay?'

'Everything's great. It's about the new children's minister. Wait 'til you see it!' Alan said.

He was sitting at the computer in the kitchen. He had a piece of paper, printed out. He handed it to me. 'See – this is what he said on the record about the Tuam babies back in 2018 when he was a councillor.'

I looked at the document. It was a printed statement from October 2018 from the Green Party, with quotes from Roderic O'Gorman, then Green Party councillor and the party's justice spokesperson.

The statement said that the Green Party welcomed the government's decision to approve a forensic excavation at the site of the former mother and baby home in Tuam, where significant quantities of human remains had been discovered.

It went on to quote Green Party spokesperson on justice, Cllr Roderic O'Gorman:

It's been over five years since Catherine Corless first
brought this shameful discovery to light, so it has taken us
a long time to get here. However, it is important that we
do this right. The government says it needs to put in place
special legislation to allow this excavation to proceed. It
also needs to ensure that experts in children's remains are
brought in to carry out the investigation and that modern
DNA techniques are used.

There is also a question as to who should be paying for
this. The Taoiseach has estimated a cost of between €6m
and €12m. As the organisation who were responsible for
the running of the home, Bon Secours should certainly be
included in this. The site in Tuam may only be the tip of

the iceberg. We don't want to see a repeat of the past where costs spiral upwards and the institutions who should be held responsible are let off the hook.

'What do you think?' said Alan, looking very excited at the find.

'It's all there in black and white,' I said. 'At least we know where he stands on the issue.'

At which point Aidan intervened. 'Or where he *stood*,' he said.

'What do you mean?' I asked.

'Well . . . it's one thing when you're in opposition,' he said, 'another when you're in government.'

Alan suggested I write to the new minister for children to introduce myself. And that maybe I should include the statement from 2018 in the letter, as a gentle reminder of what he had said before becoming minister. 'It might just jog his memory,' he said.

We decided it was a great idea. I sent a letter to the minister's office, and received a very swift reply, inviting us to meet with the minister to discuss the issue in person. I jumped at the chance. Finally, I thought. Nothing can possibly get in the way now. Maybe this will be the year that we really make progress, that things actually begin to happen for the babies. No more promises. We need action.

We arranged the meeting to coincide with a hospital appointment Aidan had in Dublin. It made sense to combine both on the one trip, seeing as we were still in a nationwide lockdown that prevented inter-county travel. We had special dispensation to travel for Aidan's medical appointment and the meeting with the minister was classified as essential work, but we wanted to limit our travel as much as possible.

Alan drove us up to Dublin and accompanied us to the meeting.

The minister's office had relocated to Baggot Street because of the pandemic. All the safety measures were put in place. We wore masks, sanitised our hands and kept a two-metre distance at all times.

We spoke with the minister for over an hour. He made eye contact with us as he spoke, rather than riffling through papers and files and avoiding eye contact, like some of the politicians did when you met with them. It made a big difference. I felt he was genuine; he was listening and he cared about what we had to say on the matter.

He told us that he had received a detailed brief from the outgoing minister, Katherine Zappone. He was working on the issue and hoped to fast-track legislation through the Dáil to allow for the reburial of the Tuam babies. Nothing of the kind had ever been done in Ireland and legislative change was required in order to exhume that number of bodies and rebury them, he told us. But he was confident it could be achieved quickly and effectively.

We left the meeting feeling reassured.

Next stop, Beaumont hospital. Aidan had been experiencing a searing pain in his back and had recently had a nerve block procedure which had brought him great relief, but he had also been experiencing chest infections regularly over the past few years so the doctors decided a full body medical exam would be a good idea, just to have a proper overall check-up.

At the hospital, I stayed in the café with Alan until Aidan was finished. Then Alan drove us back to Galway. I found long drives tough, as I was a nervous driver, and we thought Aidan mightn't be in the best form for driving after being in the hospital.

Back home, we were relieved that the meeting with the minister was so positive and that Aidan's hospital visit had gone well, and we were optimistic that we would have his test results in a few days and a plan of action to get him back on his feet.

Little did we know just what was about to unfold, for Aidan and for the minister, in very different ways.

CHAPTER SEVENTY-FOUR

There Must Be Some Mistake

⌒

We received the call on 5 October, asking us to come and meet with the doctor. They had the results of the scope, they told us, and would like to discuss it in person. We thought no more of it and made our way to Dublin for the appointment.

We arrived at the hospital and when we were called in, we sat opposite the doctor and he told us first about the tests they had carried out and how it worked.

Then he paused for a moment. His tone changed. There was something we must be made aware of, he said. He was sorry to tell us this, but the scoping exercise had spotted something they weren't expecting to find. Something quite sinister.

At first, they hadn't thought much of it, but on closer inspection one of his colleagues, analysing the images, thought he saw something in the lower oesophagus. A tumour, he said. The word rang in our ears.

Tumours usually only meant one thing.

He told us that unfortunately it proved to be cancerous.

'Cancer?' I said.

'Yes.'

Aidan was staring blankly at the doctor. Like he wasn't fully processing what was being said.

The doctor outlined the next steps. But he also warned us of the dangers associated with the treatment they were recommending – reminding us that people reacted differently to treatment, and there was no knowing how Aidan's body would take to it, until we tried it.

Chemotherapy was the proposed course of action, coupled with radiation to shrink the tumour. Then they would look at the possibility of surgery, to remove it entirely. All going well, that should work.

They told us that it had been caught early: that was a relief. And that it seemed treatable: another good word to hear. But there were no guarantees, especially when it came to cancer.

I tried to absorb it all, but I couldn't believe the words that were coming out of his mouth. Cancer. Aidan. Aidan has cancer. I tried to simplify it in my head. But the simpler version was even more frightening.

The journey home was long and very quiet. We were both lost in our own thoughts, each trying to navigate what had been said.

Over the following days I had the feeling that Aidan was trying to block out the reality of it all, that he was in some kind of denial.

The next step was to tell the children. But I needed to know first that Aidan had fully digested the news.

'You do fully understand what the doctors said, don't you?' I asked him one morning as we were having breakfast.

'I think so,' he said solemnly.

'Would we go over it again?' I asked carefully. I knew it must all be very frightening for him. Usually he was the one helping me. I felt the need to help him through this, to be his steady hand, the way he always was for me.

CHAPTER SEVENTY-FIVE

Silenced

e~~~)

Meanwhile, there was a bill relating to the commission of investigation report into mother and baby homes that was being fast tracked through all stages of the Oireachtas.

I read up on it online. It was reported that the bill would transfer a database of 60,000 records on the homes to Tusla, the child and family agency. However, the records would be sealed for 30 years, under the 2004 act under which the commission had been operating.

It was time for the Dáil to vote.

A few hours later, the result came through: 78 votes for to 67 against. The bill had passed. I couldn't believe what I was reading. After all that had happened, after everything the survivors had been through, their testimonies were now going to be sealed for 30 years.

That evening the bill went to the president. There was still a chance that Michael D. Higgins might refuse to sign the legislation, according to reports. If he deemed it somehow unconstitutional, he could summons a meeting of the council of state to ascertain its legality under the constitution. It would then go to the attorney general for review. That night as I went to bed, I thought of Michael D. Higgins sitting at his desk in the Áras, the bill laid out in front of him. I wondered what was going through his mind. Would he sign it?

The following morning, I turned on the radio. The newsreader announced that Michael D. Higgins had signed the mother and baby homes legislation.

Then followed a public outcry. Interest groups were furious at what had happened. The general public were outraged too and were letting it be known on social media and on the airwaves.

I didn't fully understand exactly what was happening.

Did this mean that the survivors' stories were not going to be heard? What, then, was the purpose of the report, I wondered? Is this really what the government was proposing? To silence the survivors all over again, after they had bravely offered up their painful testimonies to the commission, thinking that some good would come of it, at last.

I couldn't believe it. Why, at every opportunity, did the state choose to do wrong by the women and children who went through those institutions?

This was the last straw. They couldn't get away with this. And sure enough, the people of Ireland reacted. Television and radio were consumed with the news. Legal analysts questioned the government's handling of the bill.

In the midst of the pandemic lockdown, 200 people travelled to Áras an Uachtaráin to stage a protest. They tied hundreds of babies' shoes to the railings leading up to the president's house.

As I looked at the photographs of the protest, people in masks with placards and signs, risking their lives to make a stand, I thought of that much-used but powerful line in the Irish proclamation of independence – the one that promises to cherish every child of the nation equally. I thought of the day the pope gave his address in that very place – in the Phoenix Park. I thought of the thousands upon thousands of people who came to see him speak, the millions of euro that must have been spent arranging the visit, and the willingness of the government to cater to the needs of the church. When the pope spoke, millions listened around the world. And now, in that same place, a bill had been signed that would silence the mothers and babies who went through those homes.

The Green Party was coming under pressure with many of its members resigning in protest of how the bill was being handled. I wondered if this might be enough to bring down the government, the swell of public anger seemed so strong.

I read the newspaper reports, but, try as I might, I still couldn't fully comprehend what was being proposed in the legislation. It seemed to be very complicated legally.

I wondered if perhaps people had misunderstood. The government was steadfast in its defence of the bill, saying it was needed to protect the survivors and to ensure that their voices were heard. Who was right?

For now I needed to focus on Aidan. He was my priority. We only had one chance to get this right – I had everything crossed that the chemo and radiation would work.

We decided to base ourselves in Dublin for the duration of the treatment. We packed up the car, ready to leave for the city. And that's when it hit him. Aidan placed the last of the suitcases into the car, closed the door – and broke down. His body crumpled onto the car. I saw him from the kitchen window.

I hurried out to him. 'Aidan, are you alright?'

He was crying.

I hugged him close. 'It's going to be okay,' I said. 'It's going to be okay. We're going to get through this.' I could feel his tears, wet on my shoulder.

I wished with all my heart that this wasn't happening to him. Aidan, of all people. You couldn't find a kinder person with a bigger heart than Aidan. It didn't make any sense that he would be put through all this pain and suffering.

But I needed to believe that it would be okay. That he would be okay. He needed me to believe that too. I had to be strong now, for both of us.

We went inside and made a cup of tea.

I let Aidan decide when he was ready to leave. I could only imagine how he was feeling. Leaving our home was accepting that things were going to be different for some time to come. He didn't know how his body would handle the chemo, or if it would work. There was so much at stake.

The following day, Aidan went in to the hospital to begin his chemo treatment. Because of the pandemic restrictions, he had to go in alone. His cousin Michael very kindly drove him there from the house we were staying in, as I didn't trust myself to navigate the busy Dublin streets.

Aidan didn't have much of an appetite that morning. Too nervous to eat, I suppose. I gave him a kiss and wished him luck as he headed out the door. Michael was outside in the car waiting.

'See you later,' said Aidan, trying to be brave about it all.

'You'll be just fine,' I said, trying to reassure him, probably not sounding overly convincing. Truth was, neither of us had a clue how he would be. Chemo was different for everybody, we had been told. And all we could do was wait and see how it would be for Aidan.

I knew I probably wouldn't hear from him for the day. He would be busy getting his bloods taken and getting set up for his treatment. The kids rang a few times, looking for updates. I had to tell them I didn't know anything yet, but that their dad would be back soon, and I'd ring them as soon as he came in.

The day was long. I brought Shadow for a walk in Rathmines, where we were staying, then tried to pass the time going through emails. Then I went for another walk with Shadow. I was jittery. I kept watching the clock, willing the day to go a little faster.

Shadow loved all the sights and smells of the city, and all the attention he received from passers-by who were in awe of his size. As a cross between a Newfoundland and a border collie, he was bigger than any dog most people had ever seen. I laughed as children marvelled at the big black bear walking down the street. We were passing the canal – Shadow's new favourite spot, as he trotted along the well-worn path, being careful to steer clear of the hissing swans – when my phone rang. I thought it might be Aidan. I answered quickly. It was P.J., my old friend who had lived in the Tuam home as a small child. We hadn't spoken in quite a while. It was lovely to hear from him, I told him. We talked a little about how each of us was getting on, and how we were coping with the pandemic and all the restrictions.

Then he said, 'Catherine, the reason I'm calling is . . . I wanted to tell you something.'

'Okay . . .' I said, 'go ahead.'

'I got a call from Tusla,' he said.

'Oh yes?' I said.

'They phoned to tell me they had found a box with documents pertaining to me.'

P.J. told me this was most unusual as he had been contacting Tusla for years, trying to get access to his files, but without much luck.

'I'd like to show it to you,' he said. 'I really feel shook about what's in those documents. Can you meet me?' he asked.

I told him I was going to be based in Dublin for a little while, and about Aidan's diagnosis, but that I could meet him that weekend, from a distance, of course. We had decided to return home to the farm every weekend. P.J. said he was sorry to hear about Aidan's news. We made a plan to meet, and said our good-byes.

I returned to the house and heard a car pull up outside. It was Michael dropping Aidan off after his hospital appointment. I glanced out the kitchen window and saw Aidan coming up the garden path. I ran to the door, thinking I might need to help him, if he was feeling sick or weak.

He came bounding into the kitchen.

'It went so well,' he said. 'Couldn't have gone better!'

I was so relieved.

'I don't know why I was so worried about it,' he said.

As usual, Aidan was being his positive, wonderful self. I had no doubt it must have been a tough day. Initially I thought he might have been putting on a show for me, but then I realised he was genuinely relieved and happy to have the first round of chemo under his belt. One step closer to the end.

Alan phoned. 'Yes, he's just come in the door,' I told him, 'and he's in great form. It all went really well.'

I could hear the relief in Alan's voice. I knew the kids had been on tenterhooks all day too.

What I hadn't realised then was that Aidan was on steroids, to help keep up his energy and strength to ride out the chemo. The effects would last only for a day or two, and then would come the inevitable dip, Aidan explained. That's when it would hit him. We braced ourselves for a tough week ahead. But for now, we were just happy to have the first part of the treatment done. He had been through five rounds of radiotherapy and one day of chemo.

The following day we headed back to Galway. We felt a little victorious. Everything had gone well. I was looking forward to getting home, to walking the farm and to meeting P.J. We had arranged a time and place to meet, outdoors. We were being very careful about the virus, on account of Aidan's condition, and we weren't meeting other people, as a rule. But I felt I needed to meet P.J., at a safe distance. I could hear in his voice that something was wrong.

CHAPTER SEVENTY-SIX

Papers

P.J. had the cardboard box with him. He opened it carefully. 'I don't know why they have suddenly decided to give me this,' he said, though we both wondered if the impending publication of the report might have something to do with it.

He opened the box. Inside were documents that he had never known existed – proof that he had been chosen to be adopted by a couple in Rhode Island.

The papers showed an exchange of letters between the couple and the nuns at the Tuam mother and baby home. A passport had been arranged for P.J. There was also an exchange between the US embassy and the Department of Foreign Affairs in Dublin.

Then the correspondence revealed that something was missing – the Department of Foreign Affairs notified the sisters that the couple in America had not been vetted, and therefore the adoption could not take place.

I could see that P.J. was shaken by what he had seen. To see his name there, in black and white, and all this documentation proposing to send him to America, as if he were a commodity.

They would decide what life he would lead – where he would live and whom he would call his family.

Meanwhile, his mother must have been still working in Tuam, trying to save the money to buy back her son and knocking on the door of the home every few days begging for him to be returned to her. And, unbeknownst to her, a plan was being hatched to send the little boy to a far-off country – where she had no hope of ever finding him again.

Meanwhile, the cabinet was meeting again to discuss the fallout from the legislation that had been passed. From what I could gather, the government had come under huge public pressure. People were angry about this legislation. They wanted heads on plates. They were standing united with the survivors.

And so, as is usually the case, it took public outrage to force the government to change tack. A U-turn of sorts was announced, from what I could make out.

They said that they were making a clarification. They had consulted the attorney general, and it turned out that General Data Protection Regulation rules applied to the information pertaining to the adoptees. This meant that the information wouldn't be archived for 30 years.

The Late Late Show rang and asked if I would come on the programme again that Friday.

I was still feeling fragile, not quite myself. With everything that was going on with Aidan, my mind was very preoccupied. But I knew I couldn't turn down an opportunity to make the case for the babies, even though the prospect of live television still terrified me.

The researchers asked if I would be happy to talk about the legislation that had been rushed through the Dáil, and the government's U-turn.

I was honest. 'I don't actually understand it,' I said.

I told them I was finding it difficult to follow precisely what was happening, what was being proposed. But I did see that people felt very strongly about it, and I felt they should be listened to. I told them there were people better equipped than me to discuss that issue. But I was very happy to come on and discuss what had happened so far in relation to the Tuam babies.

I went on the programme. It was easier this time without the studio audience. I found it less nerve-wracking when it was just me and Ryan. He asked me some questions about progress on the report and what would happen next.

I told him that it was a basic human right for people to know their identity and that it was very important that the files relating to people's personal data be handed over to them. They deserved to know who they were.

'That's all they want, they just want information. Identity is a huge thing with them . . . to know their identity, to know where their mothers went, to know was she alright, to know how she fared out in life,' I said.

It really shouldn't be too much to ask.

As the interview drew to a close, Ryan thanked me for my work to date.

People were always very kind in their praise of me, because of the research I had done on the Tuam babies. It made me feel awkward. What I and many others who had been campaigning on behalf of the Tuam babies and survivors of other mother and baby homes had done was nothing compared to those who had been through that awful regime. It was they who deserved the praise, not me.

The show paid tribute to all those who had gone through mother and baby homes in this country, with a performance by singer Niamh Farrell. It was a song I hadn't heard before, by Kate Bush, called 'This Woman's Work'. It was beautiful.

I listened to the words of the song. I thought of Bridget, who dressed her little girl in a special outfit for her first birthday, before they took her child from her. She never even had the chance to say goodbye. I thought of all the pain she must have carried, for the rest of her life.

I thought of P.J.'s mother, banging on the door of the home, begging for her son back.

I thought of all the women and children whose lives were torn apart. Mother and child separated. I could think of nothing worse.

The lyrics echoed through the empty studio. Words of pain and regret, of moments lost between people, of words not said and time that they could never get back.

A few weeks later, news came through that the report had been given to the minister. This was a huge step forward. It would also be sent to the attorney general to read through, which was due process, and then the plan was for it to be published so that the public would have access to it before Christmas.

I could hardly believe that we were just weeks away from finally seeing what the commission's findings were. A piece of work that had been years in the making.

Aidan was feeling very tired, worn out from the chemo. But he was faring well, thankfully. We were all so grateful for that. It was very important that we isolate ourselves, the doctors told us. We had to remain vigilant against Covid-19 as Aidan's immune system was weakened by the chemo.

We were both missing the kids and the grandkids. Christmas would be very different this year. But it was different for everyone all around the world. We knew that. The best thing we could do was follow the rules and try to keep everyone safe.

We decided to stay in Dublin. Aidan was exhausted after his treatment. He wasn't able for the long drive home. We put up the Christmas lights and tried to decorate the place as best we could. We would be spending Christmas alone this year – for the first time since Adrienne was born. How strange to think that the people we loved most in the world – our kids and grandkids – were the people we were being told to stay away from.

Alan had forwarded our post.

I went through the letters as Aidan rested in the bedroom. A few bills, and administrative bits from the hospital, and an envelope with handwriting I didn't recognise. Inside was a card with a note that read: 'Dear Catherine, Thank you. You will never know what your family has done for our family.'

It was signed, 'Mary from Dublin'.

It was like a little gift from the universe. I didn't know who Mary from Dublin was or why or how our lives had interacted. And though she was thanking me, in that moment it was me who needed to thank her. 'Thank you, Mary,' I whispered.

Somehow messages from people always seemed to arrive just when I needed them most. I had been starting to feel weighed down by it all: I was on edge, nervously waiting to see how Aidan would cope with his chemo sessions while also awaiting news of the report. Mary's message reminded me that it was all worthwhile. That this was not about reports or legislation or Dáil debates. All that was red tape and bureaucracy. This was about Mary and her family and all the other families who were still struggling, to this very day. It was about justice for them, and we couldn't stop until that had been achieved. Not promises, not lip service, but real, meaningful action.

Mary's letter gave me a new lease of life, a surge of energy.

I popped my head into the bedroom. Aidan was sleeping. I signalled to Shadow and fetched his lead. He followed me out the door and we walked the streets in the cold December air. I breathed it in and let out a sigh. A mother with a pram passed me. I looked at her little bundle all wrapped up, cosy in her pram.

The mother spotted me looking at the baby. She gave me a subtle smile, and I smiled back. I felt she knew I was remembering my own children at that age. There's a language between mothers that other people don't speak. An understanding. We may be strangers, but we both know that deep love of our children, that inexplicable deep love. That's what we were talking about when we smiled at one another.

It reminded me again what this fight was all about.

My walks around the canal were keeping me going. Shadow needed the daily exercise, and so did I. It was a chance to clear my head, as I watched the swans gliding along the water amid the rushes.

I took solace in those moments of peace because I knew that a lot was about to happen. Once the report was published, we would be inundated once again with press. I was worried I wouldn't know what to say. The report was 3,000 pages long. There was no way I would have a chance to read it before the press were in touch. How would we know how to respond? Whether it was good or bad? Surely we needed to read it in its entirety.

We had been told the report would be out before Christmas, so every day that passed, I wondered if an announcement was about to be made.

Then one afternoon, I received a call from an unknown number.

'Hello?' I answered, as I was approaching the canal.

It was Minister Roderic O'Gorman.

I was taken aback. He told me he was ringing to update me on the delayed release of the report. Delayed again, I thought to myself. I asked him when he believed it would be publicly available. He explained that it was now with the attorney general for review. That it wouldn't be released this side of Christmas. Mid-January was the goal, and he was confident, he told me, that that would be achieved. I was both relieved and concerned at the same time. I had been waiting with trepidation for it to be released any day. At least now there was some sense of a timeline. I reminded the minister that, for me, the most important thing was the exhumation and reburial of the babies in a dignified manner. He assured me that he was working on the legislation to make that a reality. I thanked him for his call. I liked dealing with him. He was always very considerate. I felt he was trying his best to do the right thing.

It must be strange, I thought to myself, to be suddenly handed responsibility for a department like that. One morning you're Roderic, the next you're the minister for children and youth affairs, and all that that entails. It was a lot to take on. But it was the life politicians chose, I concluded.

I wondered what was in the report and what the government would do about its findings. Finally, we were on the cusp of some kind of meaningful change. Or so I hoped.

CHAPTER SEVENTY-SEVEN

Everyone and No one

⌒

It was Sunday, 10 January. The report was due to be published in two days' time. I got a call from a journalist. 'What is your reaction to the leaking of the report today?' he asked me.

'What leak?' I said.

'Oh,' he said, 'you didn't know?'

'No . . .' I said.

'It's been leaked to the *Sunday Independent*. It's on the front page.'

Not again! I thought to myself.

I told him I knew nothing about it. When the call ended, Aidan and I went to the local shops. I walked in the door, and sure enough, there on the newspaper rack was a photograph of me, with a headline about the report's findings. I picked it up, sheepishly, and placed it on the counter, face down, so as not to draw attention to it.

To my relief, there wasn't that much of the report in the newspaper. It simply outlined the top line – that 56,000 women were believed to have gone through the mother and baby homes in

Ireland and that 9,000 of the 57,000 children born there were believed to have died in the care of the homes.

But it was the principle of the matter. The survivors were once again betrayed by a government that was supposed to protect and serve them. Not for the first time, someone else had seen the material first. I remembered back to the day the issue of DNA testing had been leaked, when Katherine Zappone had been the minister for children.

How was it possible that the media came into possession of this information? Was it someone slipping them that information under the radar or was it a government strategy, to control the narrative before the media received the report themselves? A way of getting the word out there before anyone had a chance to analyse it and come to their own conclusions?

The minister was quick to condemn the leak, and announced that there would be a full investigation into how and why it had happened. Things were not off to a good start.

Two days later, it was time for the report to be released. I looked at the date on the calendar that hung on the wall – 12 January 2021. Ten years had passed since I had first begun my research for the essay.

The government had organised a webinar for the survivors ahead of the report's publication, so that they would be the first to know what it contained. I had been sent an invitation by email. The webinar was to be held at 1.30 p.m. In the webinar, they would brief us on the report's findings and recommendations.

At 3 p.m. the report would be published for all the world to see. Available to download on the government website. Which meant that we would have just over an hour to digest what had been said.

I tuned in, anxiously. Minister O'Gorman and the taoiseach, Micheál Martin, sat at a very official-looking table. The camera turned to the taoiseach first to make a short statement. Then over to Roderic O'Gorman to go through the report's findings. Over 500 people had tuned in, they told us.

I imagined all the survivors I knew, tuning in at home. Some of them no doubt had sat with members of the commission and told their stories. Harrowing stories of neglect. Of abuse. Of a trauma that stayed with them all their lives – the separation of mother and child. And now here they were, ready to hear the verdict. How had the commission judged their experience? What was the outcome of all this pain and hurt?

It had all amounted to this. A document being summarised, the findings spelled out in that cold room as the minister outlined the main findings of the report.

Five minutes into their summarised account, I knew this was not what we had hoped for. What they delivered was a well-thought-out summary in which we realised that it was us, society, that should bear the brunt of the blame. There was a heavy emphasis, repeated regularly, that it was the families who abandoned their pregnant unwed daughters to these homes, their only refuge at the time. By the end of the webinar, about 20 minutes later, I was in shock, in a state of disbelief, and totally deflated. They had outlined the recommendations of the report, 22 in total, but it was all quite hard to follow. They spoke of educating people about what had happened in mother and baby homes and memorialising the experience of survivors in a way that survivors felt appropriate; they spoke about access to birth records and, lastly, about some kind of reparation for the survivors. But it was all very top-level, no detail, all quite vague and nothing we hadn't heard before.

It all felt very one-sided. There was no opportunity for the survivors to speak, or to react in any way. They could only ask questions via some technical route on the computer, through a process that neither I nor many others, I dare say, would have the know-how to manage. So that wasn't much use to any of us. Four questions were read out – chosen by government staff. A mealy-mouthed attempt at 'responding to survivors' questions'. The questions related to the logistical points of where to access the report and other such trivial things.

Aidan was listening in from the front room. The moment the webinar was finished, he burst in to the kitchen, where I was still staring at the screen. He threw his hands in the air. 'What the fuck was that all about?'

That brought me back to my senses and I was comforted to know he felt the same way. It sort of validated my despair. We talked it through, and the words that kept coming up were: whitewash, waffle, spin doctors. How could they do this? I felt so angry.

The report was published half an hour later. I went to the government website immediately to download it.

We had the radio on in the background. We turned up the volume for the three o'clock news bulletin. It gave a synopsis of the now published report, which had more or less the same tone as what we had heard in the webinar. Already, from early morning, there were phone interviews lined up, where I would have to give my thoughts on the report. I felt a pressure rising, as I had no way of knowing what was contained within this enormous 3,000-page document.

Aidan and Alan had been at my side all day to help out. I had been preparing mentally for this, hoping it would be a positive outcome after such a long fight for the truth. Now, I was dreading the interviews because I didn't know what to say. I felt defeated. BBC Radio Ulster were the first to call. I tried to compose myself, to give a comprehensive account of what I thought about the report. All I could say was that from what I knew at this stage,

I was disappointed for the survivors as I felt they had not been vindicated, and I knew they would not be happy with this result. Several had already been in touch with me to let me know their feelings on it.

The interviewer introduced me as Catherine Corless, journalist and historian. That threw me from the outset. I had to correct her. I wasn't a journalist. If the listeners thought that, they might be expecting something else from me. I was just a woman who hadn't even read the report, I had only seen the government synopsis. I wasn't prepared to 'report' on that, much as I felt that's what the government was hoping for. Was all this a structured and well-thought-out way of controlling the narrative? Why did it always come back to control? Surely the survivors' lives had been controlled enough already.

I got through the interview anyway, after a shaky start. The moment I was finished, Aidan handed me the hands-free house phone. He told me that Pat McGrath from RTÉ news was at the Tuam site and wanted to talk to me. I took the phone, though I felt I was in a kind of a dream. How was a person supposed to comment on a 3,000-page report moments after it has been made public? Apart from the commission, the minister and the attorney general, all any of us knew was what we had been told, second-hand, by a careful PR team.

Pat said he was sending out a cameraman to get my views for the news bulletin. At that stage I wanted to just run away, up into the fields, with Shadow at my heels. But again, Aidan was there for me. He handed me a strong cup of tea to calm my nerves and reminded me that I still needed to speak for the survivors. Thankfully, this interview was to be a recording, rather than a live piece. It took about four or five takes as I tried to piece the right words together. Then it was back into the house for more phone calls.

From the moment the report was published, the phone was

ringing continually with journalists looking for a reaction. I tried as best I could, but I knew about as much as they did at that point, if not less.

I was invited to speak on RTÉ radio. I told the interviewer that the taoiseach and the minister for children had held a webinar to present a synopsis of the findings of the report. They had mentioned a lot of statistics, things we probably knew already, I said. They had made reference to the testimonies in the report, but the survivors knew their own stories, I continued, so there was nothing new in that. I wanted to know if the report would contain anything meaningful that we didn't already know. I hoped it would be investigative and informative.

In the webinar, they hadn't mentioned anything to do with illegal adoptions or what had happened regarding all the deaths – is the full report going to show why so many people died and why they were buried in this manner, I asked, and who was responsible for discarding little toddlers in a sewage tank. I posed the questions, because we still did not know the answers, as none of us had yet had a chance to read the report.

These were questions we had been asking ever since the commission of investigation began. I had hoped that, armed with the necessary resources, and time – so much time – the commission would come back with a complete exposé of what had happened. And that, as an independent body, it would have the gravitas to call for action and justice. So far, these things didn't seem to have happened.

We would like an apology from the religious institutions, I emphasised in the interview. A lot of blame has been put on society, I said, and that was hurtful. The government is taking responsibility, but it's not going far enough. The cruelty and neglect and why so many died – that hadn't been brought into the webinar at all.

The minister had mentioned legislation needed in order to exhume, and had said that he hoped to have that by the end of the year. We had waited three years already and now another year had been added on. That legislation was meant to be passed a long time ago. Why was it taking another year? What needed to happen that could possibly take a year, I asked. From the start of the pandemic we had seen how quickly legislation could be passed, overnight if necessary as the government had quickly passed emergency Covid legislation through the Dáil. So why did this issue always get kicked down the road? I was getting it all off my chest.

The slow rate of progress in relation to the legislation led me to think that the 22 different recommendations made by the commission, if they were to be acted upon by the government, were going to be put on the very long finger too.

Then there was the issue of the apology. They asked for my thoughts on that. I said I hoped the apology from the taoiseach would be from the heart and that it would be a proper apology. But that an apology from the state was not enough. The religious and the church must apologise too. That is what was needed to move forward, I reminded them.

A lot of survivors were very upset by the commission's report, which emphasised that society was primarily to blame. Many of the survivors were completely deflated by the whole thing. They had been hoping that at long last they were going to get the acknowledgement they deserved. They needed an apology from those at whose hands they had suffered. In addition, the report hadn't covered all the institutions that existed – there were a number of county homes that had not been included. The problem was even greater than the remit of the report.

I said that in my opinion the government needed to communicate more with the survivors, because after the webinar everyone was confused and upset.

In every interview I emphasised that survivors would never have any peace unless there was an apology from the religious orders. This was still missing. People could now read the testimonies of the women and children who had gone through the mother and baby homes. They could see for themselves the pain and trauma that was endured in those institutions. But all that was meaningless if there was no apology.

At the press conference following the release of the report, journalists asked the taoiseach and the minister if they felt that an apology should be forthcoming from the religious orders. They sidestepped the question, before admitting that it would be appropriate for the religious orders to contribute financially. The minister also confirmed that he had written to the religious orders involved following the publication of the report and had asked if they would be prepared to meet with him to discuss the issue.

But the main thread emanating from the press conference was that this was a broader issue in which society as a whole was complicit. Suddenly I felt the familiar pang of Catholic guilt come over me. This wasn't what I should be feeling, I knew that. So why was this whole performance from the government making me, and everyone else, feel guilty for what happened, rather than making people feel that it was the powerful institutions that ran the country and controlled its people who were to blame. After all, what is a society if not the reflection of those who govern and control it – in this case the government and the Catholic Church.

After several more interviews I had to prepare myself for the most difficult one, a live piece for the Six One television news on RTÉ, where I would speak to the host, David McCullagh. I was terrified at the thought.

The camera crew set everything up. I stood outside the house, as no one could come inside because of the Covid restrictions.

There was a bright light shining on me. I squinted and tried to compose myself. It was time for the interview to begin. The cameraman counted me down, then pointed to indicate that we were live on air. I could hear David McCullagh through my earphones, though I couldn't see him. I tried my best to answer his questions, but I lost my train of thought for a few seconds mid-answer. I tripped over my words and came to a stop mid-sentence.

'I'm sorry,' I said, 'I'm just a bit exhausted after the day.'

I tried to compose myself and pick up where I'd left off. I talked of how the survivors felt disappointed. They had been let down again, because, although the taoiseach had taken responsibility on behalf of the state, the emphasis on society being to blame had been particularly hurtful to the survivors. What they had wanted was an apology and an acknowledgement of what they had been through. And somehow it still felt as though church and state were hand in glove. We had expected a bit more from today, I explained.

After the interview, I went inside to Aidan and Alan, who had been watching on the television in the sitting room. I just wanted to curl up. I was so embarrassed.

'Oh God,' I said. 'Did you see it?'

I put my head in my hands. I felt like I had let everyone down. Every opportunity and platform to speak out for the babies mattered. I always felt a weight of responsibility – that somehow, through some twist of fate, I had become one of the spokespeople for such an important cause. I was always wary of that role because I had not been through a mother and baby home myself, and never wanted to seem as though I spoke for the people who had, because I didn't speak for them. I wasn't one of them, but I cared deeply about them and whatever I could do to further the quest for truth and justice, I was willing and ready to do.

I felt I had to do it, for the sake of the babies who had died. They had no voice. It was a responsibility I took very seriously. I just couldn't believe I had scuppered such an important interview. I was so shaken from the experience. Aidan and Alan sat me down. They reassured me that it had gone much better than I thought it had.

'You said everything that needed saying,' Aidan said.

'Are you sure?' I asked. 'What about when I lost my train of thought?'

'That was just for a second,' Alan said, 'and you picked it up again very quickly.'

I had to trust what they were saying. They were always honest with me, so I felt they would have told me if they thought it had gone very badly. To me, a second had felt like an eternity on live television.

I was worried that people would feel I had let them down. But Aidan reassured me by showing me the Twitter and Facebook comments full of good wishes, thanking me for the work I had done over the years, many of whom were expressing concern for my health and wellbeing, realising that it was all very taxing and exhausting.

At seven o'clock that evening my mobile rang. It was a number I didn't recognise.

'Hi, Catherine, Ryan Tubridy here. How are you?'

He had watched the evening news and had seen how frustrated and weary I looked. He said he was calling to see how I was and to remind me of the enormous good I had done for Ireland in bringing this tragedy out into the open. He talked about what this would mean to the younger generation of Irish people, that he often spoke to his own daughters about Ireland's dark history. I really appreciated everything he was saying. He told me that I should hold my head high, no matter how the report had stated its findings. That really meant a lot to me. It's what I needed in that moment. I thanked him profusely for his kindness and also for giving me a platform on several occasions on *The Late Late Show* to promote the cause of the Tuam babies.

I didn't sleep much that night. My mind was racing and I felt a deep sense of unease. I had hoped the report would bring closure, but instead it had thrown up old wounds for everyone involved. The next morning, at exactly 10.50, things finally took a turn for the better.

CHAPTER SEVENTY-EIGHT

Sorry, Forgive Me

W e were in the kitchen, talking, when Alan came bursting in.

'Sssshhhh,' he said, rushing over to turn up the volume on the radio. 'An apology from the Bon Secours!'

I couldn't believe it. We sat, rooted to the spot, listening carefully as their apology was read out. It was a four-point apology and acknowledgement for the way they had treated women and children, and – for me, most importantly – for the way the babies were buried.

Their statement said that the commission of inquiry report 'presents a history of our country in which many women and children were rejected, silenced and excluded; in which they were subjected to hardship; and in which their inherent human dignity was disrespected, in life and in death. Our Sisters of Bon Secours were part of this sorrowful history.'

Speaking about the women and children who went through the Tuam mother and baby home, they said, 'Our Sisters ran St Mary's Mother and Baby Home in Tuam from 1925 to 1961. We did not live up to our Christianity when running the Home. We failed to offer them the compassion that they so badly needed. We were part of the system in which they suffered hardship, loneliness and terrible hurt. We acknowledge in particular that infants and children who died at the Home were buried in a disrespectful and unacceptable way. For all that, we are deeply sorry.'

The statement went on to say: 'We offer our profound apologies to all the women and children of St Mary's mother and baby home, to their families and to the people of this country. Healing is not possible until what happened is acknowledged. We hope and we pray that healing will come to all those affected; those who are living and those who have died. We hope that we, our church and our country can learn from this history.'

We stood in disbelief, then hugged one another. This is what we had all been fighting for, for so long. This meant everything.

I was contacted by *Today with Claire Byrne*, *The Ray D'Arcy Show*, *Drivetime*, and RTÉ Radio 1 news, all looking for my reaction. Finally, I felt we had some sense of victory – something to be thankful for.

After ten years of beseeching them, finally the Bon Secours sisters had said sorry. It was monumental. They were acknowledging the critical part they had to play in everything. I thought of the day in 2014 when I met the nuns in the hotel outside Galway. Now, seven years later, the religious order was finally owning up and taking responsibility for what had happened. I was delighted.

Meanwhile, there was controversy brewing over the taoiseach's apology, scheduled for later that day. Many of the survivors were calling on him to delay his apology, to wait until they had had a chance to read the report, so that they would know exactly what he was apologising for. That mattered, they said. It was all happening too fast and they had not had a chance to read what had been written and published about their lives, about their experiences. They also called for the taoiseach not just to say sorry, but to ask for forgiveness from the survivors. There was a difference.

As Archbishop Diarmuid Martin said in his interview with RTÉ, saying sorry is easy, like when you bump into someone in the street and you say sorry. But asking forgiveness puts the power back in the other person's hands. It was a nuance I had never really considered before.

I watched as Taoiseach Micheál Martin rose to his feet, his speech in hand. The country was waiting to hear what he had to say, on behalf of his government, on behalf of all Irish governments.

He began: 'It is the duty of a republic to be willing to hold itself to account. To be willing to confront hard truths – and accept parts of our history which are deeply uncomfortable. This detailed and highly painful report is a moment for us as a society to recognise a profound failure of empathy, understanding and basic humanity over a very lengthy period.'

He acknowledged the bravery of the people who had stepped forward and given their testimonies to the commission. He also thanked me for my work – uncovering what had happened in Tuam, which he said directly led to the commission of inquiry. He also thanked the commission team for all their hard work.

'They have produced the definitive account of how this country responded to the particular needs of single women and their children at a time when they most needed support and protection. This should have been forthcoming from the fathers of their children, their family and friends, their community and their State, but so often it was not.'

He went on to say a great many things – talking about the

experiences of the women and children who went through those institutions, apologising on behalf of the government and promising action under four main pillars: recognition, remembrance, records, and restorative recognition.

The tánaiste and former taoiseach, Leo Varadkar, then stood up to make his speech. He apologised too, then asked for forgiveness from the survivors. It was what so many survivors wanted. Then followed a speech and apology from the minister for children, Roderic O'Gorman, who also asked for forgiveness from the survivors.

Then the floor was open to members of the Dáil to put forward their questions or statements on the matter. Several of them spoke very passionately, but Galway independent TD Catherine Connolly's speech was the most impressive of all.

She reminded the Dáil that this was not the first time we were seeing a report of this kind, of pain and suffering from a religious institution.

'I welcome the Taoiseach's apology,' she said, 'but I will place it in perspective. I will deal with 21 years very quickly. In 1999, we had an apology from Bertie Ahern for the treatment of 15,000 to 20,000 children in industrial schools, reformatory schools and what were called orphanages. I am only picking some of the reports across those 21 years. That apology was followed by the Ferns report in 2005 and the Ryan report in 2009, which found that sexual abuse was endemic in industrial and reformatory schools for boys. Girls and boys suffered emotional abuse on a great scale. In 2009, we had the Murphy report; in 2011, we had the Cloyne report; and in 2013, we had the Magdalene report of an interdepartmental committee, followed by a review under Mr Justice Quirke and the establishment of an ex gratia scheme, which was subsequently found by the Ombudsman to have been maladministered. We then set up Caranua. It was appalling to name it that and call it a 'new friend' when it was really the old enemy in disguise. This was followed in 2017 by a technical report on the Tuam site, since which nothing has happened.'

She was making the point that there was very little action following on from report after report of abuse and injustice. She also questioned the narrative of the report.

'The story jumps off the pages – the role of the church, the priest and the county council,' she said. 'Indeed, the Tuam home distinguishes itself by being one of the worst in the country, and although the county council was not actively involved, the home was under its control . . . There was even a policy there whereby if the woman got pregnant a second time, she was destined for the Magdalene laundry, not the mother and baby home. Can the Taoiseach imagine that?"

She continued: '. . .The women tell a story in this report of rape and sexual assault. Nearly 12% of the women in the homes were under 18 years of age. Some were as young as 12. However, the commission found that there was no evidence that they were forced by the church or the State. It is incomprehensible to draw that conclusion or the many other conclusions I have great difficulty with based on the testimonies of the women when they told their stories. The priest jumps off the page. Solicitors jump off the page. GPs who phoned the doctors and priests jump off the page. Some of the sexual abuse was carried out by family members, including cousins and uncles, and priests. All of that is set out in this report, but according to the commission's conclusions, there was no evidence of compulsion. Either we believe the women or we do not. If we do not, then we are adding to their hurt and their fear that they would not be believed. I will use my few minutes in this debate to say that I absolutely believe the survivors who have come forward despite these difficult memories. The commission tells us that there was no evidence of compulsion or forced adoption. All of the evidence given confirms there was.'

Deputy Connolly went on to question the 'spin' surrounding the report.

'If something bad was said, the narrative sought to balance it by finishing on a positive note. I find the whole narrative repulsive. What I do not find repulsive are the stories of the women, which I have read and with which I was familiar. The spin continues as regards the way this report was undertaken. That spin came from the then Taoiseach in 2017, which the current Taoiseach is continuing with today. The then Taoiseach stated that the nuns and priests did not come in the middle of the night and take our children. They did on some occasions, but not often because what happened was far more subtle and controlled than that. The powers that be were the church, with politicians playing a subservient role. I will use the county council in Galway as an example because it jumps off the pages. It held its meetings in the home. The absence of records and the appalling mortality rate were known at the time, but the Taoiseach is saying now that we are all responsible. I am not responsible. My family is not responsible. The people I know are not responsible. Those least responsible were those put into the homes. The Taoiseach should not stand here today and expect me to listen to him with patience when he tells us that society did that. It was done by a society composed of the powerful against the powerless.'

Her speech seemed to articulate what so many of us were feeling.

There were impassioned speeches from other TDs too, with People Before Profit/Solidarity TD Mick Barry pointing out that 'this was the Ireland that was presided over by the men whose pictures hang on the walls of the taoiseach and tánaiste. It was the Ireland of Éamon de Valera, Seán Lemass, Jack Lynch and

Charlie Haughey. The Ireland of W.T. Cosgrave, John A. Costello, Liam Cosgrave, Garret FitzGerald and John Bruton'.

This issue had spanned many governments. In some ways it was not shocking to learn that for the first 50 years after independence, while children continued to die in huge numbers in mother and baby homes and women were subjected to vilification and went through the torture of being in those institutions and having their children taken from them, and were ostracised from their communities, not *once* was the subject raised at cabinet. Not once in 50 years. That says a lot. Even though the Tuam home was owned by local government and they sometimes held their meetings there. And yet still the silence was allowed to continue.

Somehow, the manner in which the whole system was set up – with local government involved, along with the religious institutions and the health board – meant that no one was held responsible. It was a convenient system, especially when dealing with some of the most vulnerable people in society.

Next followed an apology from the archbishop of Tuam, Michael Neary. Another line in the sand.

Then came the question – now that they had said they were sorry, were the Bon Secours actually going to contribute financially in any way to the redress or the reburial? Was it just an apology they were offering, or was there a practical contribution as well?

The media must have pressed them on it, because a few hours later, the order confirmed that they would be willing to participate in any redress scheme set up in response to the report. I was delighted with this. It was progress. After all, they could afford it. The Bon Secours was one of the richest religious orders in the country and owned several private hospitals. But I was dubious too.

When we had met with Minister O'Gorman in September 2020, he had told us that no contribution to the government had been made by the Bon Secours sisters to date, although they had committed to donating 2.5 million euro to the excavation of the Tuam site back in 2018. It was said at the time that it was a voluntary contribution and not a settlement or indemnity. But yet here we were two years later, and no money, it seems, had been forthcoming.

I had seen how some of the other religious orders in Ireland had refused to contribute to reparations for the survivors of Magdalene laundries several years before this.

I had very little faith in promises anymore.

CHAPTER SEVENTY-NINE

When Everyone Is To Blame . . .

The report said there was 'no evidence of the sort of gross abuse that existed in the industrial schools.' This was the most offensive part of the final report, to say that there was no abuse. Worse still, it seemed to have been benchmarked against the violent abuse that had taken place in the industrial schools, contained in the Ryan report. I can only presume they were reporting along the lines that there was no evidence of broken bones, sexual assault, no admittance to hospital with bodily harm. It was as if the constant misery, bodies covered in rash, chilblains, boils, and toddlers with swollen stomachs from hunger did not matter. There was evidence of this, in the testimonies of mothers and survivors who attended the commission of inquiry, and also from an inspectors' report from 1947 to the Tuam home, a copy of which I personally gave to the commission. That line in particular made me furious. It belittled the whole experience the women and children had endured, in my opinion.

The executive summary of the report was extensive, but what

jumped out at me were the numbers involved. You could try to whitewash everything else, but numbers don't lie.

The report stated that 'there were about 56,000 unmarried mothers and about 57,000 children in the mother and baby homes and county homes investigated by the Commission'. But the report also conceded that the estimated numbers were actually much higher: '. . . it is likely that there were a further 25,000 unmarried mothers and a larger number of children in the county homes which were not investigated'. The commission had only looked at a certain number of homes within the scope and remit of its inquiry.

Some 9,000 children died in these institutions (the ones under investigation by the commission), accounting for about 15 per cent of the children who were in those institutions.

The report went on to say that 'the very high rate of infant mortality (first year of life) in Irish mother and baby homes is probably the most disquieting feature of these institutions. The death rate among "illegitimate" children was always considerably higher than that among "legitimate" children but it was higher still in mother and baby homes: in the years 1945–46, the death rate among infants in mother and baby homes was almost twice that of the national average for "illegitimate" children.' The conclusion being that although the homes were intended to be a refuge for mother and child, 'in the years before 1960 mother and baby homes did not save the lives of "illegitimate" children; in fact, they appear to have significantly reduced their prospects of survival'. The very high mortality rates were known to local and national authorities at the time and were recorded in official publications.

From the outset, the report laid a great deal of the responsibility on the fathers of the children and the family of the mother, saying that society in general was to blame for what befell these women and children: 'Ireland was a cold, harsh environment for many, probably the majority, of its residents during the earlier half of the period under remit. It was especially cold and harsh for women. All women suffered serious discrimination. Women who gave birth outside marriage were subject to particularly harsh treatment. Responsibility for that harsh treatment rests mainly with the fathers of their children and their own immediate families. It was supported by, contributed to, and condoned by the institutions of the State and the Churches. However, it must be acknowledged that the institutions under investigation provided a refuge – a harsh refuge in some cases – when the families provided no refuge at all.'

Compared to other countries, Ireland seemed to have a particularly bad record in terms of incarcerating women and children in this manner, as the report outlines that 'while mother and baby homes were not a peculiarly Irish phenomenon, the proportion of Irish unmarried mothers who were admitted to mother and baby homes or county homes in the twentieth century was probably the highest in the world'.

The age the women were when they entered the home ranged 'from 12 years old to women in their forties. However, 80% were aged between 18 and 29 years and this was remarkably consistent across the larger mother and baby homes.'

Though Ireland was an impoverished country, the main differentiating factor for these women and children was the issue of marriage, according to the report, which looked at why women ended up in the mother and baby homes in the first place: 'Some pregnancies were the result of rape; some women had mental health problems, some had an intellectual disability. However, the majority were indistinguishable from most Irish women of their time. The only difference between the women in mother and baby homes and their sisters, class-mates and work companions was that they became pregnant while unmarried. Their lives were blighted by pregnancy outside marriage, and the responses of the father of their child, their immediate families and the wider community.'

And this is the narrative the government was running with. But somehow, when everyone is to blame, it seems no one is to blame.

CHAPTER EIGHTY

Testimony

❧

P arts of the chapter on the Tuam home was like something
from a fairy tale. The report painted a picture of a loving
home, with flowers adorning the gardens, swings and see-saws,
and theatrical plays at Christmas; of well-fed children and love
and care from those who tended to them. This is not the picture
of Tuam I have come to know through my years of research.

Looking closely at some of the survivors' experiences highlighted in the report, I could see how such a picture might emerge.
In one example, the inquiry seemed to have used what I can only
presume is the testimony of Fr Paul Churchill and his sibling,
who speak of the impression of the Tuam home they got from
their father Paddy Churchill, who was there from 1925 to 1936
– that the nuns were so kind to him and that he was allowed to
serve mass and was in the cathedral choir, and that the food was
good and plentiful, and that he had toys at Christmas. What it
didn't say was that Paddy, in 1937, was sent to a better-class
Dublin orphanage where boys were well educated, and this was
arranged by the archbishop's secretary, Fr Fergus, who had even

travelled to the orphanage to make a special plea on Paddy's behalf, because this school was specifically for orphans only, not for illegitimate boys. Some stroke was pulled and Paddy was admitted. I ask the question: Why the special privilege?

Also singled out in the report's findings on Tuam were two girls, whom I suspect I know of, who also received special treatment in the home. One was a niece of one of the nuns, the other was born to the daughter of a very wealthy family in Galway. These were the girls who were allowed to take part in the *feise-anna* in Tuam and allowed to call to their school friends' houses. They were also given a better education, and were sent to secondary school. Their experience was very different to that of P.J. Haverty, Peter Mulryan, Tom Warde, Anne Silke, Carmel Smith, and many of the other survivors, who were adamant that even when fostered out to families, they were still victims of stigma and were not even allowed to serve mass in their communities, for example, because of their background.

That is not to say that the commission should have omitted positive testimonies about the home. I really do not think that. I am glad that both positive and negative testimonies exist and that everyone has a right to be heard, but what does bother me greatly is that it seems to me that these positive reports were given prominence over the negative. The glowing reports about the Tuam home far outweighed the two-hour-long testimonies that were given by numerous Tuam home survivors, many of whom I know personally. On page 54, for example, just three-and-a-bit lines were given to a woman of my acquaintance, whereas the *Irish Independent* devoted a full page to her ill-treatment, back in 2017.

Another part of the report which irked me was an account from Fr Fintan Monahan which referred to 'funerals' being part of the church's pastoral role at the Tuam home. Funerals? I thought to myself. If only the children that had been found in the sewage tank had been given funerals. That's all I ever wanted for them.

Then there is an account from a Fr Waldron, archivist, reiterating Fr Monahan's statement that the church had no micro-management of the home, and that the home was separated from the diocese. Yet if you go to the executive summary of the report, when the health board was going to transfer the mothers and babies to the outskirts of Galway (Merlin Park hospital grounds), the Archbishop of Tuam lashed out, declaring that it was 'undesirable in every way. Anyone who has experience of the workings of a Home for unmarried mothers will tell you that such a Home must be in a place that is quiet, remote and surrounded by high boundary walls. It is most difficult to deal with unmarried mothers. In many cases they are on the lookout to get in touch with men, and some of them cannot repress their excitement even when a man comes to the Home to deliver a message . . . Many of these unmarried mothers are anxious to get off without delay. The only thing that prevents their leaving is the strict supervision and boundary walls . . . in some cases it has been known that attempts were made from outside to get at the inmates.'

This shows the extent of the church's involvement in the decisions around what would happen to these women and children and what was being propagated about them. And the taoiseach claims that it was the families who put their daughters away? We really must question that. And we must remember too that this all happened not so long ago. The archbishop made that statement in 1959 and he was still around for my own confirmation in 1966. This is how recent all this is. This is how real and raw it is, to so many people.

One of the testimonies included was I story I knew well. The report talks of a man whose mother walked to the Tuam home for years in the hope of seeing her son. Speaking of his time in the institution he says, 'I was born twice. I was born in a prison first and I spent six-and-a-half years in it and then I was born a second time in a home where there was love and care'.

The report also included the inspection reports of Miss Alice Litster, who was an inspector with the department of health. For thirty-five years she tried to draw attention to the poor conditions of these institutions and sought improvements in the care for women and children. In her report into Tuam she highlighted the infant death rate and said that it was time to enquire into possible causes of death before the rate became higher.

I thought of her, trying to blow the whistle on these institutions. Seeing the barriers we had come up against in the present day, I could only imagine how difficult this must have been for her back then. Then I came to the part of the report that really hurt me, personally, the part that quoted from Julia Devaney's testimony. I knew that testimony so well. I had read it and listened to it many, many times through the years and had transcribed it word for word. I had given the commission all the recordings and transcripts of it. However, the report concentrated on the one small part of Julia's account of her life in the home that gave a more positive view, rather than the excerpts where she spoke of the pot-bellied toddlers who were not given proper food, even though there was an ample supply of fresh vegetables and fruit from the garden that Julia tended to along with some of the mothers.

They did not mention the mothers that the nuns sent to the Ballinasloe asylum or to the Magdalene laundry, if they gave trouble, or how Julia and the others who remained in the home all their lives (as unpaid servants) had to hide in cupboards when the inspector called, or that these women were told by the nuns that they were keeping post office account books for them in a safe for their work, but that neither Julia nor any of the others ever saw a penny from the nuns in all the time they worked there.

I felt sick to my stomach. I closed my eyes and thought of the photograph of Julia. I thought of all the things she had been through and how much she had given to others during her lifetime. Everyone who knew Julia testifies to her incredible kindness and loving way with children. She seems to have had an impact on so many children during her time in the home. To me, she represented a sliver of love and kindness in what was a cruel world for those children, born into hardship and suffering through no fault of their own.

I was angry that this representation didn't do justice to what Julia had witnessed for all those years in St Mary's. I wasn't sure what to do next. I felt that I had let her down. All the pushing, all the fighting, the quest for answers and for justice, had somehow led to this – this report from the commission of inquiry. It was a chance for Julia's testimony to stand for something, to be counted, to be heard, at last. Instead, I felt that the best bits were cherry-picked. A false reflection of her life.

I felt lost. I didn't know where to go from here. But I knew I had to do something, and I was going to do it for Julia. Her life mattered. Her testimony mattered. I was going to make sure of that.

CHAPTER EIGHTY-ONE

What They Went Through

As I read through more of the report, I saw that there were
pockets of it that told the real story, accounts from different
mother and baby homes around Ireland.

The report confirmed that children in mother and baby homes
were used in experimental vaccine trials, and that these went
ahead without the consent of the mother or the child's guardian.
This, to me, epitomised how badly these children were treated,
seen as nothing but guinea pigs to be experimented on. There is
something utterly frightening about this concept, and it is in itself
an affront to basic human rights.

Another part of the report jumped out at me, as it spoke of
the trauma of the mother, becoming pregnant in the first instance,
and then having to give her child away.

'The Committee heard from many women who were young
(some not even in their teens) when they were placed in mother
and baby homes because of a pregnancy following rape or incest.
In general, these witnesses said to the Committee, that however
young, however badly injured physically or psychologically by

rape or incest a resident was, how she fell pregnant didn't matter. The nuns and nurses in the homes showed very little empathy and understanding and the women were there to atone for their sins.'

The report went on to say: 'A witness told the Committee that she'd had to knit garments for the babies, mentioning that one of the saddest tasks she was given was that of ironing the little dresses for the babies 'to get them ready for when people were coming in to see them'.

And the part that resonated the most was the description of the babies being taken away: 'On top of the treatment they received at the hands of their carers, many mothers told the Committee that their most searing memory of their time in a mother and baby home was that of the screams of women looking through a window, through which she could see her child being driven away to a destination unknown; for many, there had not been a chance to say goodbye.'

How, then, could the report conclude that there were no enforced adoptions, I asked myself. What constitutes an enforced adoption?

It was difficult even to contemplate such a place, where mothers screamed giving birth to their children, where the child cried for the first time as he or she entered the world; then one year later, the mother's screams could be heard echoing through the cold corridors, as her child was taken away from her and the child cries, as they were separated from their mother, forever. All this, under the same roof.

Over the days that followed there were many interviews with women who had been through mother and baby homes, and their children (now adults). Their voices flooded the radio waves and the television screens. I was delighted to see and hear them. They were finally being given a voice.

One of the testimonies will always stay with me. It was a woman who was interviewed on television who had been a mother in one of the homes. She spoke of the heartbreak, every weekend, when they would hear the crunch of gravel outside, as the cars pulled up and out came the 'Sunday shoppers' as they called them – couples coming to view the children, to see which ones they might like to adopt. In an ultimate act of cruelty, the mothers were forced to welcome these strangers in and show them around.

I tried to imagine the sense of panic a mother would have felt if a couple paused and stopped to examine her child, her mind frantically willing them to move on, to pick another child. Any child but her child. The anguish and torture of watching someone taking your child must have been excruciating.

The woman spoke of that animal-like sound, which became all too familiar. That scream that echoed through the corridors. Everyone knew what that meant. Another child taken from a mother who did not even have the chance to say goodbye. She watched from the window as her child was driven away, never to be seen again. Her whole world collapsing in on itself. And she, the mother of the child, who carried them for nine months, birthed them, loved them, and cared for them for the past year, was now powerless to do anything but watch them being taken away, to an unknown place to face an unknown future.

I close my eyes and try to imagine my own children lined up in cots, with strangers looking to take them home, against our will. As a mother, you will always worry about your child, even when they are right under your nose. I cannot imagine the worry that would visit you every moment of every day, knowing that your child was out there, in the world, somewhere, and you did not know if they were being cared for; if they were hungry, happy or sad. I cannot imagine the mental torture that those women endured from that moment on, for the rest of their lives.

Another woman who was interviewed in the media about her experiences in a mother and baby home talked of the indescribable heartache of knowing you could not keep your own child.

'Nobody, unless it happened to them, will ever know what it is like to sit with your baby on your lap knowing you have to hand that child over. It scars you forever. You can't put it into words. It changes you forever in more ways than you can imagine,' she said.

She spoke about the first moment she saw her son: 'For a few moments, after my son came out, he struggled to breathe. In those moments I remember thinking: God, please let him live, even though I can't have him. I could see him from where I lay and I remember thinking he's my son and I'll never be able to keep him. There are no words.'

And then what it was like to give him up: 'I was supposed to stay for six weeks but I started having a breakdown. The night before I left I packed my bags and planned to go and take him out of his cot and leave. But where would I have gone? I had nobody to help me. I made friends with a nice girl who had arrived to have her own baby. They told me I could leave once he was christened. I arranged for her to feed my baby after I left. I made her his godmother and took a few photos.'

And then the most heartbreaking part of all: 'I kept the photo of him in his christening robe under my pillow until I met him 34 years later,' she said.

The heartache these women endured continued for their entire lives. It was the worst kind of pain – a lifelong suffering, and one which they carried in secret, afraid to tell anyone about the child they gave birth to, the one they missed every moment of every day.

CHAPTER EIGHTY-TWO

The Children

⌒

What we had hoped for was a damning report, which showed what women and children in these institutions had endured. What we got was something that seemed to justify what had happened while somehow placing the blame on the families of the women and on wider society.

So where are we now? What we need is decisive action. It is not difficult; it is not complicated.

Give people some compensation for what the state and church put them through.

Give them access to their birth records so they might know who they are and where they come from, and DNA samples of those who passed away so they may be identified.

Bury the children who didn't survive with dignity and respect – in a manner they deserve, a basic human right that was denied them.

That is as complicated as it needs to be. We've had a decade-long fight. We've had the 3,000-page report. We've had all the discussions and debates and grandiose speeches and promises. Now we need action. That is what is missing.

When will those babies be reburied?

When will people get the redress they deserve?

When will they be given their right to know who they are – who their mother was?

It pains me that I still do not have the answers to these very basic requests, and these simple questions. We can empathise with all the stories, say how terrible it was, and isn't it awful, but none of that means anything if it is not followed by action to try to rectify this terrible wrong that was done to so many people under the care of the state and the church.

If we can let this go, what else will we allow to happen to people?

What we have so far is an apology. A simple 'I'm sorry.' It wasn't much to ask for. It took a long time and a lot of pain to get there, and now the survivors have, at least, at the very least, this. And it does mean something. Words matter, at the end of the day. And actions matter.

P.J. Haverty plans to take the nuns' apology to his mother's grave and read it to her – so that she will finally know that they were sorry for what happened to her, for their part in it all. So that she will know that her life mattered, that she mattered, and that her son still loves her, all these years later. That all those times she knocked on the door of the home, begging for her child back, were not in vain because each and every knock was a testament to a mother's love for her child – and is a reminder to him, to this very day, that he had a mother who loved him. But because of external forces, their life together was not to be.

I thought of Peter, still searching for his sister, wondering if she is buried in the sewage tank with all the other babies, or if she is out there, somewhere, living her life in America, not knowing anything of her connection to Tuam and her mother's story. Or that she has a brother who is looking for her, even to this day.

I thought of Martin, and that hat with the feather in it that he placed upon my table. That little piece of his mother which he will treasure, always, and what that hat represents. All the time they did not have together.

I thought of Nora, parked outside her mother's house, hoping that one day they would be reunited.

All these people and so many thousands more are out there right now, living this reality. This is not just a scandal, it is not just a news story or a hot topic. This is their lives. And their lives are this way because of the wrongs that were done to them and to their mothers.

CHAPTER EIGHTY-THREE

Beneath the Playground

After reading the report, I felt an overwhelming urge to be with the babies. To visit them. I parked up at the housing estate and walked through the laneway, towards the site. As I walked across the playground, the swings gently rocked in the wind. The see-saw moved up and down. As if the ghosts of the children lying beneath the playground had come up to play. But there was no laughter. No children's squeals. Just an endless silence.

I looked around. For a moment I could see them, come to life again.

Mary Burke is on the swings. She's three years old. She's propelling herself higher and higher, calling out to Catherine Higgins – an adventurous little girl who is stacking sticks beneath the jungle gym. Catherine is four. Meanwhile little John Forde is coming down the helter-skelter slide. He's scared as he's still a little too small for it. He's only two.

The age they were when they died. The age they remained, frozen in time, lying beneath the ground, beside this cold tarmacadam, a crime scene pretending to be a playground.

Mary would be 68 now, had she lived. John would be 74.

The irony of it all is that little John never saw a slide in his life, nor did Mary ever see a swing. Little Catherine the adventurer never had the chance to pick up sticks and dance beneath the jungle gym. Instead, they lived in an institution. No one taught them how to walk, how to say their name; no one mothered them to sleep at night or knew what made them laugh. No one watched intently as their personalities grew day by day, discovering the world around them. Their mothers likely made to work the laundry and sent away when they were just a year old. And so their mothers never knew they died. Left them in the care of the nuns. Not 'left'. Were forced to go. 'Left' sounds optional, like a choice. There was no choice here.

For every child that was denied its mother's love, and for every mother who was denied the love of her child. There is no greater crime than to separate mother and child. The world is watching. Tonight, as I write this, the Tuam babies are lying there still.

The memory of that dream comes back to me. All of a sudden, I am a little girl again. The ground opens up beside me and there is another little girl in a hole, screaming for help. I grab her hand to pull her out, but instead I fall into the hole as well. Now we are both buried in the ground, screaming to get out, and no one can hear us.

For all the world, any one of those babies could be you or me. We are only as strong as the society we are born into. The people who make up that society, who decide the rules. Who decide who gets to live or die. Who is loved, and who is shamed. We are all responsible for this, every day. The world that we create, that affects every other living creature on this planet.

As long as the Tuam babies are ignored, as long as there is no justice for those babies, for those women, we do not live in a world I want to be a part of. Because if we turn a blind eye to this – to this injustice of the highest order – then what else are we capable of? What other cruelty will we continue to allow?

This isn't the past. This is now. Those babies are there. Their brothers and sisters are still alive. We only have one chance, now, to put this right. If it is not now, then we have failed. We cannot count ourselves as human or humane. Indeed, we are all complicit, if those men and women are not given the answers they deserve within their lifetime. Because there's no going back. Whatever we do now is the story that will be written, for all those people, for all those lives.

I do not know how to end this book, dear reader, because we have not written the end. It has been left hanging, left unanswered, unresolved. And time marches on; with every week and month that passes, we are running out of time.

I stood beside that old stone wall of the mother and baby home and remembered the red-haired girl from school, the one I had played the trick on. I was a red-haired girl and so was she. We had grown up on different sides of the wall, because my parents were married and hers were not.

This is for all the children who lived on the other side of the wall. For at any point in life, that child could be any one of us, or someone we love. Let us not build walls or ignore the ones that stand, but let us continue the fight to take them down, stone by stone, so that the inequality may turn to dust and people may rise and be as one.

I close my eyes and remember that day, as we stood in the playground calling out each child's name, one by one. No longer just a statistic behind an old stone wall.

Who knows what they would have become, who they could

have been in the world, if only they had been given a chance. A chance at life, a chance at love, a chance at all the things that make life beautiful. Instead they lie there, babies, in the ground. Dead and discarded, in the name of a church and a faith that claims to love and care.

To the 798 babies who lived on the other side of the wall, and died in the Bon Secours mother and baby home in Tuam. This book is for each and every one of you.

Names of the Tuam Babies

1925

Patrick Derrane 5 months

Mary Blake 4 months

Matthew Griffin 3 months

Mary Kelly 6 months

Peter Lally 11 months

Julia Hynes 1 year

James Murray 1 month

1926

Patricia Dunne 2 months

John Carty 3 months

Peter McNamara 7 weeks

Mary Shaughnessy
  4½ months

Joseph Coen 5 months

Mary Murphy 2 months

Patrick Kelly 2½ months

Martin Rabbitte 6 weeks

Joseph McWilliam 6 months

John Mullen 3 months

Mary Wade 3 years

Maud McTigue 6 years

Bernard Lynch 3 years

Martin Shaughnessy
  18 months

Bridget Glynn 1 year

Margaret Glynn 1 year

Patrick Gorham 21 months

Patrick O'Connell 1 year

John Carty 21 months

Madeline Bernard 2 years

Maureen Kenny 8 years

Kathleen Donohue 1 year

Thomas Donelan 2 years

Mary Quilan 2 years

Mary King 9 months

Mary Warde 21 months

George Coyne 2 years

Julia Cummins 18 months

Barbara Folan Wallace
  9 months

Pauline Carter 11 months

Mary Walsh 1 year

Annie Stankard 10 months
John Connelly 9 months
Anthony Cooke 1 month
Michael Casey 3 years
Annie McCarron 2 years

Patrick Kelly 2 months
Kathleen Quinn 7 months
Patrick Halpin 2 months
Martin McGuinness 6 months

1927

Mary Kate Connell 3 months
Patrick Raftery 7 months
Patrick Paterson 5 months
James Murray 1 month
Colman O'Loughlin 5 months
Agnes Canavan 18 months
Christina Lynch 15 months
Mary O'Loughlin 6 months

Annie O'Connor 15 months
John Greally 11 months
Joseph Fenigan 4 years
Mary Connolly 2 months
James Muldoon 4 months
Joseph Madden 3 months
Mary Devaney 18 months

1928

Michael Gannon 6 months
Bridget Cunningham
  2 months
Margaret Conneely
  18 months
Patrick Warren 8 months
James Mulryan 1 month
Mary Kate Fahey 3 years

Mary Mahon 1 month
Martin Flanagan 1 month
Mary Forde 4 months
Patrick Hannon 20 months
Michael Donellan 6 months
Joseph Ward 7 months
Walter Jordan 3 years
Mary Mullins 1 month

1929

Peter Christian 7 months
Mary Cunningham 5 months
James Ryan 9 months
Patrick O'Donnell 9 months
Mary Monaghan 4 years

Patrick O'Malley 1 year
Philomena Healy 11 months
Michael Ryan 1 year
Patrick Curran 6 months
Patrick Fahy 2 months

Laurence Molloy 5 months

Patrick Lynskey 6 months

Vincent Nally 21 months

Mary Grady 18 months

Martin Gould 21 months

Patrick Kelly 2 months

1930

Bridget Quinn 1 year

William Reilly 9 months

George Lestrange 7 months

Christy Walshe 15 months

Margaret Mary Gagen 1 year

Patrick Moran 4 months

Celia Healy 5 months

James Quinn 4 years

Bridget Walsh 15 months

1931

Patrick Shiels 4 months

Mary Teresa Drury
 1 year

Peter O'Brien 18 months

Peter Malone 18 months

Carmel Moylan 8 months

Mary Burke 10 months

Mary Josephine Garvey
 5 months

Mary Warde 10 months

Catherine Howley 9 months

Michael Pat McKenna
 3 months

Richard Raftery 3 months

1932

Margaret Doorhy
 8 months

Patrick Leonard 9 months

Mary Coyne 1 year

Mary Kate Walsh 2 years

Christina Burke 1 year

Mary Margaret Jordan
 18 months

John Joseph McCann
 8 months

Teresa McMullan 1 year

George Gavin 1 year

Joseph O'Boyle 2 months

Peter Nash 1 year

Bridget Galvin 3 months

Margaret Niland 3 years

Christina Quinn 3 months

Kathleen Cloran 9 years

Annie Sullivan 8 months

Patricia Judge 1 year

Mary Birmingham 9 months

Laurence Hill 11 months

Brendan Patrick Pender
1 month
Kate Fitzmaurice 4 months

Baby Mulkerrins 5 days
Angela Madden 3 months
Mary McDonagh 1 year

1933

Mary C. Shaughnessy
1 month
Mary Moloney 11 months
Patrick Joseph Brennan
1 month
Anthony O'Toole 2 months
Mary Cloherty 9 days
Joseph Fahy 10 months
Mary Finola Cunniffe
6 months
Martin Cassidy 5 months
Francis Walsh 3 months
Mary Garvey 4 months
Kathleen Gilchrist 8 months
Mary Kate Walsh 1 month
Eileen Fallon 18 months
Harry Leonard 3 years
Mary Kate Guilfoyle
3 months
John Callinan 3 months

John Kilmartin 2 months
Julia Shaughnessy 3 months
Patrick Prendergast
6 months
Bridgid Holland 2 months
Bridgid Moran 15 months
Margaret Mary Fahy
15 months
Bridgid Ryan 9 months
Mary Brennan 4 months
Mary Conole 1 month
John Flattery 2 years
Margaret Donohue
10 months
Joseph Dunn 3 years
Owen Lenane 2 months
Josephine Steed 3 months
Mary Meeneghan
3 months
James McIntyre 4 months

1934

John Joseph Murphy
4 months
Margaret Mary O'Gara
2 months
Eileen Butler 2 months

Thomas Molloy 2 months
James Joseph Bodkin
6 months
John Kelly 2 months
Mary Walshe 6 months

Mary Jo Colohan 4 months
Florence Conneely 7 months
Norah McCann 1 month
Mary Kelly 9 months
Rose O'Dowd 6 months
Mary Egan 4 months
Michael Concannon
  4 months
Paul Joyce 10 months
Mary Christina Kennedy
  4 months
Bridget Finnegan 2 months
Mary Flaherty 3 months

Thomas McDonagh
  4 months
Joseph Hoey 1 year
Sheila Tuohy 9 years
Teresa Cunniffe 3 months
Joseph Clohessy 2 months
Mary Kiely 4 months
Thomas Cloran 6 months
Mary Burke 3 months
Mary Marg Flaherty 4 months
John Keane 17 days
Luke Ward 15 months
Mary O'Reilly 5 months

1935

Ellen Mountgomery
  18 months
Mary Elizabeth Lydon
  4 months
Brigid Madden 1 month
Mary Margaret Murphy
  4 months
Mary Nealon 7 months
Stephen Linnane 4 months
Josephine Walsh 1 years
Kate Cunningham 2 months
Mary Bernadette Hibbett
  1 month

Thomas Linnane 4 months
Patrick Lane 3 months
Mary Anne Conway
  2 months
James Kane 8 months
Christopher Leech 3 months
Elizabeth Ann McCann
  5 months
Margaret Mary Coen
  2 months
Michael Linnane 15 months
Bridget Glenane 5 weeks

1936

Bridget Geraghty 11 days
Joseph Patrick Hynes 4 months

Martin Hannon 6 months
Martin Coyne 7 months

Nuala Mary Leech 1 year

Michael Monaghan
3 ½ months

Aiden Patrick O'Donnell
2 months

Martin Baker 3 months

Mary Browne 4 months

Angela Daly 1 year

Teresa Mary Joyce
5 months

Francis Coy 6 months

Rose Margret McLoughlin
4 months

Philomena Mary Walsh
7 months

Joan Gleeson 14 months

Joseph Michael Fahy
17 months

John Michael Walsh 7 months

Annie Corcoran 11 months

Michael Mee 13 months

Kathleen Hynes 10 months

John Coyne 16 months

Michael O'Toole 17 months

Edward Michael Feeney
13 months

Alfred Conroy 20 months

Margaret Ryan 22 months

Kate Mary O'Reilly 1 year

Patrick Joyce 13 months

Edward Munnelly
7 months

Bernadette Leech 18 months

Thomas Flaherty 3 years

Teresa Cummins 3 weeks

Desmond Edward Kilbane
2 ½ years

John O'Toole 7 months

John Creshal 4 months

Mary Teresa Egan
3 months

Michael Boyle 3 months

Anthony Mannion 6 weeks

Donald Dowd 5 months

Peter Ridge 4 months

Eileen Collins 2 months

Mary Brennan 2 months

James Fahy 5 months

Mary Bridget Larkin
8 months

Margaret Scanlon 3 years

Brian O'Malley 4 months

Michael Madden 6 months

1937

Mary Kate Cahill 2 weeks

Mary Margaret Lydon
3 months

Festus Sullivan 1 month

Annie Curley 3 weeks

Nuala Lydon 5 months

Bridget Collins 5 weeks

Patrick Joseph Coleman
  1 month

Joseph Hannon 6 weeks

Henry Monaghan 3 weeks

Michael Joseph Shiels
  7 weeks

Martin Sheridan 5 weeks

John Patrick Loftus
  10 months

Patrick Joseph Murphy
  3 months

Catherine McHugh 4 months

Mary Patricia Toher 4 months

Mary Kate Sheridan 4 months

Mary Flaherty 19 months

Mary Anne Walsh 14 months

Eileen Quinn 2 years

Patrick Burke 9 months

Margaret Holland 2 days

Joseph Langan 6 months

Sabina Pauline O'Grady
  6 months

Patrick Qualter 3 years

Mary King 5 months

Eileen Conry 1 year

1938

Mary Nee 4 months

Martin Andrew Larkin
  14 months

Mary Keane 3 weeks

Kathleen V. Cuffe 6 months

Margaret Linnane 4 months

Teresa Heneghan 3 months

John Neary 7 months

Patrick Madden 4 months

Mary Cafferty 2 months

Mary Kate Keane 3 months

Patrick Hynes 3 weeks

Annie Solan 2 months

Charles Lydon 9 months

Margaret Mullins 7 months

Mary Mulligan 2 months

Anthony Lally 5 months

Joseph Spelman 6 weeks

Annie Begley 3 months

Vincent Egan 1 week

Nora Murphy 5 months

Patrick Garvey 6 months

Patricia Burke 4 months

Winifred Barret 2 years

Agnes Marron 3 months

Christopher Kennedy
  5 months

Patrick Harrington 1 week

1939

Kathleen Devine 2 years
Vincent Garaghan 1 month
Ellen Gibbons 6 months
Michael McGrath 4 months
Edward Fraser 3 months
Bridget Lally 1 year
Patrick McLoughlin
  5 months
Martin Healy 4 months
Nora Duffy 3 months
Margaret Higgins 1 week
Patrick Egan 6 months
Vincent Farragher
  11 months

Patrick Joseph Jordan
  3 months
Michael Hanley 1 month
Catherine Gilmore 3 months
Baby Carney 1 day
Annie Coyne 3 months
Helena Cosgrave 5 months
Thomas Walsh 2 months
Baby Walsh 1 day
Kathleen Hession 4 months
Brigid Hurley 11 months
Ellen Beegan 2 months
Mary Keogh 1 year
Bridget Burke 3 months

1940

Martin Reilly 9 months
Martin Hughes 11 months
Mary Connolly 1 month
Mary Kate Ruane 1 month
Joseph Mulchrone 3 months
Michael Williams 14 months
Martin Moran 7 weeks
Josephine Mahony 2 months
James Henry 5 weeks
Bridget Staunton 5 months
John Creaven 2 weeks
Peter Lydon 6 weeks
Patrick Joseph Ruane
  4 months
Michael Quinn 8 months

Julia Coen 1 week
Annie McAndrew 5 months
John Walsh 3 months
Patrick Flaherty 6 months
Bernadette Purcell 2 years
Joseph Macklin 1 day
Thomas Duffy 2 days
Elizabeth Fahy 4 months
James Kelly 2 months
Nora Gallagher 4 months
Kathleen Cannon 4 months
Winifred Tighe 8 months
Christopher Williams 1 year
Joseph Lynch 1 year
Andrew McHugh 15 months

William Glennan 18 months
Michael J. Kelly 5 months
Patrick Gallagher 3 months

Michael Gerard Keane
  2 months
Ellen Lawless 6 months

1941

Mary Finn 3 months
Martin Timlin 3 months
Mary McLoughlin 1 month
Mary Brennan 5 months
Patrick Dominic Egan
  1 month
Nora Thornton 17 months
Anne Joyce 1 year
Catherine Kelly 10 months
Michael Monaghan 8 months
Simon John Hargraves
  6 months
Baby Forde 1 day
Joseph Byrne 2 months
Patrick Hegarty 4 months
Patrick Corcoran 1 month
James Leonard 16 days
Jane Gormley 22 days
Anne Ruane 11 days

Patrick Munnelly 3 months
John Lavelle 6 weeks
Patrick Ruane 24 days
Patrick Joseph Quinn
  3 months
Joseph Kennelly 15 days
Kathleen Monaghan 3 months
Baby Quinn 2 days
Anthony Roche 4 months
Annie Roughneen 3 weeks
Anne Kate O'Hara 4 months
Patrick Joseph Nevin
  3 months
John Joseph Hopkins
  3 months
Thomas Gibbons 1 month
Winifred McTigue 7 months
Thomas Joseph Begley
  2 months

1942

Kathleen Heneghan 25 days
Elizabeth Murphy 4 months
Nora Farnan 1 month
Teresa Tarpey 1 month
Margaret Carey 11 months
John Garvey 6 weeks

Bridget Goldrick 4 months
Bridget White 3 months
Noel Slattery 1 month
Mary T. Connaughton
  4 months
Nora McCormack 6 weeks

Joseph Hefferon 5 months

Mary Higgins 9 days

Mary Farrell 21 days

Mary McDonnell 1 month

Geraldine Cunniffe 11 weeks

Michael Mannion 3 months

Bridget McHugh 7 months

Mary McEvady 18 months

Helena Walsh 3 months

William McDoell 2 days

Michael Finn 14 months

Mary Murphy 10 months

Gertrude Glynn 6 months

Joseph Flaherty 7 weeks

Mary O'Malley 4 years

John P. Callanan 13 days

Baby McDonnell 1 day

Female McDonnell 1 day

Christopher Burke 9 months

Stephen Connolly 8 months

Mary Atkinson 6 months

Mary Anne Finegan 7 weeks

Francis Richardson
  15 months

Michael John Rice 6 months

Nora Carr 4 months

William Walsh 16 months

Vincent Cunnane 14 months

Eileen Coady 10 months

Female Roache 1 day

Male Roache 1 day

Patrick Flannery 2 months

John Dermody 3 months

Margaret Spellman 4 months

Austin Nally 3 months

Margaret Dolan 3 months

Vincent Finn 9 months

Bridget Grogan 6 months

1943

Thomas Patrick Cloran
  9 weeks

Catherine Devere 1 month

Mary Josephine Glynn 1 day

Annie Connolly 9 months

Martin Cosgrove 7 weeks

Catherine Cunningham
  2 years

Bridget Hardiman 2 months

Mary Grier 5 months

Mary P. McCormick 2 months

Brendan Muldoon 5 weeks

Nora Moran 7 months

Joseph Maher 20 days

Teresa Dooley 3 months

Daniel Tully 7 months

Brendan Durkan 1 month

Sheila O'Connor 3 months

Annie Coen 6 months

Patrick J. Kennedy 6 days

Thomas Walsh 2 months

Patrick Rice 1 year

Edward McGowan 10 months
Brendan Egan 10 months
Margaret McDonagh 1 month
Annie J. Donellan 10 months
Thomas Walsh 14 days
Bridget Quinn 6 months
Mary Mulkerins 5 weeks
Kathleen Parkinson
 10 months
Sheila Madeline Flynn
 4 months
Patrick Joseph Maloney
 2 months
Bridget Carney 7 months
Mary M. O'Connor
 6 months
Joseph Geraghty 3 months
Annie Coen 10 months

Martin Joseph Feeney
 4 months
Anthony Finnegan 3 months
Patrick Coady 3 months
Baby Cunningham 1 day
Annie Fahy 3 months
Baby Byrne 1 day
Patrick Mullaney 18 months
Thomas Connelly 3 months
Mary Larkin 2 months
Margaret Kelly 4 months
Barbara McDonagh
 4 months
Mary O'Brien 4 months
Keiran Hennelly 14 months
Annie Folan 4 months
Baby McNamara 1 day
Julia Murphy 3 months

1944

John Rockford 4 months
Vincent Geraghty 1 year
Male O'Brien 2 days
Anthony Deane 2 days
Mary Teresa O'Brien 15 days
John Connelly 3 months
Bridget Murphy 3 months
Patricia Dunne 2 months
Francis Kinahan 1 month
Joseph Sweeney 20 days
Josephine O'Hagan 6 months
Patrick Lavin 1 month

Annie Maria Glynn
 13 months
Kate Agnes Moore 2 months
Kevin Kearns 15 months
Thomas Doocey 15 months
William Conneely 8 months
Margaret Spelman 16 months
Mary Kate Cullen 22 months
Kathleen Brown 3 years
Julia Kelly 19 months
Mary Connolly 7 years
Catherine Harrison 2 years

Eileen Forde 21 months

Michael Monaghan 2 years

Mary Frances Lenihan 3 days

Anthony Byrne 6 months

Jarlath Thornton 7 weeks

John Kelly 6 days

Joseph O'Brien 18 months

Anthony Hyland 3 months

Male Murray 1 day

Female Murray 1 day

Joseph F. McDonnell
  11 days

Mary Walsh 15 months

Baby Glynn 1 day

James Gaughan 14 months

Margaret Walsh 4 months

Mary P. Moran 9 days

John Francis Malone 7 days

1945

Michael F. Dempsey 7 weeks

Christina M. Greally
  4 months

Teresa Donnellan 1 month

Rose Anne King 5 weeks

Christopher J. Joyce
  2 months

James Mannion 8 months

Mary T. Sullivan 3 weeks

Patrick Holohan 11 months

Michael Joseph Keane
  1 month

Bridget Keaney 2 months

Joseph Flaherty 8 days

Baby Mahady 3 days

James Rogers 10 days

Kathleen F. Taylor 9 months

Gerard C. Hogan 7 months

Kathleen Corrigan
  2 months

Mary Connolly 3 months

Patrick J. Farrell 5 months

Patrick Laffey 3 years

Fabian Hynes 8 months

John Joseph Grehan
  2 years

Edward O'Malley 3 months

Mary Fleming 6 months

Bridget F. McHugh
  3 months

Michael Folan 18 months

Oliver Holland 6 months

Ellen Nevin 7 months

Margaret Horan 6 months

Peter Mullarky 4 months

Mary P. O'Brien 4 months

Teresa Francis O'Brien
  4 months

Mary Kennedy 18 months

Sarah Ann Carroll 4 months

Baby Maye 5 days

1946

Mary Devaney 21 days

Anthony McDonnell
  6 months

Vincent Molloy 7 days

John Patrick Lyons 5 months

Gerald Aidan Timlin 3 days

Patrick Costelloe 17 days

John Francis O'Grady
  1 month

Bridget Mary Flaherty
  12 days

Josephine Finnegan
  20 months

Martin McGrath 3 days

Baby Haugh 1 day

James Frayne 1 month

Mary Frances Crealy 14 days

Mary Davey 2 months

Patrick Joseph Hoban 11 days

Angela Dolan 3 months

Mary Lyden 5 months

Bridget Coneely 4 months

Austin O'Toole 4 months

Bernard Laffey 5 months

Mary Ellen Waldron
  8 months

Terence O'Boyle 3 months

Mary Frances O'Hara
  1 month

Martin Dermott Henry
  43 days

Mary Devaney 3 months

Bridget Foley 6 months

Martin Kilkelly 40 days

Theresa Monica Hehir
  6 weeks

Patrick A. Mitchell 3 months

John Kearney 5 months

John Joseph Kelly 3 months

John Conneely 4 months

Stephen L. O'Toole 2 months

Thomas A. Buckley 5 weeks

Michael John Gilmore
  3 months

Patrick J. Monaghan
  3 months

Mary Teresa Murray
  2 months

Patrick McKeighe 2 months

John Raymond Feeney
  3 months

Finbar Noone 2 months

John O'Brien 21 days

Beatrice Keane 5 years

Mary P. Veale 5 weeks

Winifred Gillespie 1 year

Anthony Coen 10 weeks

Michael F. Sheridan 3 months

Anne Holden 3 months

Martin Joseph O'Brien
  7 weeks

Winifred Larkin 1 month

1947

Patrick Thomas Coen 1 month

Mary Bridget Joyce 8 months

Geraldine Collins 13 months

Mary Flaherty 5 days

Vincent Keogh 5 months

John Francis Healy 10 days

Martin J. Kennelly 1 month

Patrick Keaveney 2 months

Philomena Flynn 2 months

William Reilly 9 months

Margaret N. Concannon
 1 year

Patrick J. Fitzpatrick 14 days

Joseph Cunningham
 2 months

Mary J. Flaherty 13 months

Kathleen Murray 3 years

John O'Connell 2 years

Alphonsus Hanley
 21 months

Bridget P. Muldoon
 11 months

Patricia C. Higgins 5 months

Catherine B. Kennedy
 2 months

John Desmond Dolan
 15 months

Stephen Joynt 2 years

Catherine T. Kearns 2 years

Margaret Hurney 2 years

John Patton 2 years

Patrick J. Williams
 15 months

Nora Hynes 8 months

Anthony Donohue 2 years

Brendan McGreal 1 year

Anthony Cafferky 23 days

Nora Cullinane 18 months

Kathleen Daly 2 years

Nora Conneely 15 months

Mary Teresa Joyce
 13 months

Kenneth A. Ellesmere 1 day

Mary P. Carroll 4 months

Thomas Collins 17 months

Margaret M. Moloney
 3 months

Josephine Tierney 8 months

Margaret M. Deasy
 3 months

Martin Francis Bane 3 months

Bridget Agatha Kenny
 2 months

Baby Kelly 1 day

Mary Teresa Judge
 15 months

Paul Dominick Bennett
 3 months

Mary Bridget Giblin
 18 months

Sarah Carroll 8 months

Francis Brehony 1 year

Patrick Kelly 2 years 6 months
James McDonnell 4 months

Anne Conneely 6 weeks
Josephine Staunton 5 days

1948

Kathleen Madden 2 months
Mary P. Byrne 8 weeks
Joseph Byrne 4 months
Joseph Byrne 11 months
Kathleen Glynn 4 months
Augustine Jordan 9 months
Michael F. Dwyer 18 months
Noel C. Murphy 14 months
Margaret McNamee 6 months
Patrick Grealish 6 weeks
Bernadette O'Reilly 7 months
John Joseph Carr 3 weeks
Paul Gardiner 10 months

Simon Thomas Folan
  9 weeks
Joseph Ferguson 3 months
Peter Heffernan 4 months
Patrick J. Killeen 14 weeks
Stephen Halloran 7 months
Teresa Grealish 5 months
John Keane 4 months
Mary Burke 9 months
Brigid McTigue 3 months
Margaret R. Broderick
  8 months
Martin Mannion 3 months

1949

Mary Margaret Riddell
  8 months
Thomas J. Noonan 7 weeks
Peter Casey 10 months
Michael Scully 3 months
Baby Lyons 5 days
Hubert McLoughlin 4 months
Mary M. Finnegan 3 months
Nicholas P. Morley 3 months
Teresa Bane 6 months
Patrick J. Kennedy 5 weeks
Michael Francis Ryan 3 days
John Forde 2 years

Mary P. Cunnane 3 months
Margaret P. Sheridan 4 months
Patrick Joseph Nevin
  3 months
Joseph Nally 5 months
Christopher Burke 3 months
Anne Madden 7 weeks
Bridget T. Madden 7 weeks
Thomas Murphy 3 months
Francis Carroll 2 months
Bridget J. Linnan 9 months
Josephine Staunton 8 days
Mary Ellen McKeigue 7 weeks

1950

Mary J. Mulchrone 3 months

Catherine Higgins 4 years

Catherine Anne Egan
 3 months

Thomas McQuaid 4 months

Dermott Muldoon 4 months

Martin Hanley 9 weeks

John Joseph Lally 3 months

Brendan Larkin 5 months

Baby Bell 1 day

Mary J. Larkin 7 months

Annie Fleming 9 months

Colm A. McNulty 1 month

Walter Flaherty 3 months

Sarah Burke 15 days

Mary Ann Boyle 5 months

John Anthony Murphy
 5 months

Joseph A. Colohan 4 months

Christopher Begley 18 days

1951

Catherine A. Meehan 4 months

Martin McLynskey 6 months

Mary J. Crehan 3 months

Mary Ann McDonagh
 2 months

Joseph Folan 22 days

Evelyn Barrett 4 months

Paul Morris 4 months

Peter Morris 4 months

Mary Martyna Joyce
 18 months

Mary Margaret Lane 7 months

1952

John Noone 4 months

Anne J. McDonnell 6 months

Joseph Anthony Burke
 6 months

Patrick Hardiman 6 months

Patrick Naughton 12 days

Josephine T. Staunton 21 days

John Joseph Mills 5 months

1953

Baby Hastings 1 day

Mary Donlon 4 months

Nora Connolly 15 months

1954

Anne Heneghan 3 months

Mary Keville 9 months

Martin Murphy 5 months
Mary Barbara McDonagh
  5 months
Mary P. Logue 5 months
Margaret E. Cooke 6 months

Mary Ann Broderick
  14 months
Ann Marian Fahy 4 months
Anne Dillon 4 months
Imelda Halloran 2 years

1955

Joseph Gavin 10 months
Marian Brigid Mulryan
  10 months
Mary C. Rafferty 3 months
Nora Mary Howard 4 months

Joseph Dempsey 3 months
Patrick Walsh 3 weeks
Francis Martin Heaney
  3 years 10 months

1956

Dermot Gavin 2 weeks
Mary C. Burke 3 years
Patrick Burke 1 year
Paul Henry Nee 5 months
Oliver Reilly 4 months

Gerard Connaughton 1
  1 months
Rose Marie Murphy 2 years
Peter Folan 4 months

1957

Margaret Connaire 4 months
Stephen Noel Browne 2 years

Baby Fallon 4 days

1958

Geraldine O'Malley 6 months

1959

Dolores Conneely 7 months

Mary Maloney 4 months

1960

Mary Carty 5 months

Acknowledgements

CATHERINE CORLESS

I would like to thank the following:

Ciara Considine, publisher/editor at Hachette Books Ireland, for giving me the opportunity to record the truth of what happened in the Tuam Mother & Baby Home. Thanks also to Publicity Director Elaine Egan and all at HBI.

Co-writer Naomi Linehan for her professionalism in weaving my story together.

My husband Aidan who believed in me and supported me throughout my struggle for the truth, and my wonderful family who did likewise.

University College Dublin, Trinity College Dublin, National University of Ireland Galway, for their doctorate awards in recognition of my research.

Rehab Ireland for the honour of Person of the Year Award, and Galway Rehab for the County Award.

The Bar of Ireland for the Human Rights Award.

Newsbrand Ireland for their Journalism Award.

Trinity FLAC Award. SAOL Project Award. Psychological Society of Ireland – Presidential Citation.

I would also like to thank the Hardiman Library NUIG and Library headquarters Nun's island Galway for their help and patience in finding maps which were crucial to my research and discoveries.

To Anne Glennon of BDM Registration Office Galway who

accumulated the 796 deaths in the Home and for her continuing help.

I am grateful to all the Tuam Home Survivors who came forward to recount their life stories to so many national and international TV crews/documentary makers/radio/journalists, etc. Their courageous accounts were the backbone of the research I had documented.

Thanks to all the decent people of Ireland and beyond, who offered support, gratitude and kindness in their hundreds through letters, cards and tokens.

Also, many, through their grief for the Tuam babies, brought various type gifts to decorate the site and to give them recognition.

Others through their talents created poems, dramas, songs, crafted items, sculptures, exhibitions, all to remember the Tuam babies.

On the political front, thanks in particular to former Senator Trevor O Clochartaigh who was always at hand for advice, and also to Cllr. Colm Keaveney, and Deputy Catherine Connolly who gave a voice to the Tuam babies in their Dail speeches.

Finally, I want to thank Sadie Cramer, who first initiated the idea of holding a vigil at the Tuam babies' site, which in turn became an annual occasion, and to all those who assisted in every way they could, especially Amanda, Carmel and Denise. Also to Valerie Jennings who organized the Relay Lantern vigil from Islandeady, Co. Mayo all the way to Tuam to the babies' site.

Not forgetting the many professional people who assured me that help was at hand should I need them – you know who you are. Heartfelt thanks, one and all.

Acknowledgements

NAOMI LINEHAN

To Catherine, for your strength and courage. Your determination to do for others, to fight for justice against all the odds, is incredible. You are a remarkable person and I am truly honoured and extremely grateful to have had the opportunity to work with you. Thank you for sharing your story with the world. It is a true testament to what is possible when people choose to take a stand and fight for what is right.

To Ciara Considine, who is the driving force behind so many important stories being told in this country, so many voices being heard. For making all this possible and for your vision and unwavering support. And to all the team at Hachette Books Ireland who work tirelessly to bring these stories to light.

To all the survivors of mother and baby homes and the many people who have been involved in this long struggle for justice – you are an inspiration and you deserve so much.

To my family – to Ben, my husband. Thank you for being you. You make the world a better place for all who know you. Thank you for being on this adventure of life with me – for all the love and laughter. For all that you are and all that you do, and for all the ways you made this book possible.

To Laura – for being the incredible person that you are. I am constantly in awe of your kindness, generosity of spirit and the way you are there for all the people in your life. Thank you for all your support through this project. You and Dallan have such an adventure ahead of you, and there is no better duo in this world to take it all on.

To Mum, who was the first of my family to read this book, a constant support and source of encouragement. Thank you for being my mother – for the life that you gave me and the love and bond we will always share.

To Dad, two years since you passed away. We love and miss

you every moment of every day. For teaching me the love of writing, and for being my hero in so many ways. I was very, very lucky that you were, and always will be, my Dad.

And to all the Linehans, Dillons and Kitchins – I am so lucky to count you as my family. You are always very close to my heart. With a special note for my Grandmother who passed away some months ago – a missing part in all our lives.

For the past year, we lived in a cocoon in a little pocket of Sligo where much of this book was written. Thank you to Robert and Carmen for letting us into your oasis when we needed it most and for being incredible friends to us through it all. To Rosemary and Anthony, Chris, Dor, Debbie, Moyna, Roo, Neassa, Cloe, Lea and the kids – for all the ways you welcomed us in and helped us along the way. We will always be so thankful for that time together.

To all the friends we've missed over the past year during the pandemic – we have learned to cherish the moments all the more. Thank you for your friendship – it means more than you'll ever know.

During the writing of this book, I had a child. His name is Oliver. He is a beautiful, healthy baby boy. We have since found out that we are expecting twins – our family of three, soon to be five. We cannot wait to meet you little ones - to show you the world, and introduce you to your big brother. As I write this I can feel you move within me – those little kicks, with all the promise of new life. We love you already – your Dad and I. We are connected and always will be. As those mothers from Tuam were connected to their babies. It is a bond that should never be broken.

As the days, weeks and months passed, I have watched Oliver grow – watched him become the person he's going to be in the world. Watched him explore with wonder and delight all the things this world has to offer. He loves looking for bok boks (chickens) through the magic door in the kitchen, reading stories, and making funny noises. He loves his Dad and he loves his Mum. He laughs with all his heart and feels things so deeply. His first birthday was in November. That day, as I dressed Oliver, I felt a pull on my heart. I thought of the mother in Tuam dressing her daughter in a special outfit for her birthday, then being called into the head nun's office where she was told that she was being sent away, and would never see her daughter again. Her bag was packed and she was not even allowed to say goodbye. I held Oliver close that day as I imagined the torment that that mother must have felt. I thought of all the mothers in the Tuam mother and baby home who were forced to leave their babies on their first birthdays. I thought of all the babies who never saw their mothers again. Every day of our lives that we have together after your first birthday Oliver, is a gift we would not have had, had our circumstances been different – had you been born in a different time and had I not been married to your dad. By accident of birth, we have been given the gift of time, the gift of a relation-ship, the gift of family. We are so lucky.

My wish that day as Oliver blew out his candle, was that all the babies from Tuam who were denied so much – who were torn from their mothers on their first birthdays – that they would receive some kind of justice and truth, for all the time and love that was stolen from them. And their mothers too. It is the *very least* we can do. Oliver, this one's for you.